COLUMBUS BEER

Recent Brewing & Deep Roots

CURTIS SCHIEBER

AMERICAN PALATE

Published by American Palate
A Division of The History Press
Charleston, SC
www.historypress.net

Front cover: Randall L. Schieber.
Back cover: German Village Society August Wagner colleciton; *insert*: Randall L. Schieber.

First published 2017

Manufactured in the United States

ISBN 9781626199101

Library of Congress Control Number: 2017948449

For my mother, Marion Lillian Schieber, who read everything I wrote about anything until her passing in 2015 and my wife, Martine, and children, Evan and Flannery, who endured my distraction for nearly two-and-a-half years.

CONTENTS

ACKNOWLEDGEMENTS

While my gratitude goes out to all the interviewees whose memories shaped this story, I must admit the stories from Scott Francis, Angelo Signorino, Lenny Kolada, Vince Falcone, Allen Young, Victor Ecimovich III, Dick Stevens and Ben Pridgeon were personally meaningful. I was a friend to all of them as they created history in Columbus and was motivated to write this book, in part, to celebrate their accomplishments.

My journey began when, during a downturn in the available hours at my full-time job at Barnes & Noble and in search of freelance writing work, I contacted old pal Bill Eichenberger, now editor-in-chief at the Ohio History Connection's quarterly magazine *Timeline*. He led me to The History Press, whose editors looked to add a chronicle of Columbus brewing to their series of regional interest books.

Research began in the dining room of Jay and Genie Hoster's home. Jay was the first and one of the few descendants of the original line of German brewers I was able to find. Thanks to Jay for his stories, photos, documents and pictures of his memorabilia. When Jay's family closed shop on the brewery, he said, they took nothing with them. He has had to acquire most of his fine collection of his own family's history from collectors, especially David Foster. Hopefully, this book will help get some of that history back into circulation.

When I first contacted Russ Arledge, curator of archives and facilities at the German Village Society, he was still cataloguing the August Wagner archives, donated by the estate of the storied brewer's daughter Helen.

Arledge was very generous with his time and the society's copyright, allowing me to publish the collection's photos and documents in this book. Interestingly, in conversations with David Foster, I discovered not only that Helen had become Foster's friend but also that she had granted him rights to use the Gambrinus brand, the names of its signature brews and even the artwork from the originals when he began his own Gambrinus Brewery in 1993.

A year and a half into this project, when I was already six months past my first contracted deadline and was about to wrap up the research phase, I finally located David Foster, beer memorabilia collector, amateur historical sleuth and, for part of the 1990s, professional brewer. He had put his extensive collection, historical archives and brewing ambitions in storage and had become an antiques dealer.

He and his wife, Carla, still share a passion for beer history, which was reawakened when I arrived, unannounced, at their home in southeast Columbus in the spring of 2016. I was hoping I could just get a couple stories out of him and a recollection of his time resurrecting the Gambrinus brand twenty years before. I was ecstatic when he offered to open his collection, research and memory in order to further a project he had hoped to accomplish himself years ago—to publish a book about the rich history of brewing in Columbus.

Similarly, my chance meeting with Columbus Brew Adventures' Jim Ellison—he spotted me taking a picture of King Gambrinus on Front Street one day and introduced himself—opened a new window on the city's brewing history. Jim connected me with Chris and Alex Hostettler, whose father and grandfather were essential brewmasters during nearly all of twentieth-century German brewing history. Alex's experience brewing for mainstream breweries, especially Anheuser-Busch, gave me a much-needed respect for the skill of the mega-company's brewers. Jim also connected me with Reid Wasserstrom, vice president of the realty division of the Wasserstrom companies, who took me on a memorable tour of the unused nooks and crannies of the old Hoster Brewery building.

While my initial investigation included, fittingly, the Ohio History Connection, I found the collections at the Columbus Metropolitan Library, and especially the help of librarians Julie Callahan, Nick Taggart and Nancy Kangas, essential in my education. Westerville Public Library's Anti-Saloon League Museum and its collection of propaganda were downright eye-opening.

INTRODUCTION

Brewing in Columbus, Ohio, for decades has been dominated by the mammoth Anheuser-Busch plant at the north end of town. Its first brewery was founded in the United States by German immigrants in St. Louis in 1852 and became Anheuser-Busch at the end of the Civil War. AB first came to Columbus in 1966. But this book is about Columbus's own breweries established by locals, whether they were English and German immigrants or central Ohio born; pioneer brewers of the nineteenth century; or the wildly creative craft brewers of today. These breweries began in the community to which they were to add a rich tapestry of lore and impressive commerce.

Brewing in Columbus began just after the city, designed from its start in 1812 to be the state capital, was founded. The earliest brewers were of English descent. Beer making started humbly in a structure little more than a log cabin but, interestingly, right in the center of the area that would become the hub of Columbus brewing for another 160 years and grow to its turn-of-the-century heyday. Names such as Hoster, Born, Schlee and Wagner would forge national and international reputations from that neighborhood, making Columbus an industry hub. Called the Brewery District today, it was also the site for local brewing's demise in 1974 and return in 1989.

While AB continues to—as local craft brewers have been heard to joke—spill more beer than the upstarts produce in a year, the town today has a brewing scene that has earned national notice again, with thirty-seven microbreweries and brewpubs currently operating and several more due to open this year. (It is interesting that this number was sixteen when I first sketched this introduction in the fall of 2014.)

Reading Tom Acitelli's book *The Audacity of Hops: The History of America's Craft Beer Revolution*, I was taken with the idea that the not widely known national history of the current brewing renaissance might make a good documentary. The story has all the elements for such a project, including colorful characters, a David-and-Goliath struggle at its center and a front-row seat during the emergence of a wide-ranging and influential subculture, one that threatens to go mainstream as we speak.

Then I realized that I was reading a protohistory of craft brewing in Columbus, Ohio, and how its evolution mirrored the national emergence, first as a cult-sized interest and later as a cornerstone of current youth culture and a very real economic challenge to the gigantic beer industry. Acitelli's book begins with the appliance—and, more important, gourmet cheese—heir Fritz Maytag loving and then buying a decaying old brewery/restaurant in San Francisco called the Old Spaghetti Factory, which brewed and served a beer called Anchor Steam. As the book backtracks a bit to recount the stories of a couple of servicemen stationed abroad and an Englishman, all three of whom wished to drink European-style beers in America, we find the roots of home brewing, formal brewing education and the birth of modern brewing experimentation. Maytag employed an unknown hop grown in the Yakima Valley of Washington State for his crucial Liberty Ale in 1974. It was later named Cascade, and its floral resins came to be the signature flavor note distinguishing American-style craft beers to this day.

Ben Pridgeon, brewmaster at Columbus Brewing Company in the mid-1990s, may have been the first locally to employ that floral bouquet and push it to a new level of assertion. Certainly, craft brewers in Columbus haven't looked back since, playing to the youth market that demands hoppy IPAs and responds to increasingly creative brewing recipes.

There's a good chance you are a fan of today's hop-forward American styles and are reading this book in large part to discover the roots of the current explosion. This book begins with the genesis of that current boom, as it is immediate, lively and stands as a history of its own. The book ends with the present and the future, making no attempt to make sense of the ever-evolving current scene, which is spreading like wild hop rhizomes throughout central Ohio. Hopefully, though, it will inspire an interest in the "ancient" history, as well. It is one that is not gone and forgotten. One short walk in the Brewery District, along streets with names such as Hoster and Blenkner, past the imposing, colorful statue of King Gambrinus, between the tall restored structures built by the nineteenth-century beer barons, will show you that.

1

THE CLASS OF 1989

For much of the mid-twentieth century in Columbus, Ohio, the beer of choice was Gambrinus. Imagine a classic film noir shot in central Ohio, say, 1955: Guy walks into a dimly lit bar. He bellows, "Bartender, give me a beer." Likely, he's going to get a Gam. In fact, if he is in downtown Columbus, he might have seen the giant "Give Me a Gam" sign outside, dominating the northeast corner of Broad and High Streets.

If he walked into that bar after 1974 and got a Gam, he would have entered the "Twilight Zone."

August Wagner's Gambrinus was out of business, his brewery levelled by the end of that year. His was the last brewery in a 160-year tradition of local, independent brewers. Between 1974 and 1989, Columbus didn't have a single independent, Columbus-based brewery. Beer manufacture in the city was solely represented by the large, international corporation Anheuser-Busch, which opened a 1.5-million-barrel facility in Columbus in August 1968. So lopsided was the new history compared to the old that Jay Hoster, great-great-grandson of seminal nineteenth-century brewer Louis Hoster, wrote a damning piece of history for *Columbus Monthly* magazine in 1976. In it, he pointed out the disparity between the old and new beer markets nationwide. Where less than one hundred years before there had been thousands of small, local and regional breweries—the biggest making a couple hundred thousand barrels of beer a year—by 1976, there were just a handful of major corporate brewers, their facilities producing many millions per year.

Columbus, a classic nineteenth-century brewing city, wasn't alone in witnessing the decline—in our case, demise—of independent, localized brewers. Cleveland lost its last, Schmidt's, in 1983; Cincinnati saw its last independent, historic brewery, Hudepohl, shuttered in 1999. According to the Brewers Association of America, there were 4,131 breweries in the United States in 1873. By 1978, there were just 89. More significantly, they were owned and operated by just 51 companies. Prohibition had dealt the first, biggest blow, leaving just 756 breweries to resume production in 1934, a year after its repeal; consolidation and its partner-in-arms—bland, uniformly flavored beer—finished the job a few decades later.

August Wagner's Gambrinus was the last to go in Columbus, in 1974. Wagner had opened his own brewery in 1905 after being brewmaster for the Hoster Brewing Company, Columbus's longest-running and first major brewery, opening in 1836 and running until 1920. Wagner's own brewery suffered through Prohibition by marketing cooking-grade malt extract, ostensibly for "baking," though it was significantly more valuable in home brewing. Like many other brewers of the time, he also made "near beer" (extremely low-alcohol brew) and soft drinks.

After Prohibition, the brewery hit its stride. Gambrinus, or "Gam," as it was affectionately called, was the first choice for decades to follow in central Ohio. After Wagner died in 1944, his secretary, and then his daughter, took the company's reins. In the 1950s and '60s, under president James Amento, it staved off the consolidation that was taking most of the nation's other independents into the wings of majors such as Anheuser-Busch and Miller. After several financial reorganizations, though, it closed its doors in early 1974; its Front Street building was demolished later that year. The statue of King Gambrinus that graced the brewery's entrance survived and still holds court in the neighborhood, on a grassy knoll in front of the Kroger grocery store at West Sycamore and Front Streets.

The King has exacted his revenge, though. Today, there are more than thirty independently owned craft breweries in central Ohio. Though it seems to have happened overnight, it doesn't represent simply a rebirth of Old World brewing tradition. Rather, it has mirrored—albeit perhaps a decade behind—the national trend of a changing American palate, one obsessed with variety, detail and local sourcing.

More than perhaps any other figure, Alice Waters turned the tide of fast-food America back toward thoughtful cooking, locally sourced ingredients and slow, pleasurable meals. She studied at UC Berkeley and then in France, returning in 1971 to open Chez Panisse, one of the most significant establishments in the foundation of a new American cuisine.

Dutch immigrant Alfred Peet was there just a few years before, opening his first Peet's Coffee and Tea in Berkeley in 1966 and several more in the area soon thereafter. A coffee roaster in Europe before the war, Peet thought American coffee tasted like World War II rations. His shop jump-started the popularity of custom-roasted beans that led directly to the establishment of Starbucks and the modern American coffee roasting movement.

Then there was Fritz Maytag, heir to not only the washing machine dynasty but, more notably for our story, also the Maytag Dairy Farms and its world-famous Maytag Blue Cheese. The Stanford grad lived in San Francisco, where he found an old brewery called Anchor that changed his life and brewing history in America. He bought the place in 1968, making his the first of what was soon to be called a modern "craft brewery." His incorporation of experimental, American hop strain no. 56013 in his 1975 landmark strong Liberty Ale established the course of American craft brewing followed today. The hop, later named Cascade, is the cornerstone of today's American IPA, its floral notes the signature flavor of modern brewing.

In 1978, home brewing became legal in the United States. Perhaps in response, Charlie Papazian and Charlie Matzen founded the American Homebrewers Association that same year. Like many other budding beer fans in America, they were inspired by British beer writer Michael Jackson's *World Guide to Beer*, which, from the time it was published in 1977, set the international beer scene in Technicolor. Tom Acitelli's book *The Audacity of Hops: The History of America's Craft Beer Revolution* includes a short chapter on Jackson, nestled among all the other pioneers who figured in the rebirth of brewing in this country. They ranged from world travelers to academics, adventurers to frustrated expats.

Like the pioneers in the craft brew movement on the West Coast, most of the local professional brewers began as home brewers. In Columbus, Scott Francis and his wife, Nina Hawranick, bought the Winemaker's Shop in 1974—coincidentally, the same year that Gambrinus went under.

The accent was on wine making because, as Francis recalled recently, ingredients to make good beer simply were not available. "There was Blue Ribbon malt, Red Top and Gold label. Those were the three malt extracts you could buy. They were terrible, baking-quality extracts and the recipe was you put five pounds of white table sugar and a pack of red yeast [and the malt]. It was just like Prohibition." In fact, during Prohibition, home brewing

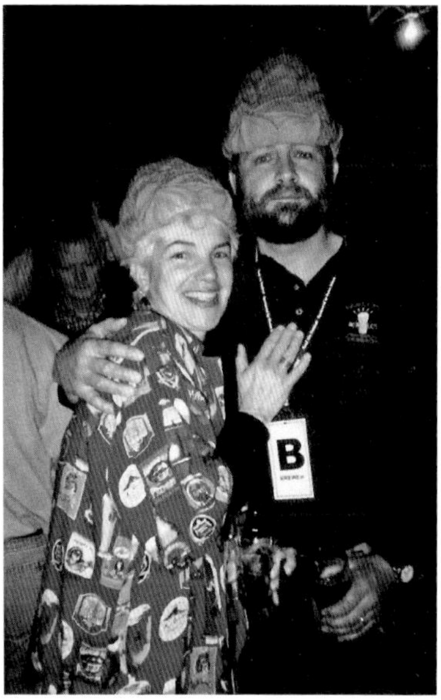

Scott Francis and his wife, Nina Hawranick, paying tribute to the spirit of the hops in the early 1990s. *Courtesy Nina Hawranick.*

flourished, supported by shops run by the likes of Columbus's Wasserstrom Company (see sidebar in chapter 9).

By the end of the 1970s, perhaps in response to the official legalization of brewing, whole grains, fresh hops and, most important, brewing-quality live yeast became available. Suddenly, fans of the import beers that had begun to come into the market in increasing numbers in the previous two decades were able to imitate them at home. When Francis and Hawranick bought their business, the focus was on wine making, partly because the previous owner had established it that way, but also because of the low grade of beer-brewing ingredients.

Then high-quality extract became available. Francis bought it from Lee Beetle at Specialty Products in Chapel Hill, North Carolina. Whole grain followed in the late 1970s, but the biggest advances were made when fresh yeast and hops came on the market for home brewers. "These two guys started these companies," Francis remembered. "Dave Wills started Freshops, and I still deal with Dave. Then Dave Logston, who was a brewer at Hood River Brewing (likely Full Sail Brewing Co.), started this little yeast company on the side, Wyeast. I was the first, maybe the second customer Dave had. I was the first customer for Freshops."

Francis continued: "When I would get the packages from Freshops, Dave would send me these bricks of whole hops that were wrapped in plastic, but he would stuff some bottles of West Coast craft beer, stuff that wasn't available here, Anchor and Pyramid. So I started to taste these beers. That was really an eye-opener."

Soon, Francis began to dream of opening a real brewery like those beginning to pop up on the West Coast. Coincidentally, the brewery district once populated by thriving breweries one hundred years before caught the imagination of a local developer. In this case, it was the developer's son, the recent college graduate Jeff Edwards, who convinced his dad, Pete, to invest in the neighborhood on Front Street, south of Livingston. By the late 1980s, their Multicon Development Company built a twelve-story office building, several restaurants and apartments on the east side of Front and had visions of larger improvements across the street, including a theater, shopping center and more apartments.

Where the elder Edwards had devoted much of his company's resources to building developments in the suburbs, Jeff was the impetus for shifting to the Brewery District. He had seen what could be done in historic districts while visiting former fraternity brothers in grad school in Pittsburgh. Jeff thought it would be very interesting to rehab the old buildings that populated the district beginning at Livingston and heading south on Front. He met with several landlords to see if they would sell the largely uninhabited buildings.

His first project was the malthouse from the nineteenth-century Schlee Bavarian Brewery, which he turned into apartments, and the stable behind, which became offices. With high school buddy Brian Gibson, he opened Gibby's bistro to the north; just south, the former Schlee brewery building itself was coming along, too.

By that time, Multicon was not the only one interested in developing the area. For a brief time, Cleveland developer Jeff Jacobs envisioned an outdoor music arena in the area, an idea that faltered only after the city hesitated in its support. The idea to build a sub-stadium-sized outdoor music venue was a popular one in big cities and larger markets. The proposals would float from one location to another and be introduced by several local and regional business concerns before bearing fruit north of town with the Polaris Amphitheater, which opened in 1994.

Francis encountered Edwards in 1986 and later met with Multicon about a brewery, confessing he didn't have the money to do it himself. Edwards had another high school friend whose sister designed the labels for Boston's Harpoon Lager, so he had some knowledge of the oncoming craft beer movement. He decided to give Francis the opportunity to do it at home.

The tiny space behind Gibby's at 476 South Front Street—situated about where the Hoster bottling plant had been a century before and Double Happiness nightclub is today—was the site for the new Columbus Brewing Company, which opened in December 1989. (The business was founded in 1988 after Francis and Hawranick copyrighted the name in 1986.) It produced exclusively English ales. The choice of style was easy, as the couple were big fans of British rock 'n' roll and especially folk-rock pioneers Fairport Convention, not to mention of English ales. The brewery was tiny, producing just two thousand barrels per year and selling its Gold pale ale only in the area at first.

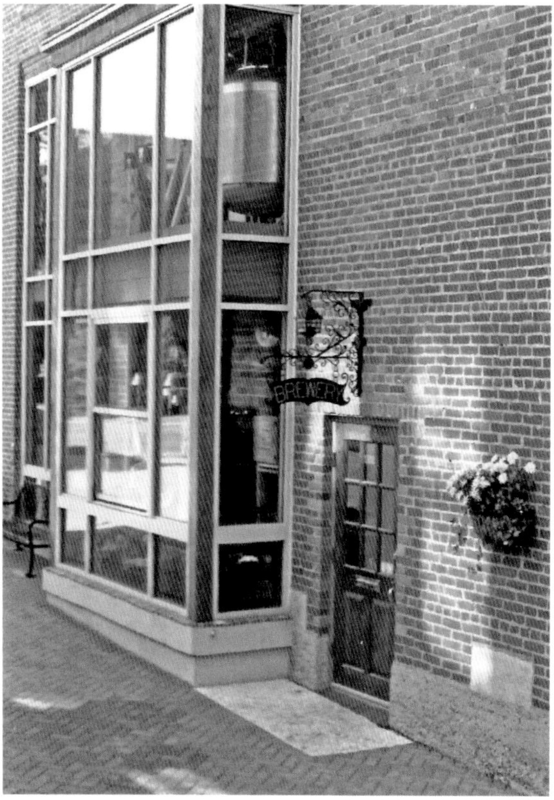

Left: The original location for the Columbus Brewing Company at 476 South Front, in the back of Gibby's. The bar was the primary source for the company's English ales when they rolled out late in 1989. The Gibby's space is now Double Happiness nightclub. *Courtesy Nina Hawranick.*

Below: Scott Francis, the godfather of Columbus craft brewing, in Gibby's, adjoining the newly founded Columbus Brewing Company in the historic Brewery District in the early 1990s. *Courtesy Nina Hawranick.*

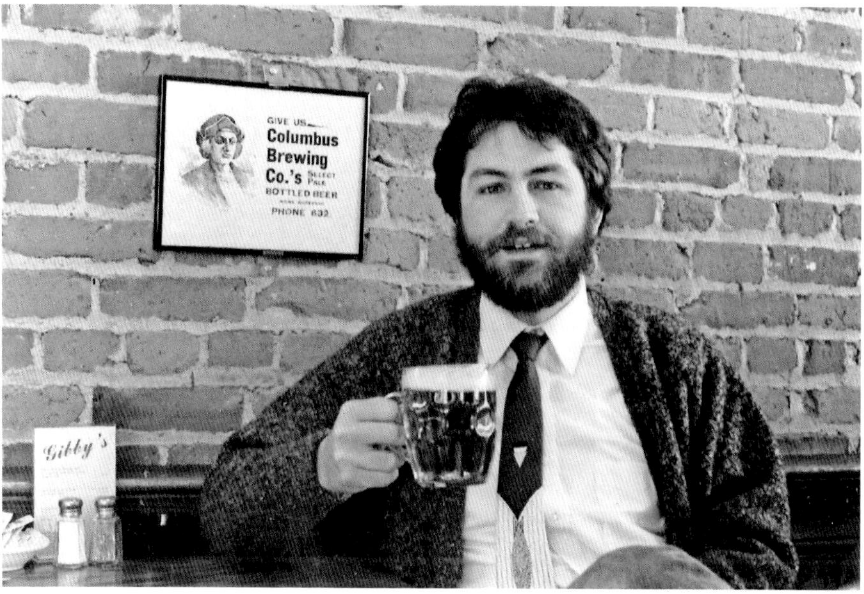

The brewing space, as Edwards recalled, was around 1,350 square feet and had no loading dock. Francis had to haul heavy tubs of malt extract and bags of grain upstairs to dump them into the system. Production and distribution began small, but unbeknownst to everybody, the little brewery was about to spark a revolution. Interestingly, the same day that the *Columbus Dispatch* broke the news about Columbus Brewing Company, it also ran a story about Anheuser-Busch still having room to grow after two expansions that boosted its capacity to 6.2 million barrels per year.

As CBC restarted the history of brewing in Columbus, it fell in line with the nascent national boom in craft brewing that has continued for nearly thirty years. The floodgates were open. The year 1988 saw fifty-five new breweries open nationally, forty-four of them brewpubs. Today, there are more than four thousand craft breweries.

Among the first of Francis's helpers at CBC was Vince Falcone, a college dropout who played in a band called Monster Truck Five. Falcone vividly remembers signing on with Francis. It happened at Stache's, Columbus's alternative music mecca and one of the first and best outlets for CBC, where Falcone was painting the bathrooms for owner Dan Dougan. When Francis, who liked to hang out there during happy hour on his way home from the brewery, announced he was looking for help, Dougan said, "Hey, Vito. You're looking for a job, right?" It was a fortuitous meeting, as Falcone eventually took over as head brewer, helped establish the Elevator brewery in 1999 and continues to brew today for various hot craft companies on the West Coast.

Meanwhile, Francis missed having regular interactions with the people who drank his ales. He still feels that way today, as he has taken his show to a new brewpub called Temperance Row in Westerville just north of Columbus. In 1992, though, that was a long way off.

Lenny Kolada was an architect inspired to take up home brewing under the guidance of Francis and Hawranick at the Winemaker's Shop beginning in the late 1980s. His mind was blown and palate enriched while on business in St. Louis, where he sampled the Danish import Carlsberg Elephant Beer at a local eatery. The arrival of Anchor Steam in Columbus around that time cemented his love for flavorful drink. Then, in 1989, during a trip to Boston, he happened into the Cambridge Brewing Company. Today, he says the experience was something like the transition from black-and-white to color when Dorothy finds herself in Oz. Cambridge had pale ales, stouts, porters and a firkin on the bar as well as cask-conditioned beers.

Kolada set about to found such a joint in his own town. One day, he took a walk and popped in on Francis at CBC, who took his offer to come on board to establish an honest Columbus brewpub. Though Barley's Brewing Company and Ale House No. 1 opened in the Short North in 1992, it wasn't the first—the new Hoster Brewing Company's brewery and restaurant in German Village scooped Kolada by a little less than a year. The two fledgling brewpubs not only coexisted peacefully at opposite ends of High Street's downtown stretch, they also complemented each another and worked together. Interestingly, both were located on or near beer-themed streets, with Hoster settling in at the corner of South High and Hoster Streets (the latter named for early brewer Louis Hoster) and Barley's on North High Street, just a block from the large cross street Goodale ("good ale."). Their enemy was the same, after all: bland beer brewed by the behemoth AB corporate brewery north of town.

Barley's on North High Street stuck to English ales, even brewing its pilsner-style beer with ale yeast, while Hoster's on South High brewed traditional German lagers. Kolada remembers the era as "one of the purest, coolest things that's happened in Columbus beer history."

Early on, Francis was stretching himself thin, overseeing CBC (with Falcone doing the day-to-day tasks) while brewing at Barley's. He had opened a nano-brewery in the New Albany Country Club in June 1992 to enable the club to take advantage of a legal loophole in order to get a liquor license. Then Barley's opened in November 1992. Francis built similar club nano-breweries in Hideaway Hills in '93 and two more over the next year or two. Angelo Signorino, who started home brewing in March 1991 and began working at the Winemaker's Shop that September, joined Francis just after Barley's opened.

Working together creatively, Francis and Signorino made the finest examples of classic English ales brewed in the city, beginning with pale ale and porter. (It should be noted, though, that English-style ales were among the very first brewed in the city—180 years earlier in a log cabin southwest of Front and Livingston Streets and a couple of decades later by a brewery also called Columbus.) They made a damn fine variation of the Czech pilsner, too. Signorino then pitched the idea of a Scottish ale created with a trick from the classic brewers. Much to Francis's chagrin, he first heated the brew kettle with just enough water to protect the bottom and quickly replaced the water with a bit of raw barley liquor, called the wort. The scorched wort lent the style's distinctive caramel flavor note to the end product. The unique brew became one of Barley's most popular items.

Other innovative styles included the Centennial IPA. The big ale, derived from one of Signorino's homebrewed batches, was created for the brewery's one-hundredth batch and for the first time with Centennial hops. Cascade and Centennial feature the floral hop note that most strongly identifies the American style of pale and IPA today. By contemporary standards of hoppiness and alcohol content, the Centennial IPA was, according to Signorino, rather "pedestrian." Back then, he said, it was "mindboggling" and a tough sell. Signorino, an avid bike rider, said that quiet time in the saddle is where many of his best ideas are germinated. One day on his way to work, he thought about brewing an Imperial IPA. He first inventoried the hops on hand and then made it with generous doses of Cascade, Centennial, Chinook and Columbus hops. It was called Four Seas.

With Kolada, the three brought a host of other traditions to Columbus as well, from the shaker pint to firkin and cask conditioning. Firkin' Friday featured a keg on top of the bar with a minimal cooling sleeve that poured from gravity and slowly let air into the cask. As the weekend wore on, the flavor would change slightly as the beer oxygenated. Cask-conditioned beers were filtered less and carbonated naturally in the keg. Barley's annual homebrew competition, begun in 1996, was a good PR move and a way to inject yet another beer style and origin into the mix. The winner of each year's competition gets to have that beer brewed on premises and served at the next year's event.

The Barley's story wasn't so different from that of Hoster's. As Jeff Edwards reinvented the Brewery District, another businessman, Dean Skillman, led a quintet of developers from Toledo in search of a location for their brewery. They landed in an old streetcar trolley barn at the corner of South High and Hoster Streets, a couple blocks away from CBC. The street was named for Louis Hoster, founder of the city's first major brewery, which opened in 1836 and dominated central Ohio brewing for most of the following century. Given the address, it was only fitting that his new business should be named Hoster Brewing Company (the copyright to the Hoster name had lapsed, according to Skillman). Skillman said that Louis's great-great-grandson Jay Hoster had continually renewed copyright to the name until the year the Toledo concern went looking for it. The new Hoster opened in 1991 and, within six months, went in search of a new brewer. The first one, Greg Beaston, made "crap product," according to Skillman. When his replacement came, said Skillman, "we boiled up a bunch of water and threw in some bleach and bleached and cleaned the whole brewery." Beaston, apparently, was not skilled at brewing's number one rule: cleanliness.

Allen Young had not only won awards as a homebrewer in California, he also went to college in San Francisco during the mid-1970s brewery

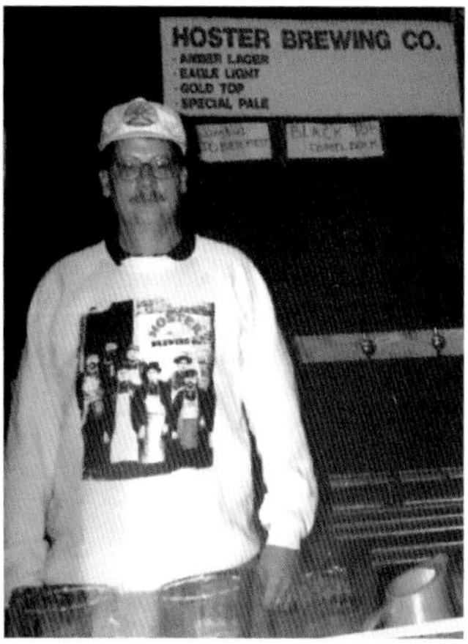

Allen Young, officially the second brewmaster at Hoster's beginning in 1992 but the first to bring the rigor of traditional German brewing back to Columbus. *Courtesy Allen Young.*

boom. A tour of the Anchor Steam Brewery in its original location was for him a turning point. He left determined to become a brewer. He took brewing classes at the UC Davis Extension. (The program, the first of its kind in the United States, was begun by microbiologist Michael Lewis in 1970.) From there, he apprenticed with German braumeister Wolfgang Roth at Virginia Beach micro Chesapeake Brewing Company, an early entrant in the craft brew movement. Young recently remembered, "I was classically trained to brew German style beers according to the Bavarian Purity Law, and that's what I brought back to German Village."

Before coming to Columbus, about which he knew nothing, Young found a recounting of the town's brewing history in a small volume called *A Brief History of the Breweries of German Village*, written by Wayne David Foster. Found today in the Columbus Metropolitan Library, the book resembles a self-published poetry chapbook. Still, it was perhaps the only general history of Columbus's rich brewing past available in book form at the time. Young read the abridged history on the plane when he came to interview for the brewmaster job at Hoster in 1992

He ended up at Plank's Bier Garten for dinner the night he arrived. There he observed two men meeting about a brewery and introduced himself as a visiting brewer interviewing for a job at Hoster. When Young asked if the two knew of the author of the brewing history book he'd been reading, one revealed that he was its author, David Foster. Young would get to know Foster well over the next few years, as a collector of local brewing memorabilia at first, and as an assistant later. Young was about to reinterpret the German brewing tradition of the original Hoster Brewery, established in 1836.

Foster became a fellow brewer a few years later when he opened a nano-brewery that attempted to recreate Gambrinius's German lagers.

Though Young never saw any of the original Hoster's recipes, he set about recreating them with newer beers in the spirit of Hoster's famed Gold Top, Wiener Beer and Eagle Dark. According to Young, the old brewers chose to write down as little as possible in order to guarantee the secrecy of their specific technique. Jay Hoster has said that nothing was saved

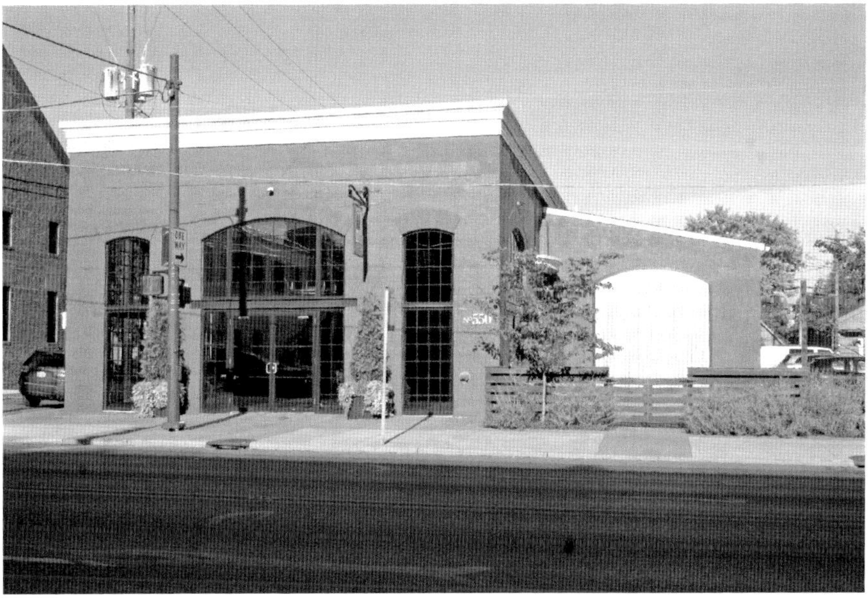

The building at 550 South High Street that housed the reborn Hoster Brewing Company in the 1990s. *Photo by the author.*

from the old brewery when his forefathers walked away from it in 1920. For its interpretation, the new Hoster's brought in traditional brewmaster Karl Strauss, who based the new ones on styles he had brewed in Germany before the war. Then Young convinced Skillman and his partners to turn Hoster into a brewpub, bringing Chef Charles Langstaff into the fold after an introduction made by Doral Chenoweth (aka local food reporter the "Grumpy Gourmet").

In the meantime, Foster parlayed his adolescent interest in collecting beer cans, bottles, memorabilia and history into a brief but deeply rooted brewing career. He got to know Ed Heller, the last brewmaster at Gambrinus before its demise in 1974, who befriended him and later taught him to brew. Foster met Alexander O. Hostettler, the grandson of Hoster and Wagner brewmaster Alex Hostettler; Foster interviewed and acquired books and recipes from Peter Wittman, the last brewmaster at Washington Brewery, which closed in late 1952.

Foster is most proud, though, of getting to know Helen Wagner, August's daughter and heir to the business after his death in 1944 and its vice president in the 1950s and '60s. Helen, who took brewing classes herself, was not only an inspiration to Foster but also helped him take the first steps toward

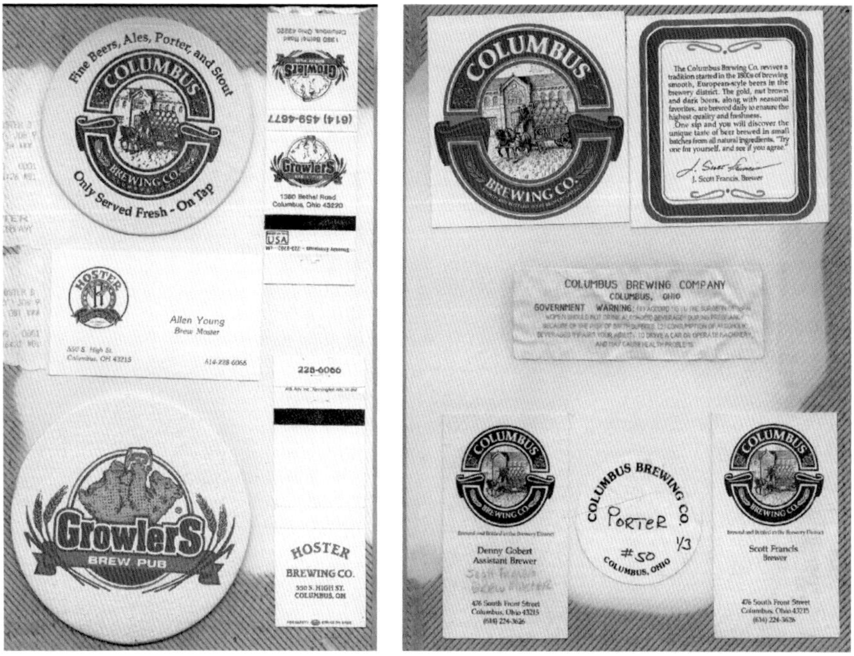

Promotional items and memorabilia from the rebirth of craft brewing in Columbus, including matches from Hosters and the short-lived brewpub Growlers, Allen Young's business card, coasters from Columbus and Growler's and a keg sticker for CBC's fine porter.. *Courtesy David Foster collection.*

opening his own brewery. She introduced him to Fred Holdridge, co-owner of Hausfrau Haven with his partner Howard Burns and the unofficial mayor of the German Village neighborhood that grew up around the nineteenth-century breweries. Foster was invited to display his collection at the area's annual Octoberfest celebration, where he met Andy Schmidt of Schmidt's Sausage Haus.

In the late 1980s, Schmidt revealed to Foster that his family was planning an addition to their classic German restaurant chain in Westerville, just north of Columbus. The idea, according to Foster, was to make it a brewpub, so Schmidt invited Foster to run the brewery. He employed the hopeful brewer in the German Village restaurant while plans took shape. The brewery was never built.

By the time Schmidt's abandoned its scheme, sometime after 1992, Hoster's was running full steam under the direction of Allen Young, who hired Foster as his assistant. After a year or so there, though, Foster left to aid in the move of the failed Growlers Brewpub from Bethel Road in Columbus to Dayton.

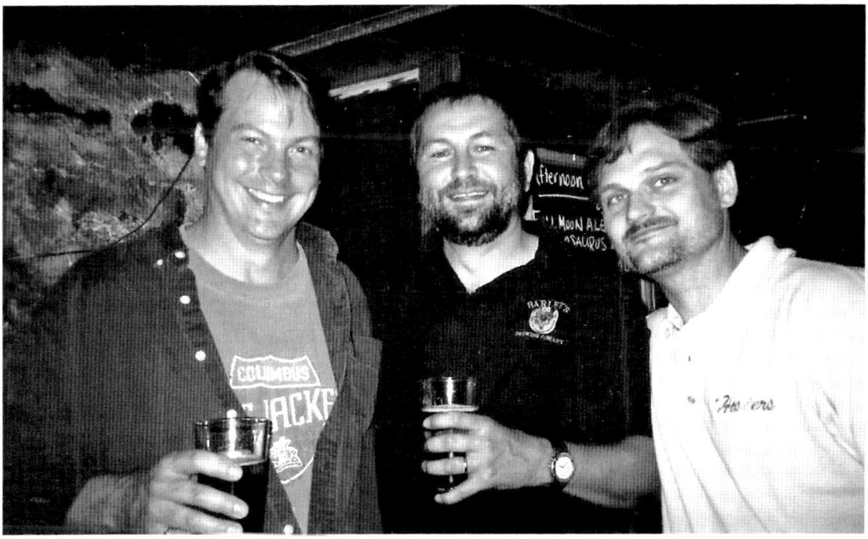

Brewing "summit," mid-1990s, including from left to right: Ben Pridgeon, who would lead CBC into the modern American styles of craft brewing; Francis; and Hoster brewmaster Victor Ecimovich III. *Courtesy Nina Hawranick.*

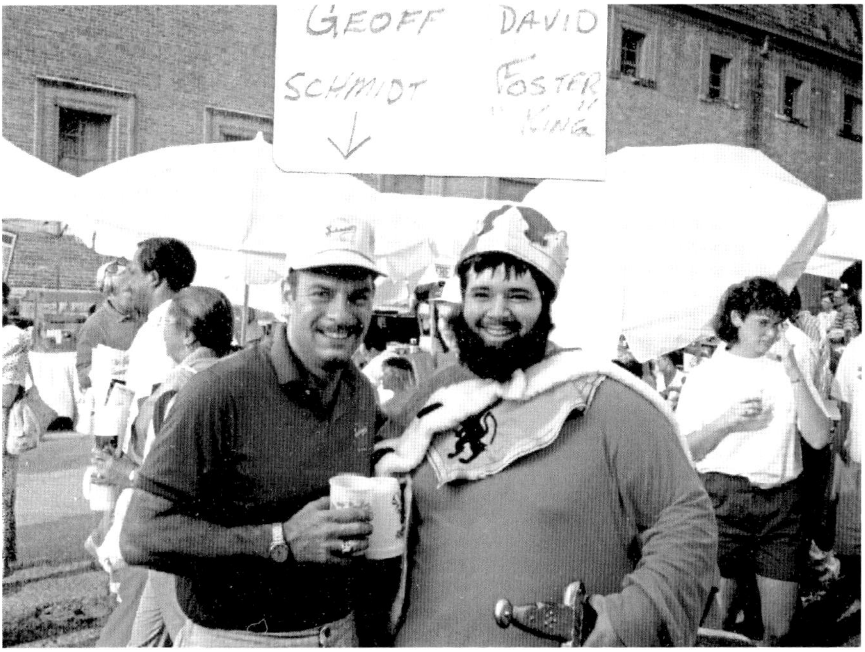

David Foster with Geoff Schmidt, who would plot a failed plan for a Schmidt's brewpub in Westerville. *David Foster collection.*

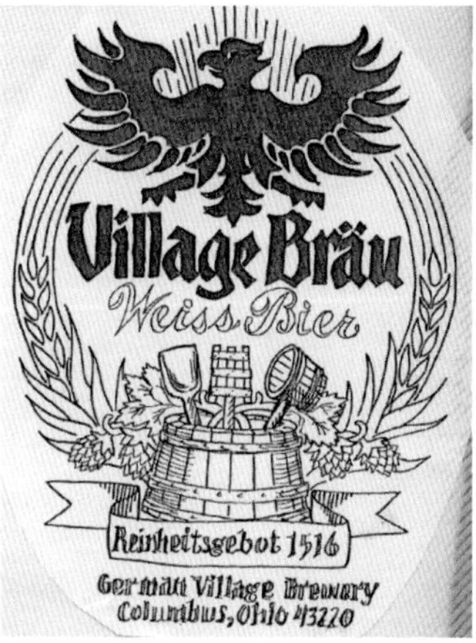

Proposed logo for Schmidt's brew, including a tribute to the German brewing purity law of 1516. Planned for Westerville, the brewpub was never built. *David Foster collection.*

In the fall of 1993, Foster came to realize his dream, a culmination of decades collecting brewing history and several years as a brewer learning the traditional trade. With the blessing of Helen Wagner—and legal use of the Gambrinus name, labels and legacy—he opened the Gambrinus microbrewery in a small warehouse space behind the White Castle at High Street and Greenlawn Avenue. Not only did Foster register the brand (the copyright for which apparently had lapsed since the Pittsburgh Brewing Company acquired the Gambrinus assets for the final years before its demise), but he also had Helen Wagner's promise to sign off on any legal conflict in the use of the original labels and artwork.

With a 3.5 barrel (bbl.) brewhouse and 7 bbl. fermenters culled from a failed California micro, he began brewing Gambrinus, producing Augustiner, Gambrinus Quality Pale Ale and Gambrinus Bock, among others.

Foster was counting on the legacy of the Gambrinus brand—and the continuation of one-hundred-year-old habits of beer drinking. Francis and Young were on the forefront of a reinvention of European traditions to come, a movement that would be inspired by traditional English ales and German lagers but evolve to establish a distinctly American style of brewing, marked by rule-breaking creativity, the improvisational spirit of the emerging new American cuisine and, eventually, the restless millennial palate.

It is hard to imagine today, with the explosion of craft brewing in Columbus, that in the 1990s it was very much still an uphill battle to find a market. Foster's Gambrinus never made it to the new golden era, succumbing in 1998 to the fading of traditional style. But CBC, Barley's and Hoster were part of the generation of brewers popping up across the nation that initiated the dialogue about flavorful, locally brewed beer, ushering in an era when what they brewed soon came to be called "craft beer."

In the early 1990s, they were mostly winging it, though. Reflecting the camaraderie that still exists among brewers, Young and Francis took their show on the road in those days, tag-teaming for tastings at local pubs. "We

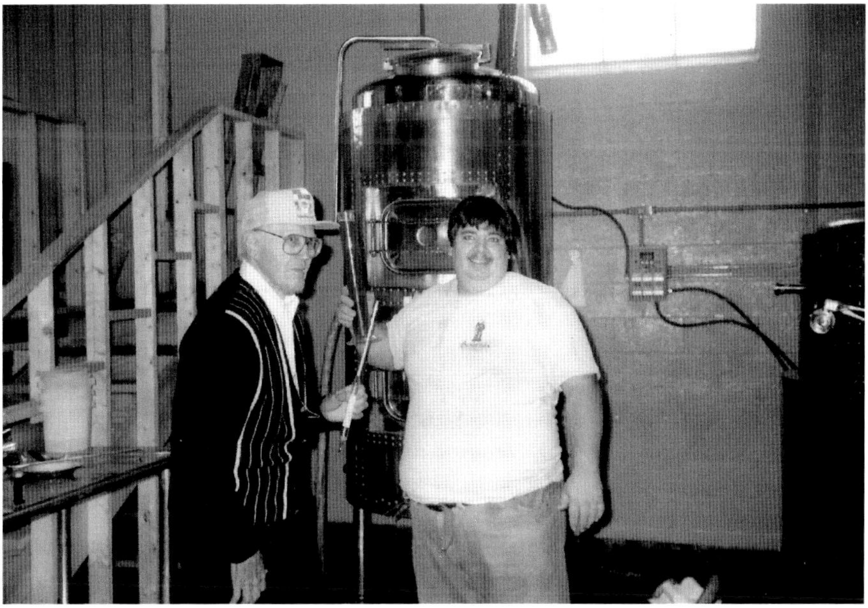

Foster brewing the first batch of the revived Gambrinus brand with advice from Ed Heller, the last brewmaster at Gambrinus. *David Foster collection.*

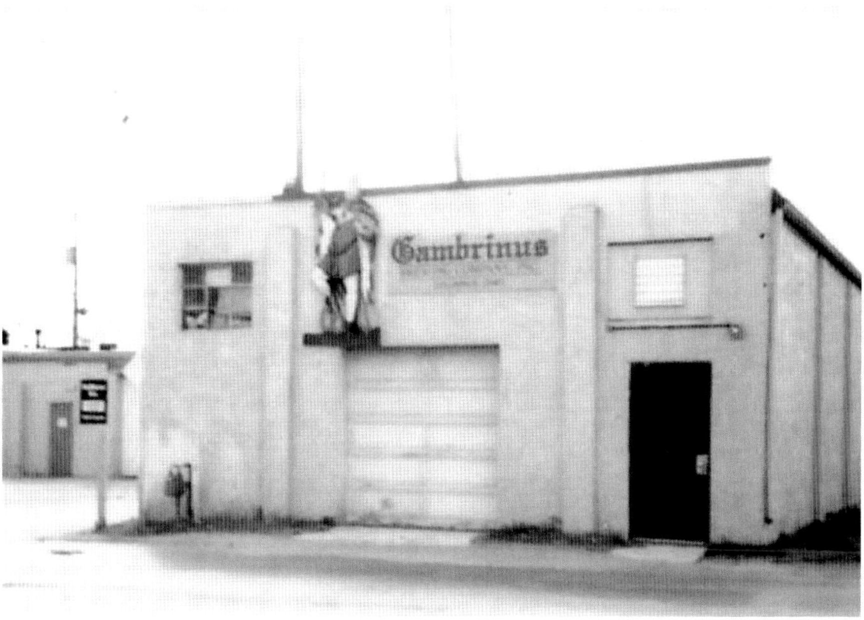

The new Gambrinus brewery, behind the White Castle on Greenlawn and High, where Foster attempted to rejuvenate the brand with the blessing of August Wagner's daughter Helen. *David Foster collection.*

had a great two-man show worked out after a few sessions," said Young. "They were great times we shared."

"We weren't fighting the big breweries," Francis remembered. "We were fighting the low mentality of bar managers. The demand wasn't there. Allen and I would drive around in my pickup truck with a couple kegs of his Gold Top and a couple kegs of my Columbus Pale Ale, and we'd stop in bars. Allen and I would do beer tastings at pubs and bookstores together, because at that time you are trying to show the public that there's something other than what you know. I couldn't give kegs of beer away."

Francis continued selling his ales in select locations locally. The hip and now-legendary club Stache's was among his top customers. Distribution at first for his ales, which tasted nothing like the corporate American pilsners that dominated the shelves at carryouts, grocery stores and in bars, was left to one man and one small pickup. Young's Hoster product, which in a couple of years included twenty-ounce, hand-sealed bottles as well as kegs, also depended on the brewery crew to get around town.

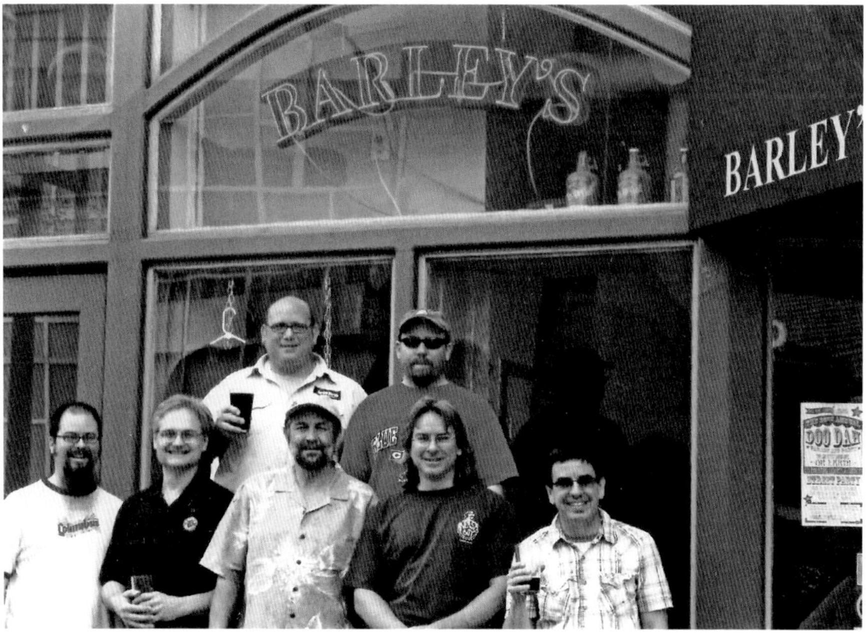

"Afternoon with the Brewers," 2009. *From left to right, top row*: Chris Alltmont (Gordon Biersch) and Vic Schiltz (Elevator); *lower row*: Eric Bean (CBC), Victor Ecimovich III (Hoster's), Scott Francis (Barley's, etc.), Jay Wince (Weasel Boy)and Angelo Signorino (Barley's) in front of Barley's. *Courtesy Nina Hawranick.*

About the time that CBC introduced Columbus 1492 Lager, though, Hill Distributing picked up the brewery's distribution. The 1492 product was based on a recipe Francis created but had contract-brewed by FX Matt Brewing Company, a family brewery in Utica, New York. Its sales topped the company's projections, even though its production life pretty much coincided with the 500th anniversary of America's discovery by the Spanish.

A few West Coast microbrewed ales, most notably Anchor and later Sierra Nevada, began to come into the Columbus market about that time, thanks to Robins Wine & Spirits, which already had a respectable portfolio of English ales, German lagers and a couple of Belgian ales.

Robins was the first to get the idea that there just might be something to this new brew thing. The company picked up both CBC and Hoster for distribution in Columbus. Dan Tarpy, who worked for Robins until it was sold to Glazer's Distributors recently and was part of Tarpy's Beverage and Delicatessen in the Kingsdale shopping center, remembers that it was a tough sell.

Tarpy conducted innumerable beer tastings at the family's deli, during which he found grad students and professors from Ohio State generally more worldly and open to the flavorful beer. He mixed local and American microbreweries with imports such as Samuel Smith's and a few Belgians. Occasionally, he would pop a Budweiser and serve it alongside a Guiness stout, just to make the point that alcohol strength and the amount of grain that goes into a beer is not necessarily directly proportional to the perceived flavor intensity.

With distribution at Hoster, Young began bottling more beer, and production grew to a breaking point. Young landed equipment for a new expansion and then moved on, becoming first the U.S. rep for Germany's Beraplan brewing equipment company, the supplier of Hoster's new brewhouse.

Victor Ecimovich III replaced Young at Hoster in 1995. He finished the expansion, pushing even further into bottling and off-site distribution. The new equipment went in smoothly with the help of a German village architect/contractor team. Though Victor and his crew had to work twelve-hour days seven days a week for a couple of months, they filled every order.

Plus, he expanded the stylistic variety, adding English and Belgians, tapping considerable previous experience heading the likes of Millstream in Amana, Iowa, Summit in St. Paul and Goose Island in Chicago. Ecimovich, in fact, is the grandson of a brewer.

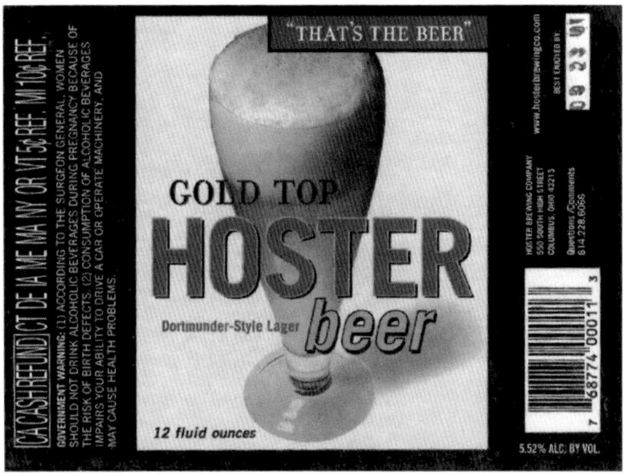

A bottle label from Hoster's revival of the Gold Top brand, circa 2001, the old brewery's top seller before Prohibition and the signature brew for the reborn marque nearly a century later. Note the expiration date in the corner. *Courtesy Jay Hoster.*

Ecimovich didn't plan to overthrow Young's vision but, rather, simply to augment it. He began brewing ales, especially Belgians, including a fine Saison. He diversified the German selection, as well, adding a traditional Kolsch to the mix. Though the last one can be found in a few contemporary local breweries, his was strict, echoing the exquisite, refreshing examples he had in Cologne, where the style originated.

Ecimovich remembers the educational curve as still pretty steep in the mid-1990s. "Most people either drank liquor or wine or they drank Budweiser or Miller," he remembered. He was reassured to see folks who'd traveled enjoy his beer and was thrilled to watch older drinkers who'd been in the service overseas find a brew they liked better than corporate American suds.

The larger resistance began to evaporate by the end of the millennium, though. Barley's was doing well enough by then for Kolada and business partner Ron Jezerinac to plan a spin-off. In the summer of 1998, they opened Barley's Smokehouse & Brewpub, initially Ale House No. 2. When Kolada cashed out of Barley's in 2013, the newer business was renamed Smokehouse Brewing Company. It continues to produce many of the beers first brewed there, including Alexander's Russian Imperial Stout, MacLenny's Scottish Ale and Bombshell Blonde Lager, designed by brewmaster Scott Francis. Scott's son Alex worked there as well and continues today to work with his father at Westerville's Temperance Row.

In 1999, though, things didn't go as planned, and the business was shuttered about a year after it opened. Kolada took over full ownership, and it reopened several months later. At the Smokehouse without partners, Kolada was able to be more creative again. Special programs have included more than a dozen years of the Mini Real Ale Festival and several years of a special night honoring Scottish poet Robert Burns.

Signorino became head brewer when Francis left in early 2011. He continued in that role for two years after Kolada's separation from downtown Barley's. After the arrival of Sam Hickey from Boston's Mystic Brewery in 2015, Signorino devoted himself full-time to Barley's. Hickey, originally from central Ohio, brought his experience with unique fermentation and hop recipes to the Smokehouse. Thus far, he has experimented with a gruit—a beer substituting botanicals for hops—and is developing a yeast strain sourced locally to be used in a future brew. In 2015, he brewed Old School Barleywine, a high-gravity, high-alcohol ale that is so traditional it features hops of the unknown strains that grow outside the brewery windows. Those hops were planted more than eighteen years ago by Francis and Nina Hawranick, both of whom, according to Kolada, have forgotten the original strains.

Signorino's stint at Barley's, which continues still, represented the next wave of craft brewers, most of them veterans of operations headed by Young and Francis.

Ben Pridgeon, a brilliant local musician and avid homebrewer, worked for Francis while the groundbreaking local brewer moved most of his energy into Barley's. Pridgeon spent some time in New York City, returning to Columbus in 1992, where he ran into Francis and began almost immediately to work with him and Falcone. Pridgeon accompanied the master brewer to five different breweries, learning about a diverse set of equipment on the job. When Falcone left, he took over as head brewer for the company and oversaw its move to a new building at the west end of Liberty Street in tandem with an independently owned restaurant also sporting the name Columbus Brewing Company.

Pridgeon remembers Francis's distaste for the nuts and bolts of a production brewery. "Scott was never intrigued with the idea of a production facility," he said recently. "Tracking cooperage, negotiating wholesale contracts, introducing bottled products, etc. I was fascinated with all of that."

So when Pridgeon took over in 1995, he negotiated, designed and oversaw building of the new facility, which opened the next year. Impressively, he also undertook a seven-week tour with local band R.C. Mob that year. Pridgeon is likely also one of the first to brew a hoppy, American-style ale in Columbus. His brother had lived on the Oregon coast, where Ben became familiar with Rogue, Pyramid and Redhook, early purveyors of the now-dominant new style. He also got CBC in the mammoth, venerable Community Festival, where during three days in

June the brewery would sell about 250 kegs. Still, Pridgeon admits that imagining that the American IPA would be the fastest-growing style in the United States today was inconceivable in the mid-1990s.

It would have been further from believable in 1994, when Pridgeon was still working with the English ale recipes developed by Scott Francis. These brews, though, had won accolades as far away as England in the favorable notice that famed English beer writer Michael Jackson gave Columbus Brewery in his *Pocket Guide to Beer*, a portable tour of breweries around the world.

On March 3, 1994, Pridgeon answered a knock on CBC's Brewers Alley door, only to find Jackson, his own rumpled self, popping in for a visit. After a leisurely conversation, Pridgeon insisted that Jackson go to Barley's to meet the godfather of Columbus brewing, Scott Francis. Select members of the press, including myself, were tipped, and a long, very pleasant afternoon was had by all in Barley's over a bunch of fine ales.

Vince Falcone, who began with Francis and was soon "stolen" by Young, would go on to be the head brewer at Elevator Brewing, which opened in 1999 and was the last of the early phase of the brewing rebirth in Columbus. While he was with Young, Falcone learned the tradition of German brewing

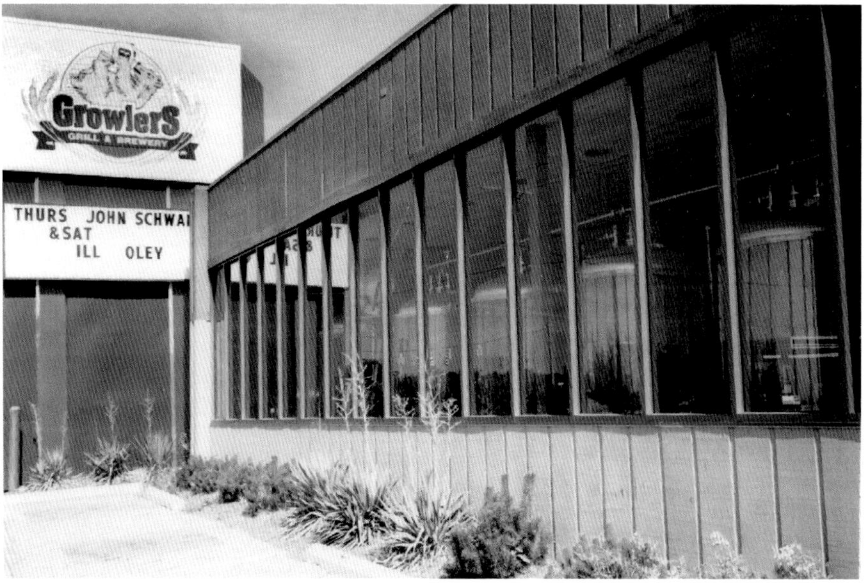

Growlers Grill and Brewery, likely 1991, on the city's unhip north side, didn't stand a chance, with unskilled brewers and a relatively unreceptive audience. *David Foster archive.*

from a master. When Victor Ecimovich took Young's place, the education continued along slightly different, nonetheless traditional lines. In addition, Ecimovich began experimenting with a hoppier, American-style pale ale. Falcone remembers wondering just what the brewery's Rev. Purley Ale would taste like after they first brewed it, because it had so much more hops in it.

Falcone met Ryan Stevens's roommate while working at Hoster's in the mid-1990s. When Falcone needed to find an apartment a few years later, he went to Stevens's father, Dick, then a successful real estate owner. Dick Stevens asked Falcone if he'd like to open a brewery in Marysville in conjunction with a restaurant named Elevator Company built in an old grain elevator. The existence of the brewery would allow the restaurant to have a complete liquor license as well as sell its beer. A structure was added to the building, and the brewery began production in September 1999.

The relationship between the two entities was never very good, according to both Stevens and Falcone. Both remember delivery trucks filling the restaurant with major corporate beer from the day Falcone finished his first batch. It became clear that the brewery was just the means to an end for the restauranteurs. Falcone did his own distribution for a time, driving the beer to Columbus.

In March 2000, Stevens and a couple of partners opened the Elevator Brewery and Draught Haus in downtown Columbus in the old Clock building at 161 North High Street. A nano-brewing system downstairs in the restaurant allowed it to get its own liquor license.

Falcone began by brewing seven beers deriving from both the English and German traditions he'd learned from his iconic Columbus mentors, including a light lager, helles lager, pale ale, ESB, hefeweizen, doppelbock and porter. Interestingly, the Elevator Restaurant was about midway between Barley's and Hoster, and it brewed a mix of both of those companies' traditions. Dick Stevens named the restaurant with the English spelling of "draft" and the German spelling of "house." He designed a couple of clever tasting programs around the range of styles available from his brewery, called MBA (Master in Beer Appreciation) and PHD (Professor of Hearty Drinking.)

Opening the restaurant and trucking beer to Columbus took its toll on Falcone, as did the loss of Chris Wilson, Falcone's best friend and lead singer in his band, Monster Truck Five. Falcone left Elevator in 2002, returning home to Cleveland for a time. After working for a couple of breweries in northwest Ohio, he returned to Columbus in 2007 to head a bold experiment in Reynoldsburg called Mulholland. The brewery, which produced all the styles Falcone had interpreted over the years, tried a few new ones, as well, only in a small suburb on the eastern edge of Columbus.

Falcone remembers the burg embracing his beer. Management, investment and timing all conspired to sink the project within a year of its establishment, though. Falcone said the project was underfunded, the "financial manager was of dubious ethics, and we were week to week as far as paying the bills and payroll." He added, "The executive chef assaulted a server and was jailed on the third night of operation."

The nascent local scene and the blossoming national craft scene in the late 1980s and early '90s needed distribution to take it all to the next level. The time was right for a local distributor to specialize in craft beers, bring the new world of beer to Columbus and take the results of central Ohio's first steps beyond the city.

Robbins took on CBC and Hoster's by the mid-1990s, so when Ron Wilson opened Premium Beverage Supply in 1995, he focused on fine new breweries across the United States. He began with just six: Birmingham Brewing from Alabama; Gritty McDuff's and Casco Bay Brewing from Portland, Maine; American River Brewing from Auburn, California; Sudwerk Brewing from Davis, California; and H.C. Berger from Fort Collins, Colorado. He scooped up Foster's Gambrinus to support the locals. Though they were the purview of Robbins in Columbus, Premium also handled Cleveland's successful Great Lakes in Dayton and Cincinnati and CBC outside of Columbus in the late 1990s.

Wilson cut his teeth at a distributor in Chicago, so he already understood the business and had contacts with new breweries. The first years often posed an educational challenge, he remembered, especially in traditional carryouts and bars where he had to "shoehorn the damn beer in and hold it like crazy" because the Bud and Miller guys would pitch a fit. He found specialty outlets eager to carry his product. It was easy for him to bring in hip craft beers from all over the country because, unlike Cleveland and its iconic Great Lakes, Columbus didn't have a local brewery presence strong enough to "guard the gates" to keep the nationals out.

Even though his business didn't take off as fast as he would have liked, Wilson looks back on the late 1990s as an exciting time, one in which the brewing world seemed reborn and selling craft beer was something like presenting the gospel to neophytes. Everything seemed possible. He got in on the ground floor with brands such as Bells, Founders and Southern Tier, all of which were producing just a few thousand barrels a year then. He brought in Flying Dog in 1997 and Abita in '99. Today, they're among the big dogs of regional craft.

Then, mysteriously, at the turn of the millennium, craft beer growth stalled. CBC felt it, Jeff Edwards noting that imports began to take back some of the admittedly still meager market share. Ron Wilson felt it, as well. "I thought it would move a little quicker in those first five years than it did," he said. "It kinda got going and then it stalled a little bit, late 1990s."

Perhaps that downturn after the initial blush also had something to do with Hoster's gradual failing, with the restaurant closing in 2001 and the brewery following soon after. Ecimovich cited a couple of factors that may have played a role, including the brewery's switching distributors, causing interruption in the beer's availability, and Hoster's having to compete with a new portfolio for attention. The city's nightlife focus was shifting as well, he said, to glitzy new suburban shopping areas such as Easton and Polaris. Intermittently since the brewery closed, copyright and recipe owners Ecimovich and Dan Meyers have contracted the brewery's classic Gold Top, itself a re-creation of the original brewery's early 1900s flagship, to regional breweries in Toledo and Cleveland and, in late in 2016, to Springfield's Mother Stewart's Brewing Company, making it available in short supply.

The early twenty-first century was an uneventful time for craft brewing in Columbus. In fact, Elevator would be the last significant new opening in town for another dozen years, at which time a whole new, bigger wave of brewing barnstormed Columbus and a handful of new faces came on the scene. Though Barley's continued with Signorino at the helm, Elevator and CBC found new brewers who ushered them into the current phase of craft brewing, allowing all three breweries to successfully bridge the subtle but substantial changes in brewing that had occurred since its local rebirth in 1989.

During the lull, Hops Restaurant, Bar & Brewery, a chain of more than sixty such establishments nationwide, opened locations at Polaris Town Center in 1999 and Easton Town Center in 2000. Small nano-breweries on the premises brewed stock recipes provided by the chain's master brewer. Financial problems forced chainwide belt-tightening, and both locations closed by 2002. On the upside, though, Hops' closing set brewer Vic Schiltz free, sending him packing and looking for a new gig. He landed at Elevator in the mid-aughts, first driving the delivery truck and soon taking over as brewmaster. He oversaw the brewery's move from Marysville to its current location at 165 North Fourth Street, just a couple of blocks from the restaurant. He continued to expand its stylistic offerings until summer 2017.

Gordon Biersch opened a chain pub and brewery in the Arena District in 2001 that, while it must be counted among new brewing operations, as a chain it had as much in common with big business as it did with the burgeoning craft brew movement. Though it featured refined, traditionally styled brews produced on the premises, it relied on a national business model and limited experimentation.

On the plus side, Biersch gave Columbus brewer Eric Bean, who would take the helm at CBC in 2006 and lead it into the next phase of craft brewing when he bought in at 40 percent soon thereafter. In 2010, Bean and his wife, Beth, bought the rest of the brewery and took it to the next level of success, maxing out the 525 Short Street location and making plans to dramatically expand the brewery by moving it to the west side in 2015. Eric and Beth look to the new location to be good for at least fifty thousand bbl. per year.

2

EARLY DAYS

A small ad appearing in the *Western Intelligencer* of May 4, 1814, and dated April 26, announced Columbus's first brewery: "Hops Wanted. The subscriber will pay the highest price in cash for good HOPS, WHEAT or, BARLEY, delivered at his Brewery in Columbus. John M'Coy [*sic*]."

John McCoy's plot, just north and a little west of today's corner of Front and Liberty Streets, interestingly staked out a foothold in the area that would become the brewing center of Columbus for the next century and a half beginning with Louis Hoster's City Brewery in 1836.

It contained a log cabin, twenty-five feet by twenty-five feet, in which records indicate lived a distiller. The ad above and a few historical references indicate that he brewed there as well. His structure was on the low side of Peters Run, which was spring-fed and likely the water supply for his activities. Little more information is available about the brewery and its product, though it is likely that McCoy was brewing English-style ales. Mention is made in various documents from the time of a distillery located on Front Street on a parcel around today's Liberty Street that may have doubled as a brewery. His brew, like that produced since colonial days, was probably as much a source of pure water as refreshment.

Columbus was still wilderness as the nineteenth century began. Franklinton had been founded by Lucas Sullivant in 1797 to the west of what was to become the capital city. A bit north, Worthington flourished since its establishment in 1803, the year Ohio became a state. Franklin County was created by the first general assembly of Ohio in 1803.

Worthington was designed by its founder, James Kilbourne, who led a group of settlers from the Farmington River valley in Connecticut and Massachusetts to the site in 1802 and mapped sixteen thousand acres precisely to function as a village. Before Columbus was even founded, Worthington, about fifteen miles north, had not only a newspaper office that doubled as a library but also a general store with imported goods and, soon, even a school.

Columbus's frontier plot was more generally planned in 1810 around the idea of centrally reestablishing the state capital, which formerly had been situated in Chillicothe and for a short time in Zanesville. A quartet of landowners, Lyne Starling, John Kerr, Alexander McLaughlin and James Johnson, proposed moving the state capital to a new town just south of the center of today's city, for which they would contribute plots. The plan was accepted by the state legislature in February 1812, with parcels set aside for a square with public buildings, including a statehouse and a penitentiary, the latter to provide inmate labor to build the new town. Sale of lots in the new capital began on June 18, 1812, the same day as the formal declaration of war with England.

Almost as quickly, Columbus gained a physician, Dr. John M. Edmiston, in 1814; lawyers David Smith, Orris Parish, David Scott and Gustavus Swan around 1815; and a subscription school in the winter of 1813–14. A Presbyterian congregation began meeting in a log cabin on Spring and Third Streets, and a Methodist Society formed on Town Street beginning in 1814.

The area saw its first newspaper established, the *Freeman's Chronicle*, published in Franklinton beginning in 1814 and folding two years later. Worthington's *Western Intelligencer* moved to Columbus in 1814, becoming the *Western Intelligencer and Columbus Gazette* in 1817. Columbus and Franklinton remained separate towns, though the first bridge over the Scioto linking the two was built by Sullivant in 1816. Columbus took over as Franklin County seat from the older settlement in 1824. Franklinton wasn't officially annexed into Columbus until 1870.

Public records, newspaper advertisements and historical documents show that at least three more brewing concerns were active in the area after McCoy and before Hoster's City Brewery was founded in 1836. In this chapter, we will look at the two English ale establishments; the first German brewery will appear later.

Charles Truman owned a grocery on High Street likely just north of State and High, with a brewery north of that. An announcement appeared in the *Columbus Gazette* on January 17, 1822, informing the public that "the brewery belonging to Charles Trueman [*sic*], north of the State House, in Columbus, is in full operation, where may be had PORTER, ALE, AND STRONG BEER, of superior quality." The ad, which also offered cash for six hundred bushels of barley, was signed "THOMAS Brenden, Brewer."

His brewery was short-lived. Truman must have died the next year, as probate court documents list items in his estate in August 1823, including brewing equipment, some of which was sold at an estate sale in October.

The recently revised edition of Donald M. Schlegel's well-researched and finely detailed *Lager and Liberty: German Brewers of Nineteenth Century Columbus*, names John Abbott's Columbus Brewery, established at the northwest corner of Spring and Front Streets in 1832, "the first of what one might call the 'professional' breweries of Columbus, with a substantial building designed and erected for that specific purpose." Though Pennsylvania native Abbott founded the brewery—another source says in 1830—the property was owned by Elijah Converse, leading to the building, according to Schlegel, sometimes called "Converse's brewery."

It went up for sale in 1835 in order to dissolve the partnership of Abbott and Converse. The listing in the *Ohio State Journal* of November 27, 1835, is significant for several reasons, including the building's structure of brick and stone; the brewery's capacity of two thousand to three thousand barrels per year; and on-hand stock including two thousand bushels of barley, one thousand bushels of malt and twelve hundred pounds of hops. The kiln was covered in English tile, the malt floors flagged and grouted. An added come-on included the use of the newly opened Ohio Canal feeder line to supply surrounding towns.

It didn't sell but continued operating. Ads in the *Ohio State Journal* in 1837 and 1838 solicited barley and advertised beer, ale and porter for sale. During a series of complicated financial arrangements, during which John Keating briefly took control, the property and business finally limped to a collapse. It was auctioned and ended production late in 1842.

The brewery was notable in employing Louis Hoster in 1835 and providing the springboard for Hoster's City Brewery, the iconic early German brewery founded the next year. Hoster's was the first large-scale Columbus brewery and the one that lasted the longest, from 1836 to 1920.

A more complicated history accompanied the North Brewery, perhaps founded in 1834 by John Marcy. The property at the corner of Front Street and Mulberry Alley was owned by James Woods beginning in 1826, but a tax record from 1831 mentions equipment for a brewery valued at $300.

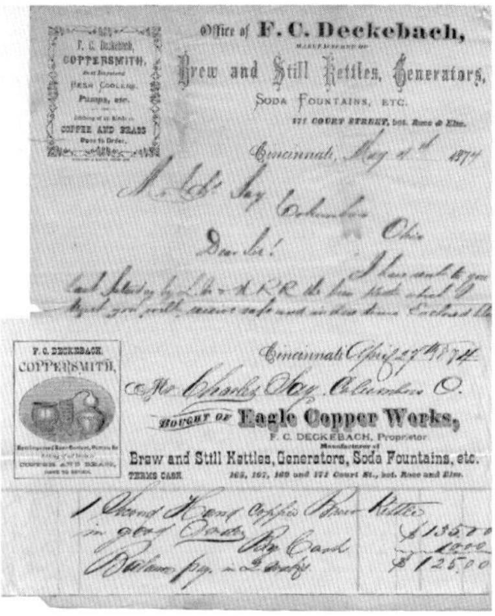

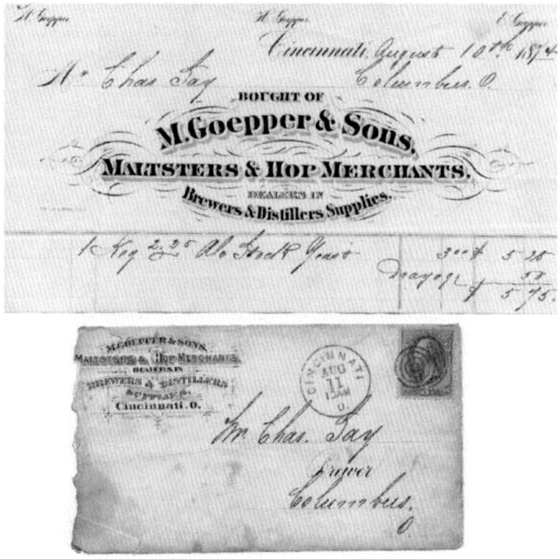

Left: Receipt for brew kettle construction for the Say Brewery, dated 1874. David Foster found this treasure-trove of history in a trunk at a yard sale. Note the price of the custom-built kettle: $125. *David Foster collection.*

Right: More Say memorabilia, including a receipt for ale stock yeast from a maltster in Cincinnati. *David Foster collection.*

Though Marcy is an English name, according to Schlegel he was German, arriving from Hamburg in the mid-1820s.

Marcy's brewing days were short-lived, as he died on January 4, 1836. His property was purchased by real estate dealer Christopher Niswanger, who did not brew there. Production resumed in 1849 when Niswanger sold the holdings to three of four English brothers, William, Joseph and Charles Say. Named North, it was located north of the brewing center, farther south on Front Street. Producing "Say's Ale," the partnership continued until 1852, when William and, later, Joseph sold their interests. Still, an article in the *Ohio State Journal* in 1860 tagged the brewery's production at ten thousand barrels per year. The city directory for 1864 lists only Charles brewing at the Front and Mulberry address. A year later, Charles sold the North Brewery to John T. Davis and Daniel Cushing, who ran it as Davis & Company. After a partial sale to Joseph H. Nevett, the company was named Nevett & Company.

William Say, meanwhile, set up a brewery at a small location on Hickory Alley, then closed it in 1867 and opened another behind his house at 76 East Third Avenue in 1870. His brother Joseph took it in 1872 and continued until 1880.

Charles returned to brewing in 1876 at a location currently Neil Avenue and Spruce Street. Perhaps he was encouraged by the reputation his fine English ales and porters held in a city dominated by German lagers. The book *Industries of Ohio* (1878) declared: "Twenty years ago his beverages were the most popular in the market, and one hundred barrels a week were necessary to supply the demand.…Two years ago he resumed his former business, and is again rapidly regaining his old customers and former prestige…his ale and porter consisting of the choicest malt and hops, devoid of the least admixture of anything beyond pure spring water—not a physician in the city failing to attest to its remarkable adaptability to the sustenance of invalids."

3

EARLY GERMANS

The short and simple narrative explaining today's German Village is that the breweries were on Front Street, south of Livingston, and the workers lived just east and across High Street in the tiny, shotgun-shaped homes that make up the bulk of the contemporary neighborhood. The largest homes farthest east, in today's Old Town East and on Broad Street, belonged to management and company owners.

But in the earliest years, Germans in Columbus settled a bit north and east, closer to what now is the heart of downtown, mostly north of today's Livingston and largely east of High Street. Bernhard Burck was among the first, signing a deed for two lots on the north side of East Fulton Street between High and Third in April 1838. (The homes and brewery are long gone, replaced today by the Franklin County offices' parking garage.) Though there is evidence he developed his lots, proof of Burck's brewing is tangential, according to Donald Schlegel, as the city council granted him a license to sell beer, ale and porter in 1834. Names associated with his business and brand include the Washington Brewery (34 East South in directories of the late 1840s and early 1850s).

Burck was born in Baden, Germany, and came to Columbus in the early 1830s and married Maria Rader here in 1834. Though Rader's family was Lutheran, Burck was Catholic. He was a respected member of that community and significant in the establishment of the first Catholic church, St. Remigius, around 1837. For several years before that, Catholic mass was performed in one of several buildings on the Burck compound

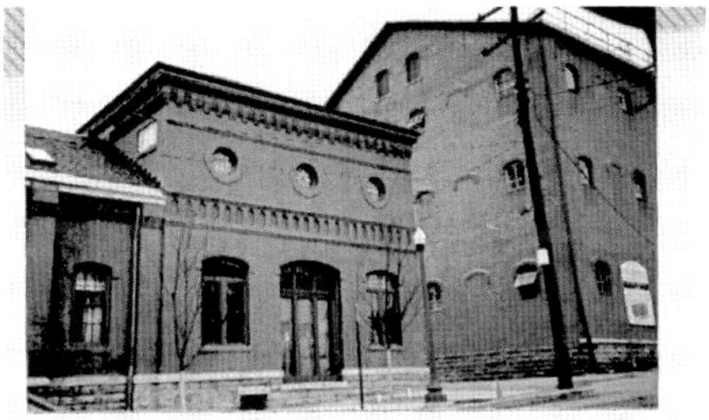

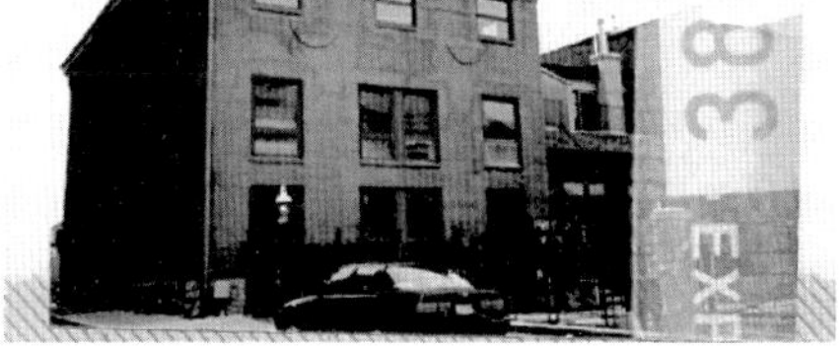

The former Zimmerman brewery building in the 1990s. It operated for a short time in the 1860s; the building was absorbed by Schlee's company in 1885. *David Foster collection.*

for the small but growing Catholic population, according to Schlegel's *Lager and Liberty*.

His brewing activities in another of those structures was revealed in the settlement of his estate following his death on August 29, 1849, including horses, a beer carriage, charcoal, malt, barley, hops and barrels and kegs. Various copper boilers and other equipment were included. Among the appraisers is listed Louis Hoster, the first of the significant German brewers to leave a lasting mark in Columbus.

The brewery was taken over by Bavarian immigrants Frederick Zimmerman, Franz Wuerm and John Hartman in 1850. Wuerm and Burck's widow, Maria, married in 1850, and the new husband took over operation of the brewery. After a couple of years' financial failure, the couple signed the business over to Zimmerman, who operated the brewery as a lease until 1855. He turned it back over to the Burcks, in this case Maria and Bernhard's daughter Margaret and her husband, George Lederer. When Lederer's partner Fred Bauman left in 1858, first Zimmerman came back to run the brewery, then the former Bucyrus brewer Johan Moerch. Finally, Erhard Stoker took the lease in 1865 and continued for a few more years.

Zimmerman, Moerch and Stoker would go on to found breweries of their own.

Zimmerman's first experience brewing was not at Washington Brewery. He and his wife, Phillipina, who with their daughter emigrated from Bavaria, lived at 101 North Front Street, right around the corner from the North Brewery, run by English brothers named Say. It is likely that he worked there and, after he ran Washington, in the bigger breweries in what is today the Brewery District. The family first built a house on the corner of Front and (now) Hoster and later a brewery just east, naming it the Frederick Zimmerman Ale Brewery. The brewery lasted about four years, after which Zimmerman returned to work for the Born brewery across Front Street. He died in Germany during a visit in 1884. His brewery was sold to Nicholas Schlee and was blended into Schlee's Bavarian Brewery complex in 1885.

Moerch, also from Baden, had settled in Bucyrus with his mother, Eva, about 1840. Moerch bought a chunk of land south of town in 1843 with his mother on which he built a brewery. He was successful enough to raise a family, which would eventually include twelve children. A devastating fire destroyed the business in 1857, prompting the sale of the property and a move to Columbus a year later.

Moerch ran the Washington Brewery from 1860 until he opened his own Scioto Brewery, fittingly close to the Scioto River. His mother had purchased the property wedged between the Ohio Canal feeder and South Canal Street (now the center of Bicentennial Park) in 1861 where he began brewing the next year. In a retrospective article in the *Citizen Journal* nearly a century later, writer Ben Hayes said the scuttlebutt back then was that Nicholas Schlee, whose own huge brewery was a favorite in Columbus, preferred to drink Scioto's lager.

The family lived at the brewery for a few years until 1866, when they built a mansion on the other side of what is today Civic Center Drive. The house had the added bonus of a spring in the basement that ran underground to the Scioto and kept the basement cool enough to brew cool-conditioned lagers during the summer.

The good times didn't last very long, though. The day after Anna Maria Moerch birthed the couple's twelfth child, the baby died. Its mother died a dozen days later. Though Moerch remarried less than a year later, he had lost his desire to own a brewery. It was put up for sale in March 1868. Moerch's sons and a son-in-law bought the brewery and continued for a couple of years, but son John's health and subsequent death of tuberculosis prompted the partners to sell it back to the elder.

Moerch senior next sold the business in 1871 to Henry Biehl and George F. Hummel. German immigrants both, Biehl and Hummel had brewing experience, the former at City Brewery, the latter at Bavarian Brewery and Scioto. (City and Bavarian will figure in the next part of our history.) Hummel sold his half to Beihl, and the latter then sold the whole thing back to Moerch. With his money, Biehl bought into City Park Brewery (also featured later in this book.) The elder Moerch closed the brewery in the late 1870s, retired and then died in 1893 at the age of seventy-three.

Erhard Stoker was the last to lease Burck's Washington Brewery, beginning on September 19, 1865. Also an immigrant from Baden, he ran a saloon at 18 West Broad, next to Wall Street where One Columbus stands today. With his son Ferdinand, he began brewing on the premises, with a five-month permit each year. They began brewing full-time in 1865, the same year the hardworking Stoker leased the Washington Brewery. After the lease ran out at the Washington, the Stokers concentrated on their Brewery and Lager Beer Saloon. According to tax records, the capacity was about five hundred barrels per year. In 1868, he built homes for himself and his son on a property he'd bought on Front and Perry and a new brewery behind them, on Bank Alley. The river provided ice to store in order to get the brewers through the summer months.

Their timing was terrific, as the Columbus and Hocking Valley Railroad was laid just west of the brewery about the time it opened. The railroad would take the place of the nearby canal and elevate the district's brewers to a new level of production. The new brewery's capacity was around six hundred barrels. Stoker's death in 1875, a fire in the brewery earlier that year, crippling debts and a failed public auction left the brewery abandoned. According to an article in the *Columbus Dispatch* of July 12, 1879, about the property's destruction the night before, it had changed hands "five or six times" and its then-unknown owner lived in Cincinnati. The cause of the fire was a spark coming from a passing train. The train sparks also caused Fred Stoker's nearby home to catch fire briefly. It is ironic that the rail lines that gave the Stoker brewery its initial boost should bring it down years later.

4

LOUIS HOSTER

1836–1905

Brewing in America received a big boost in the early and mid-1800s from the uncertain political and economic climate in Germany. The resulting influx of immigrants changed the stylistic emphasis of American brewing—from English to German—and established new brewing centers, situated in cities where German immigrants first settled. That had everything to do with transportation, specifically waterways. In the pre–Civil War years and just after, St. Louis benefited from the Mississippi River, Cincinnati from the Ohio River and Milwaukee from Lake Michigan.

For Columbus, it was the Ohio Canal that brought an influx of new population and a big boost in business and trade. With its opening in 1831, the German population that had come up the Mississippi to St. Louis and then via the Ohio suddenly had easy access to central Ohio and the state's rapidly growing capital.

Louis Hoster was the iconic German-born brewer in nineteenth-century Columbus, the most successful and best known of the earliest generation. His brewery, which established the center of Columbus beer making on Front Street south of Livingston, was the longest lasting of all, succumbing to Prohibition in 1920 after an eighty-four-year run. When craft brewing returned to the Capital City in 1989, it began again a few hundred feet across the street from Hoster's first brewery, next to the site of his bottling plant, with the Columbus Brewery. It continued a couple of years later with the revival of the name Hoster Brewing Company with a brewpub located on High and Hoster Streets just two blocks away.

THE CANAL

Perhaps the earliest of Columbus's breweries failed not only because their business affairs seemed to be in disorder but also because the city lacked a good network to transport supplies and product, forcing them to rely on local producers for supplies and local consumers for sales. The evidence for some of their activity, newspaper ads soliciting grain and hops, would suggest that they relied on local farmers for ingredients.

The transportation issue was settled on September 23, 1831, with the opening of the Columbus feeder, joining at Lockbourne with the Ohio Canal, which linked Lake Erie with the Ohio River through 309 miles. The Columbus Lateral ran 11 miles from the main canal to the Scioto River just south of Broad Street. It made the area where John McCoy had done the city's first brewing nearly twenty years earlier uniquely suited to bringing in the raw materials for beer, as well as access to a vastly larger market, through the spur, down the canal and into the Ohio River. McCoy's spring was equally well situated, a block or two south of the closest docks on the canal, to supply crystal clear water for the new breweries that were to follow.

According to Randall and Ryan's *History of Ohio* (1912): "Those waterways were the great controlling factors of increasing commerce, manufacture and population. Through their influence villages became cities, towns were built where forests grew, farming developed into a profitable enterprise, and the trade and resources of the world were opened to Ohio."

It wasn't quite as stimulating to business and immigration as the Ohio River was for Cincinnati, which had a big jump on Columbus in commerce in general and brewing in particular. But it gave the city a mighty boost.

In addition, the canal transported new settlers. Columbus's population grew from 2,437 in the June 1830 census to nearly 20,000 just twenty-seven years later in 1857. A large portion of those new residents were from Germany, perhaps partly the result of the 1848 German revolution and economic depression. The first German newspaper appeared in 1833. It is estimated

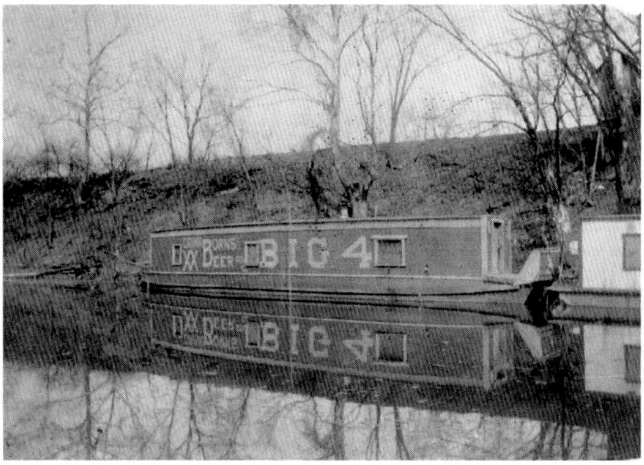

A rare picture of the canal with a barge advertising Born's brew. *David Foster collection.*

that after midcentury, nearly a third of Columbus was of German descent.

Among those immigrants likely was the consumer for the new German beer in Columbus and, perhaps, some of the families whose names would dominate the industry in Columbus for the next one hundred years. They included Berhnard Burck, Louis Hoster, John Blenkner, George Michael Schlegel and Conrad Born.

There was no bigger boon to the industry, specifically brewing, in Columbus until the arrival of the railroads in 1850 and the first station in 1851. It took some time, though, for the iron horse to conquer the slow barge.

Louis Hoster was born on September 6, 1807, in Dielkirchen in the Rheinpfalz region of Bavaria in southwestern Germany. The brewing tradition in that region centered on ales, generally amber to dark ones, brewed according to the Reinheitsgebot purity law of 1516, established first in Bavaria and eventually applied, with exception to local styles, to the rest of Germany. It stipulated that beer could only be produced with water, barley and hops. (Yeast, the other key component, hadn't been identified at the time.)

Hoster came to America in the early 1830s. Multiple sources recount the legend that on his way to Brown County in southwest Ohio on Independence Day 1833, he dined in a downtown Columbus hotel and heard a series of patriotic speeches from the governor and other state dignitaries and witnessed a celebration that impressed him. According to his obituary in the *Columbus Dispatch* from July 4, 1892, "He was sufficiently acquainted with the English language to understand it all, and the experience was a novel one to the immigrant." Two years later, on his way to Canton to seek work, he again visited Columbus. This time, he put down roots, landing a job at the Columbus Brewery at Spring and Front, sometimes known as Converse's brewery.

On May 6, 1836, he opened the City Brewery with partner George M. Herancourt, also an immigrant from the Rheinpfalz, who had studied brewing before coming to America in 1830. Their brewery was built just northwest of Liberty and Front Streets, where John McCoy had operated a still and brewery more than twenty years earlier.

Hoster lived around the corner in a large house on Livingston and walked to work every morning, doing most of the work himself, while Herancourt continued to run a shop on High Street that he had established in 1834. The brewery's output was a mere 300 barrels per year. (For a little perspective, at the turn of the century, Hoster's brewery produced about 1,000 times that, or 300,000 barrels a year.)

A lot of growth and innovation came between those markers, not to mention personal history. Hoster married Philippine Ambos in 1838, with whom he had five children: Louis Peter, Elise, George J., Emma and Lina. Herancourt married Ambos's sister Louise. When she died from childbirth in 1843, Herancourt retired from the business, placing half of his interest in a trust for their daughter and selling the other half to Jacob Silbernagel, another immigrant from the Rheinpfalz. Silbernagel and his brother were both brewers, and the injection of new blood into City Brewery inspired growth. The company expanded south on Front Street with additions in 1848 and 1856.

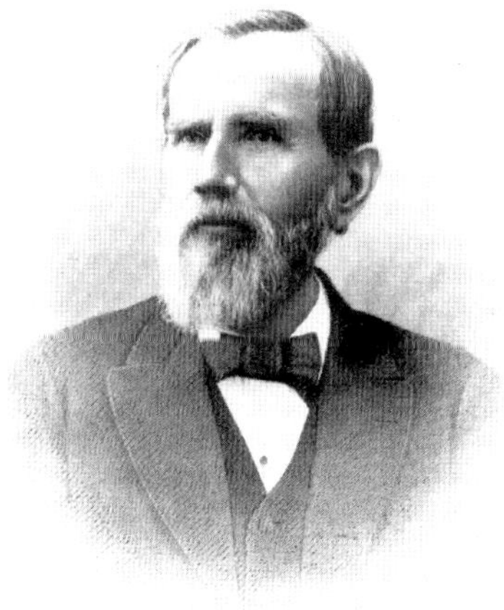

Louis Hoster was born in Dielkirchen in Rheinpfalz on September 6, 1807, and came to America in the early 1830s. His brewery, opened in 1836, was the first major German brewery in Columbus, beginning a tradition that would last nearly 150 years. *Courtesy Columbus Metropolitan Library.*

The business structure of Hoster also changed. Silbernagel sold his part back to Hoster in 1858, joining in a partnership with Conrad Born Sr. and providing the brewing know-how for Born's new Capital Brewery just two blocks down on Front. (Much more

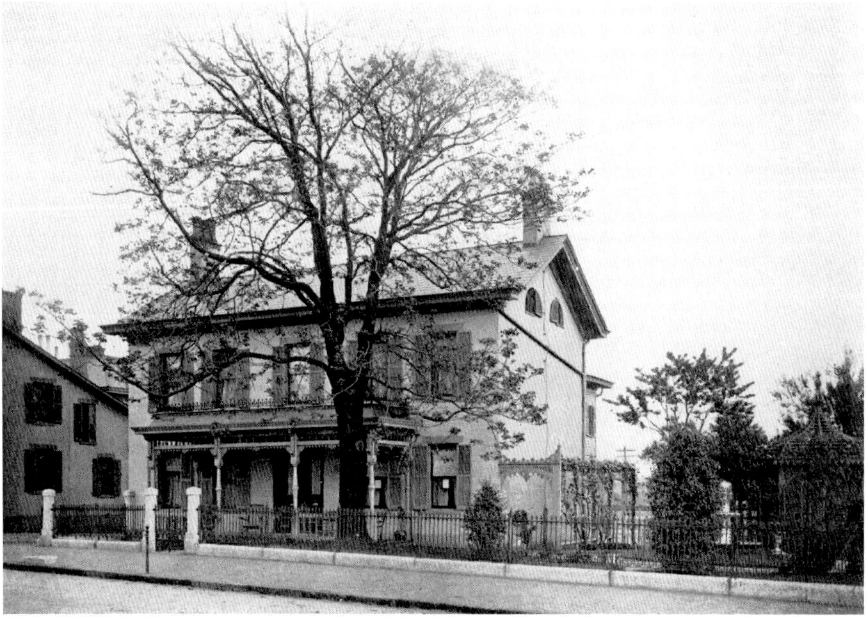

Louis Hoster lived around the corner of his brewery, at 29 West Livingston Avenue, so he could walk to work. *Courtesy Jay Hoster collection.*

about Born in chapter 5.) Generally reflecting those changes and the Hoster kids' coming of age, the brewery changed names several times, including Hoster, Son & Company; L. Hoster & Sons; L. Hoster & Sons & Company; and L. Hoster Brewing Company. Louis's sons Louis P. Hoster and George Hoster bought half the business from their dad in 1864 after Louise, Herancourt's daughter, sold her part.

By 1850, before all those changes, the brewery's output showed a modest gain, to about 1,600 barrels and employing eight men. Hoster was still brewing top-fermenting ales, traditionally associated with both German and English styles. During that time in Germany, though, brewers began to develop lager yeasts, which ferment at the bottom and at cooler temperatures. Lager—the term roughly translates "to store"—also requires more time to age. Nonetheless, when Hoster began producing lagers in 1856, the business grew more rapidly.

Hoster's earliest lagers may have been relatively dark in color, like the earliest German ones, similar to today's "Dunkel." According to an extensive article on lagers written by Michael Jackson—the late world-renowned beer writer, not the singer—and published on his website The

Beer Hunter, golden lagers were developed in 1842 in Plzen, in Bohemia. This is the origin of the term *pilsner*, the parent style of nearly all mass-produced corporate beers today.

A history of St. Louis brewing puts the first lager in that city in the early 1840s, while other major markets were a little slower to embrace the new, bottom-fermented yeast and its attendant conditioning period.

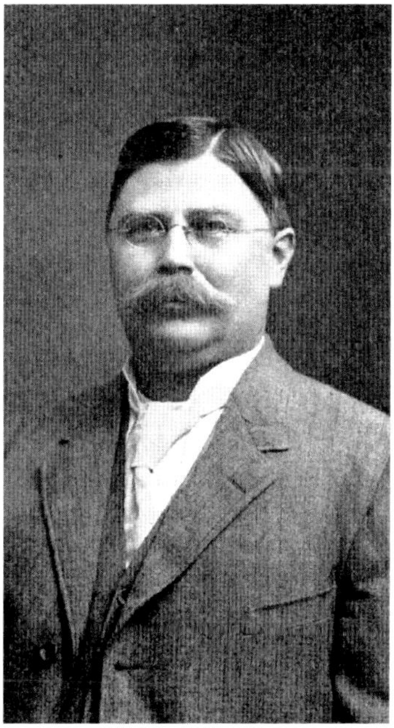

Carl L. Hoster, son of Louis Hoster's brother George, joined the family business in the mid-1880s. *Courtesy Columbus Metropolitan Library.*

After Hoster's business was incorporated in 1885, with capital stock of $500,000, Louis's two sons became more significantly involved. With Louis president of the new corporation, Louis P. was treasurer and George J. the plant's general manager. Carl L. Hoster, nephew and son of Louis's elder brother, also George, became secretary. George J. studied brewing in Cincinnati's Lafayette Brewery in 1861, according to an 1892 *Columbus Dispatch* article, the same place his father had years previously. If George was the most serious brewer among the Hoster children, their father was apparently an adept businessman and upstanding citizen. He was a member of the city council from 1846 to 1857 and served on the school board from 1869 to 1873.

While on vacation in Deer Park, Maryland, on July 3, 1892, the patriarch died suddenly and surprisingly of liver disease. Up to that time, he had continued to work every day. Less than two months before he died at age eighty-four, the *Dispatch* celebrated him thus: "We believe unquestionably [Louis Hoster is] to-day [*sic*] the oldest living brewer in active business life in the United States, if not in the world." Alfred E. Lee's history of Columbus discusses Hoster: "A gentleman long associated with Mr. Hoster says of him, 'I never knew a more perfectly honorable man or a more perfect gentleman.…He made every cent of his large fortune honestly, and he was a model citizen in every way.'"

After Louis's death, his son George, then forty-eight, became president, with Louis P. vice-president, Carl L. treasurer and George's son Carl J. secretary, and another of George J's sons, Louis Ph., the plant's

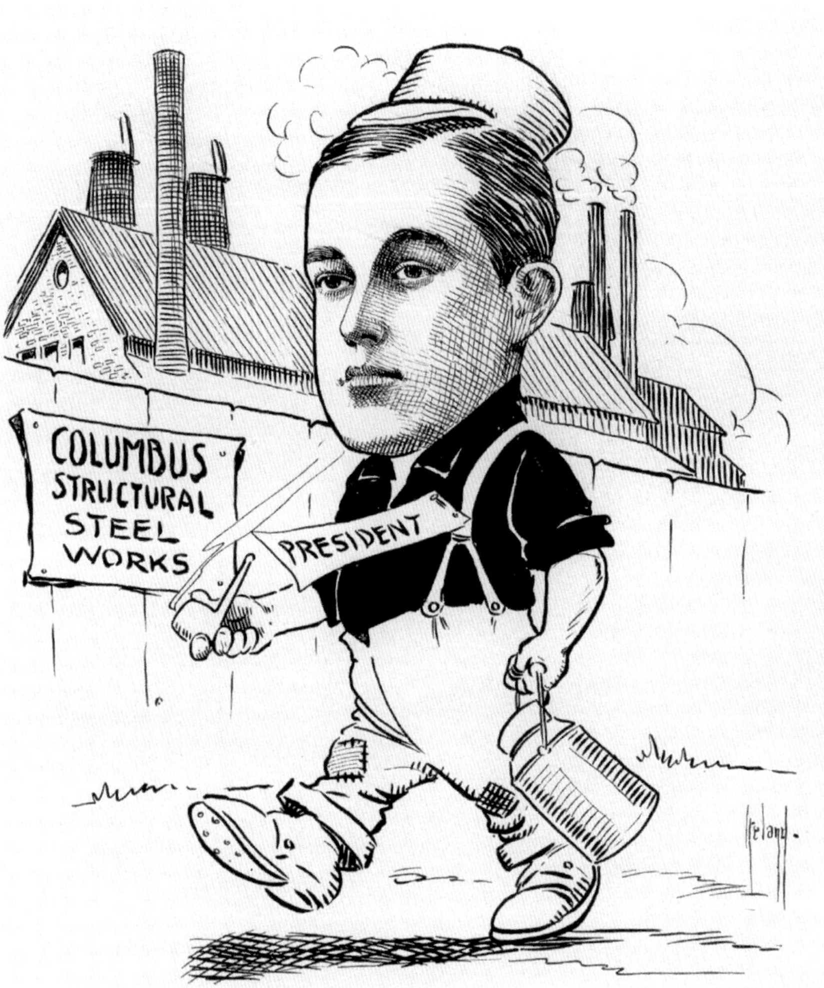

Louis Ph. Hoster, grandson of founding brewer Louis, like many of the children and grandchildren diversified and became an icon in Columbus society and business. *Courtesy Columbus Metropolitan Library*.

superintendent. The business flourished before and just after his death, largely the result of technical innovations and the expansion of the railroad.

Jay Hoster, great-great-grandson of Louis, noted two innovations toward the end of the century that likely added a boost to business. Of the first, he said, "His son George went to the Philadelphia Centennial Exposition in 1876 and there is this new process, where you could pasteurize beer. That allows you to ship the beer."

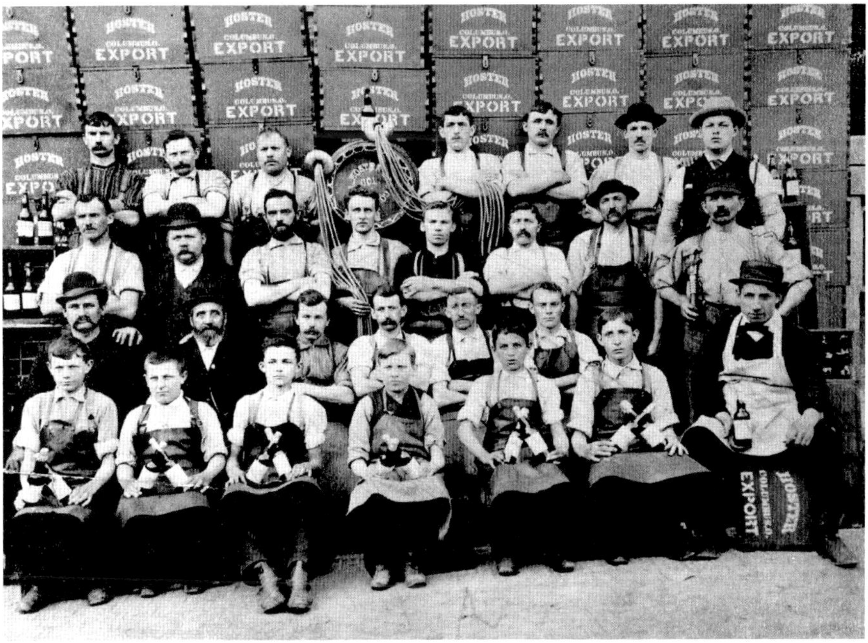

The Hoster brew crew, likely around the turn of the last century. Note the youngsters, who also worked long, punishing hours at the plant. *David Foster collection.*

The brewery grew across the street with a new bottling plant with a capacity of sixty thousand barrels. Connected to the brewery across Front by a tunnel under the street, the bottling house was expanded in 1899. (Annheuser-Busch began bottling in 1872, Hoster in 1876, according to the 1903 book *100 Years of Brewing*.)

Regarding the second important innovation, Jay Hoster also credits George with likely upgrading the Hoster brewery with its first ice machine, in 1880 or 1881, ending the industry's reliance on ice cut from the river in the winter and stored in cool basements during the summer. *100 Years of Brewing* notes that the company installed two 25-ton ammonia ice systems as early as 1883, augmenting them with three 220-ton machines in 1892. Hoster erected a large building dedicated to that purpose in 1892, an impressive and attractive structure across Ludlow Alley west of the main plant. It stands today, redesigned inside and housing landscape architecture and urban design firm MKSK. A crisp, well-proportioned brick archive of late-nineteenth-century design, it reflects a sophistication and modernity surely not anticipated by its builders.

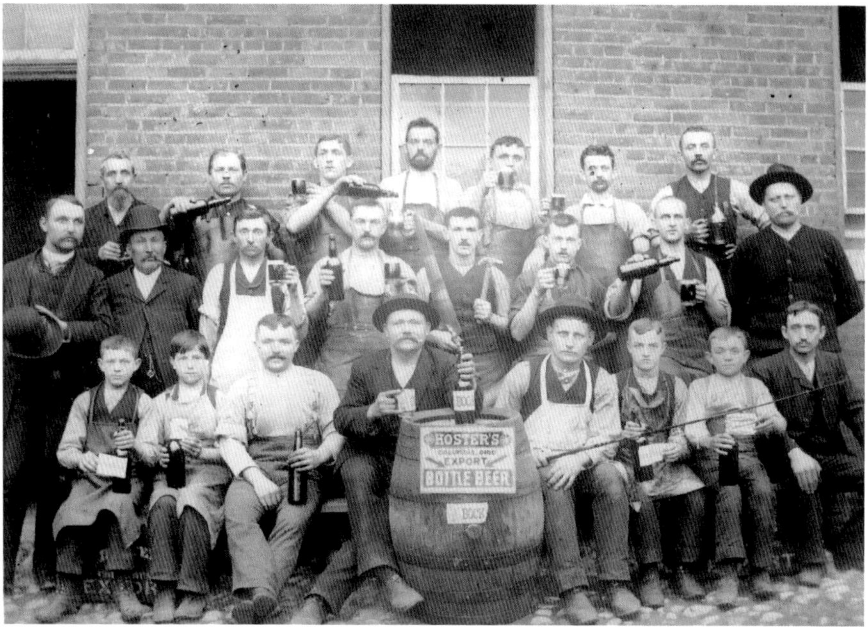

Another Hoster crew shot from the turn of the last century, complete with more young workers. *Courtesy Jay Hoster collection.*

An ad for the Anheuser & Company Bavarian Brewery from the 1860s reproduced in the excellent new history *St. Louis Brews* looks amazingly like the Hoster Brewery logo at the turn of the century. The architecture of the St. Louis breweries is similar, as is the complex of interlocked buildings. That Anheuser was at that level about thirty years before Hoster serves to illustrate the large difference between breweries in major and minor markets even then. After Prohibition, with the consolidation of regional breweries into a few majors, that difference was considerably more striking.

Hoster continued expanding south, constructing an unusual-looking building with turrets at its corners at the corner of Front and Liberty Streets in 1893 to house its 125 horses. The striking structure is called the Worly Building today and has housed a radio station, an international beer bar and a music hall–inspired theater troupe. In 2016, half of it became the restaurant and tavern for Lancaster's terrific Belgian-style Rockmill Brewery. The stables building was followed by a power plant in 1896, a wash building 1898 and additions to its brewhouse and cellars by 1900.

With these innovations and an increased output, Hoster quickly went to the top, with a capacity of 100,000 barrels per year in 1892, about twice

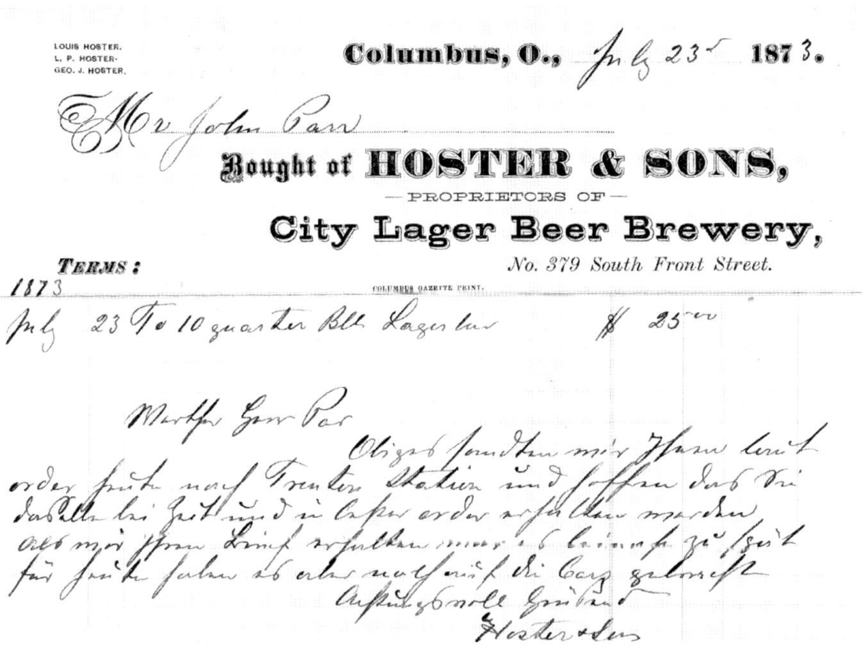

LOUIS HOSTER.
L. P. HOSTER.
GEO. J. HOSTER.

Columbus, O., July 23 1873.

Mr John Parr

Bought of HOSTER & SONS,

— PROPRIETORS OF —

City Lager Beer Brewery,

No. 379 South Front Street.

TERMS:

COLUMBUS GAZETTE PRINT.

1873

July 23 To 10 quarter Bbl. Lager beer $ 25.00

Bill for Hoster beer, likely sold to a saloon in 1873. Note the company name, Hoster and Sons, and the children in question (*upper left*) Louis P. and George J. *Courtesy Jay Hoster collection*.

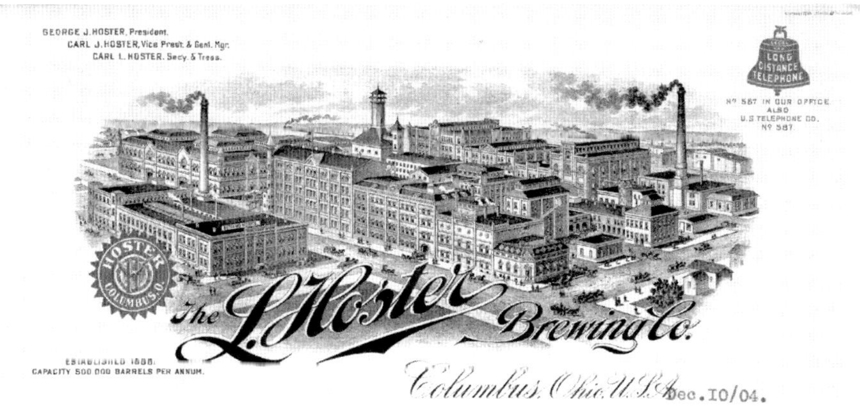

Hoster letterhead in 1904, when the plant was at its height, with a capacity to produce a half-million barrels of beer per year. *Courtesy Jay Hoster collection*.

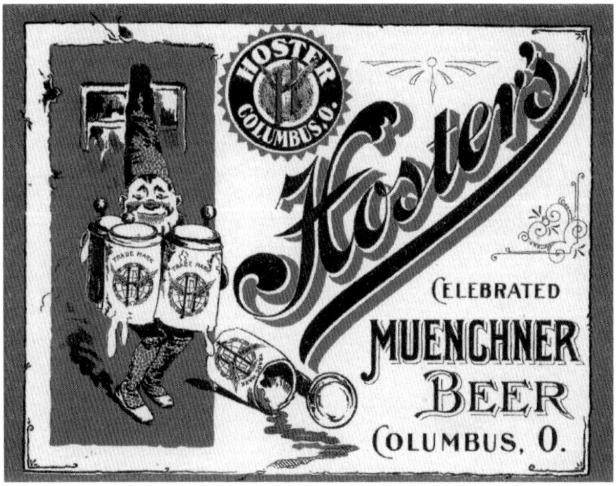

Bottle label for Hoster's classic Muenchner beer with the famed flying "H" logo, around the turn of the last century. The style's spelling has varied but refers to a dark lager developed in Munich. *Courtesy Jay Hoster collection.*

that of its nearest competitor, the Born Brewery. In 1890, in fact, Hoster was among the ten biggest brewers in the country. By 1896, producing 175,000 barrels, Hoster was the third largest in Ohio, behind Moerlein and Windisch-Muhlhauser, both in Cincinnati. According to *Franklin County at the Beginning of the Twentieth Century*, the plant brewed "about a quarter million barrels" a year in 1901. Hoster clearly dominated central Ohio and had a considerable presence in West Virginia and Virginia, with bottling plants throughout West Virginia. The beer went into Indiana and Kentucky, as well.

All of this growth and change is reflected not only in the official company name but also in the company's ads, listing first City Brewery, then L. Hoster & Company and soon Hoster & Sons. The artwork speaks volumes not only about the company's increasing budget but, more important, also changes in the national culture. Simple ads with very little other than block letters and a few lines of text began to yield to elaborate designs with whimsical illustrations late in the century. Cartoons of goats engaged in odd, human activities; suave, stylish couples enjoying a cold one; and boastful headlines interspersed with special holiday-themed ads. The brewery's marketing department was cranking out constant variations as well as wildly kooky ones. One ad from about the turn of the century shows a little guy drinking from a mug a foot taller than he and declaring, "Small People Drink Lots of Hoster's Famous Beer / Large People Drink Lots More."

Interestingly, as the country's attention turned toward temperance in the late 1800s, the ads started spinning the supposed health benefits of drinking beer. One of the more spectacular appeared in the *Ohio State Journal* in 1907, proclaiming, "Beer is adapted to the organism of the adult in much the

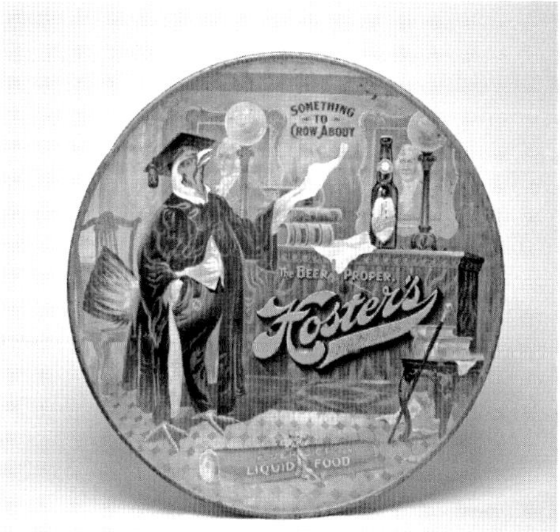

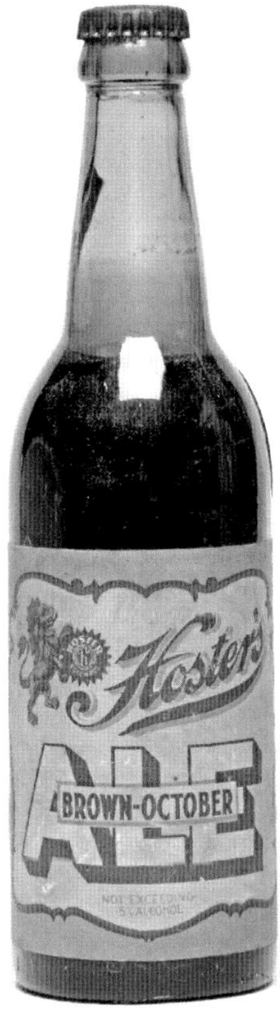

Above: Lacquered tray from the turn of the last century, illustrating a couple of promotional strains of the time, including the insistence that beer is "liquid food." *Jay Hoster collection, photo Randall L. Schieber.*

Right: Still-sealed bottle of Hoster seasonal offering. From the turn of the last century, its contents are less than fresh. *Jay Hoster collection, photo Randall L. Schieber.*

same way as milk is to that of the infant," and comparing the two beverages' relative nutritional makeup in a two-column chart.

Another ad declares in a large headline, "No Alcohol Brewed in Our Famous Liquid Food Beverages." The fine print confesses, "Months after, during the fermenting stages only, we get two things—carbonic acid gas and a very small quantity of alcohol, never over 3½ percent."

Though the Hoster brewery succumbed to Prohibition in 1920 (we'll take up that story in chapter 9), its history, brand and physical structures continue to be a presence today. Reflecting the brewery's stature in Columbus brewing history, it remains the best-known of the original German companies. A couple of recent stories and a tour of the old brewery buildings recall past glory.

Chris Hostettler's grandfather Alex joined the Hoster Columbus Associated Brewing Company in 1905, as the dark clouds of Prohibition were just beginning to gather. (He replaced August Wagner, who left to

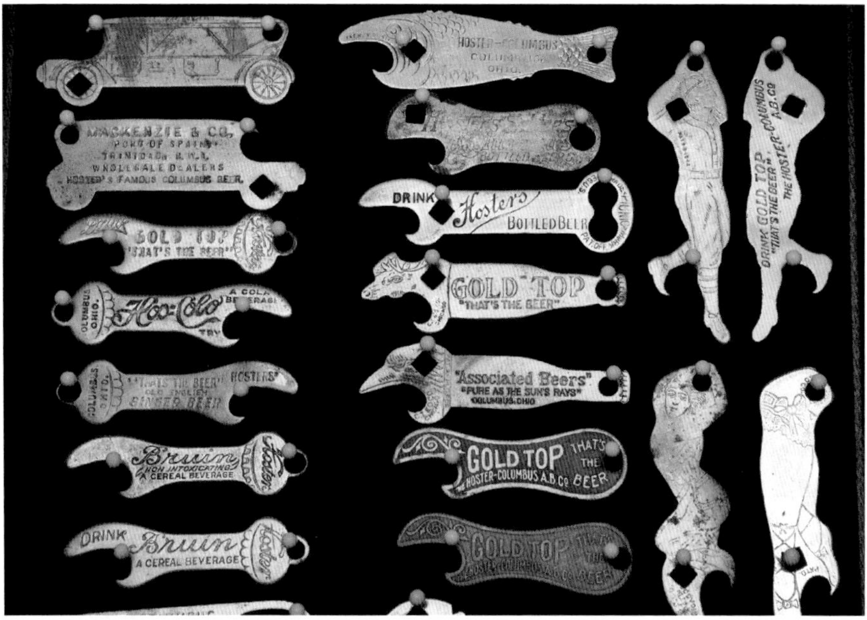

Bottle openers in stunning variation and internationally sourced (one created for Trinidad), and including nonalcoholic brews from the Prohibition era. *Jay Hoster collection, photo Randall L. Schieber.*

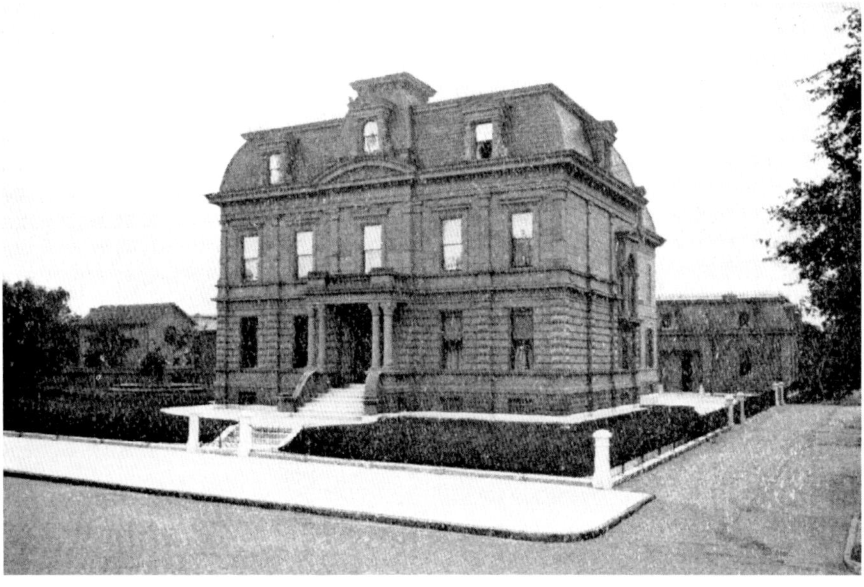

Louis P. Hoster residence on Rich Street. As the wealth trickled down to second and third generations, the homes moved farther from the factories. *Courtesy Columbus Metropolitan Library.*

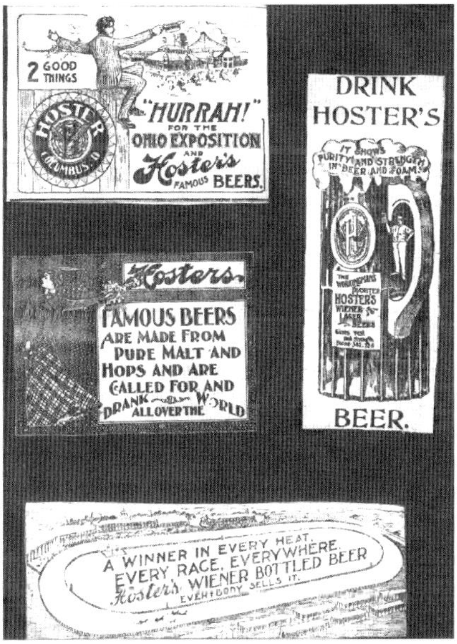

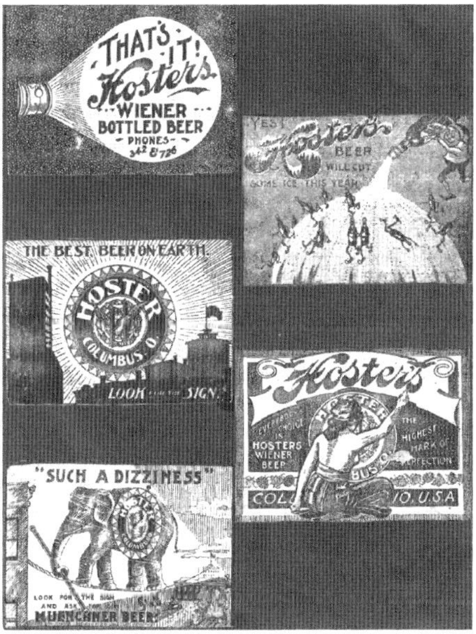

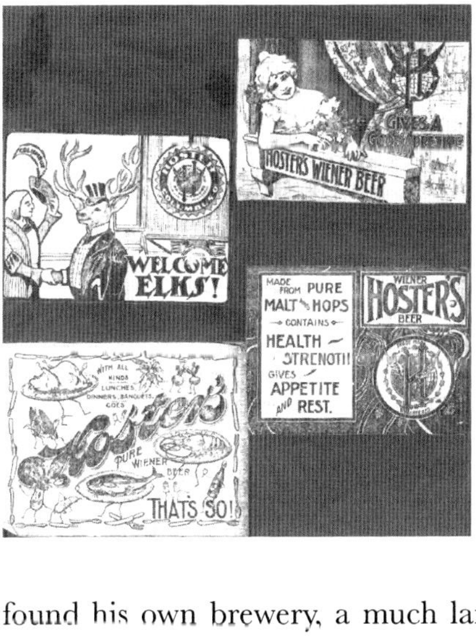

Top left grouping: Late-1800s Hoster ads. The brewery began to tie its product to the leisure lifestyle of the time, including horse racing. *Courtesy of David Foster collection.*

Top right grouping: Another collection of Hoster ads from the late 1800s, tapping a strange selection of subject matter. *Courtesy of David Foster collection.*

Group at left: Yet another selection of Hoster ads from the turn of the last century. Note the addition of health benefits in a couple, predicting the Temperance movement. *Courtesy of David Foster collection.*

found his own brewery, a much larger story for later in this book.) The brewmaster and his family lived in the brewery, according to Hostettler, who said that his father was born in the Hoster complex. Interestingly, Chris is CFO of MKSK, a landscape architecture firm whose offices are in the old Hoster icehouse.

The remains of the largest complex of buildings were bought in 1962 by the Wasserstrom Company, which leveled the front and built an office. A fascinating tour led by Reid Wasserstrom, vice-president for the realty

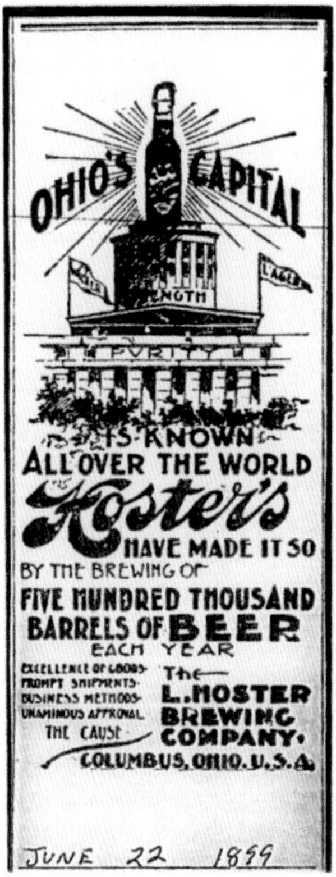

division of the company, suggests the function of individual parts, many barely renovated. Most telling are the upper levels, with wide-open spaces and smooth, flat floors surrounded by regular rows of thick, round pillars. Resembling the vast warehouse spaces devoted to malting floors in traditional German breweries, they seem to be fed by regularly spaced round chutes in their ceilings, about a foot in diameter.

Perhaps the raw grain was fed from above, distributed on the smooth floors and wetted and heated for the malting process, wherein

Left: Using the state capitol building as a prop, Hoster's touts its national distribution in an 1899 ad. *Courtesy Jay Hoster collection.*

Below: Worly building in 2015, erected for Hoster Brewing's stables, inhabited much later by radio station CD101, then World of Beer and today Rockmill Brewery's taproom and restaurant. *Photo by the author.*

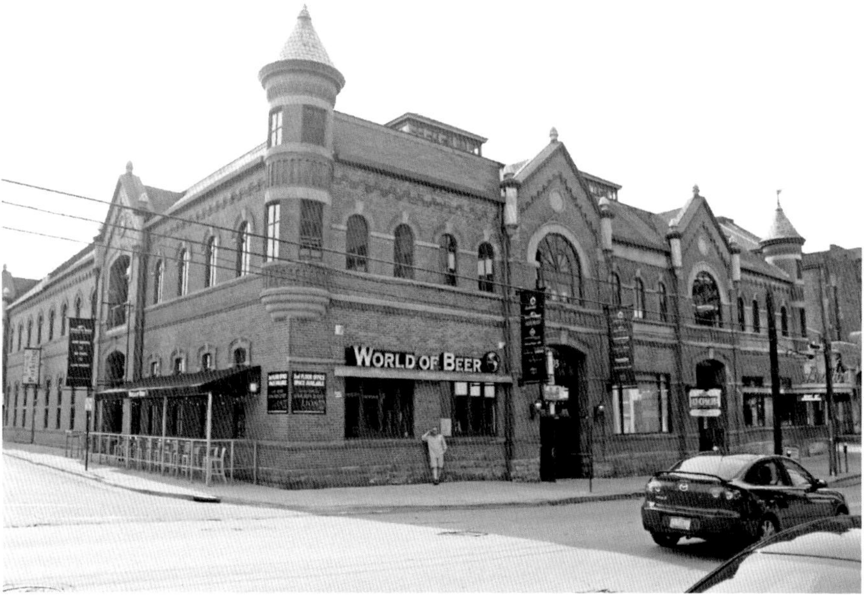

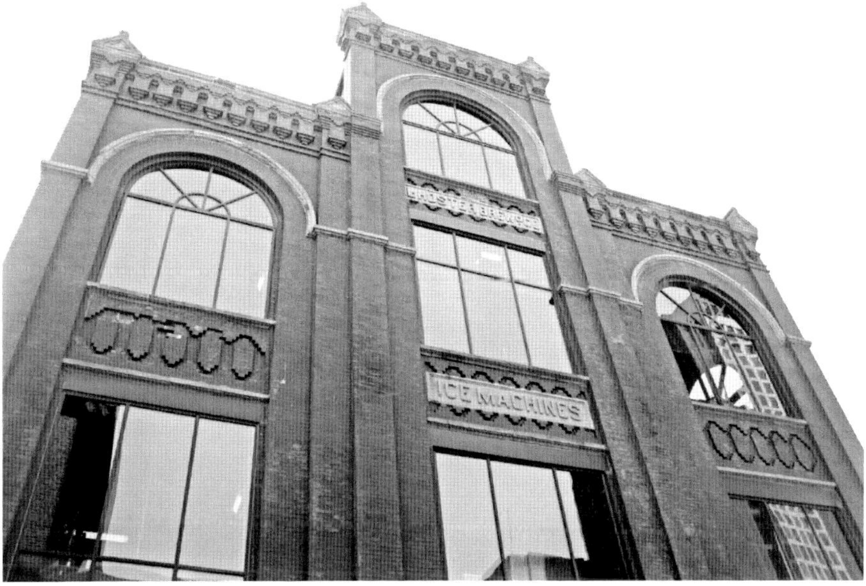

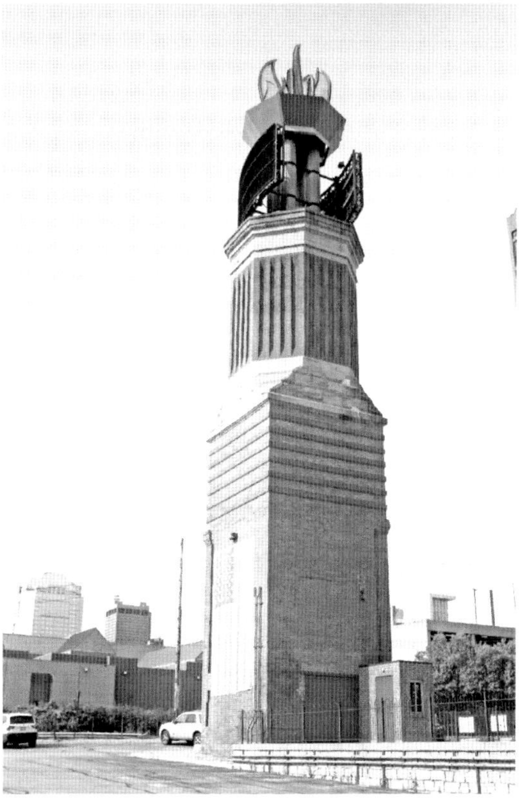

Above: Hoster Brewing Company's Ice House, today the offices of landscape architecture firm MKSK, 462 South Ludlow Street. *Photo by the author.*

Right: The largest of Hoster's smokestacks, originally two hundred feet, six inches, is not so tall today, lopped off years ago and today a prop for electronic advertising. *Photo by the author.*

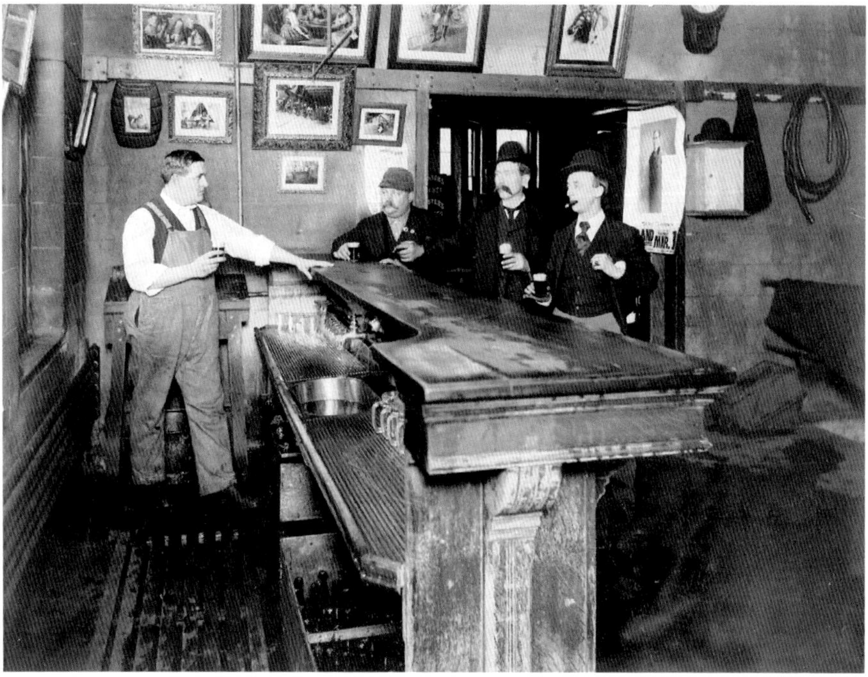

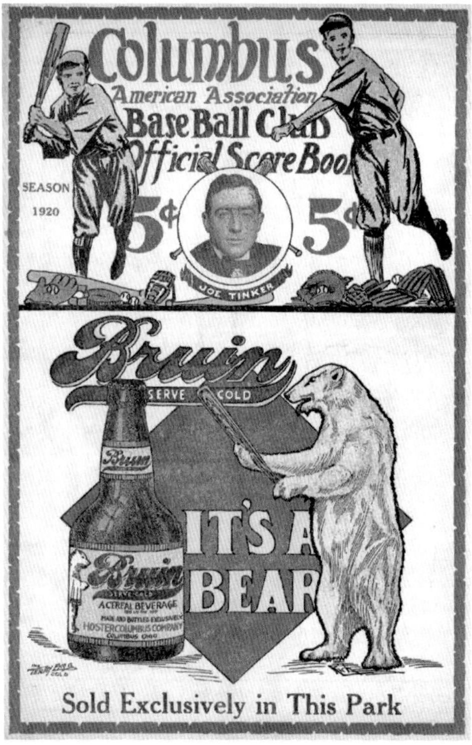

Above: Bar at the Hoster Brewery, early 1900s. *Courtesy Jay Hoster collection.*

Left: Scorekeeping book from American Association of Baseball Clubs' 1920 season. Bruin cereal drink in ad below signals the beginning of Prohibition. *Courtesy Jay Hoster collection.*

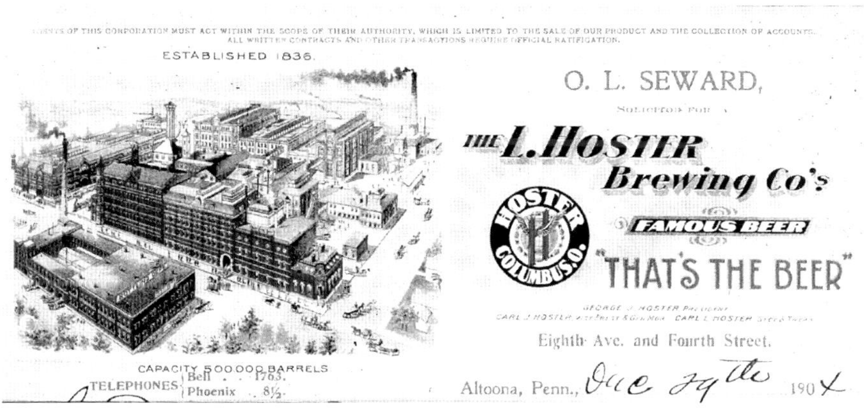

Another Hoster letterhead, this time in color from 1904. The illustration makes the complex seem massive, which it was, producing half a million barrels. *Courtesy Columbus Metropolitan Library.*

grains are briefly sprouted to produce key enzymes and then dried and ground before they are mashed for brewing.

The rabbit warren of tunnels and secret rooms that characterize the basement were likely lagering rooms. Along with the high-ceilinged, European-style brewing floor, they are today vivid testament to the labor of the company brewers and the tradition they maintained. The earthquake-defying structure, built on four-foot walls in the lower portion, is—like a bank building's giant columns suggesting permanence—a testament to the empire Louis Hoster built.

My 2016 tour was a fortuitous one. According to *Columbus Business First* of December 2016, Wasserstrom announced that it would be selling the entire 140,000-square-foot property for a mixed-use redevelopment and would be moving its offices to East Broad Street.

5

CONRAD BORN

Conrad Born came to the United States in 1837, settling in Utica, New York, then Cleveland, Circleville and, finally, Columbus in early 1839. He was born on March 1, 1812, in Herxheim in Rheinpfalz, in the same general area of Germany from where Louis Hoster hailed. A butcher by trade, he also did well in the real estate business in Columbus. The portrait that emerges from documents about Born is of a self-made man, a hardworking, no-nonsense immigrant who lived the American dream. He opened his butcher business on March 16, 1839, reputedly with a mere ninety-five cents. His foray into real estate began in 1841. If he didn't found his brewery as a member of the German brewing tradition, he did so as a businessman who sensed a receptive market.

Born married Mary Ann Rickly, born in 1817 in Switzerland, and they had eight children. Conrad Born Jr. was born in Columbus on September 21, 1844, and educated in Columbus schools. Conrad Jr. was a godsend, a young man who developed a passion for brewing. He studied the tradition for four years beginning in 1860 at age fifteen at Cincinnati's great Moerlein Brewery under Christian Moerlein himself. About that time, George J. Hoster was studying in Cincinnati, at Lafayette Brewery. For the next couple of years, Conrad Jr. apprenticed in St. Louis and Chicago. When he returned to Columbus in October 1864, he rejoined his father's business. In 1869, he married his teacher's daughter Lena Moerlein. Conrad Jr.'s joining the firm coincided with the elder Born buying out his partner Silbernagel the same year. The company name was changed to Born & Company.

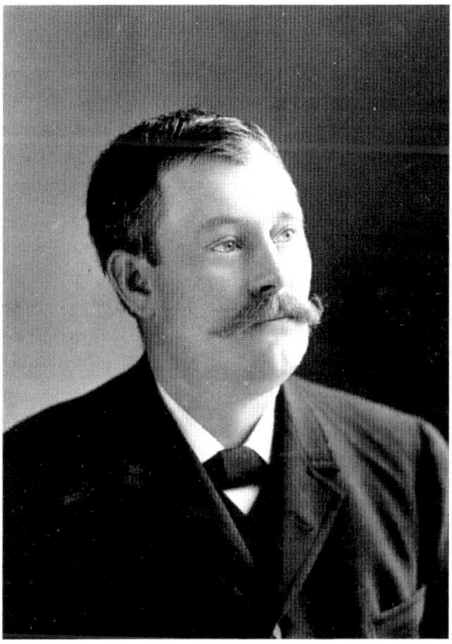

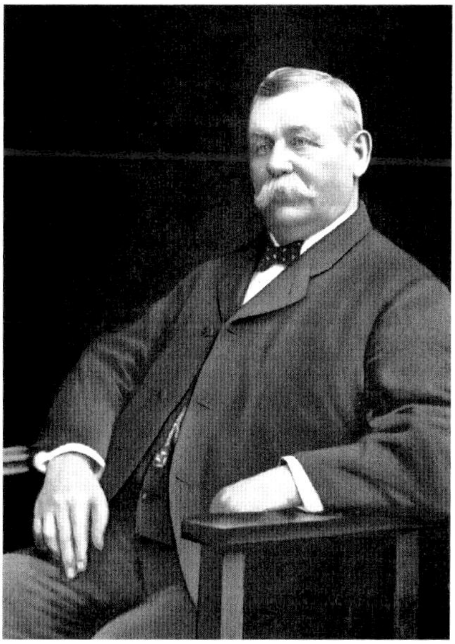

Left: Conrad Born Jr., the brewer of the Born family, studied in Cincinnati and Chicago, married a Moerlein and led the company in innovation. *Courtesy Jay Hoster collection.*

Right: Conrad Born, a butcher by trade, would establish the second great German family brewing dynasty in Columbus. *Courtesy Columbus Metropolitan Library.*

Brewing became a central part of life for the Born children. Anna was wed to Louis Hoster's son George J., and Jacob married Katharine P. Jung, whose uncle was an officer at Moerlein. Not only did it set up a détente that might have aided—spoiler alert—a merger with Hoster much later, but it also strengthened the relationship with Cincinnati's Moerlein. Carl Jr., in fact, became a large stockholder in the Moerlein brewery.

Unlike Hoster, who had some brewing training before he came to America, Conrad Born Sr. did not. In fact, he didn't do much of it himself at first and later left it to his son Conrad Jr. Instead, he took a partner, another Rheinpfalz native and brewer named Jacob Silbernagel, who had owned half of Hoster's City Brewery in the 1840s and '50s. Silbernagel must have used that inside information and the knowledge that City, combined with Georg Schlegel and John Blenkner's Bavarian Brewery, couldn't keep up with the demand for the new, popular lagers that were making their impact in the United States after taking hold in Germany a decade before, in his decision to join with Born to open the Capital Brewery in January 1860.

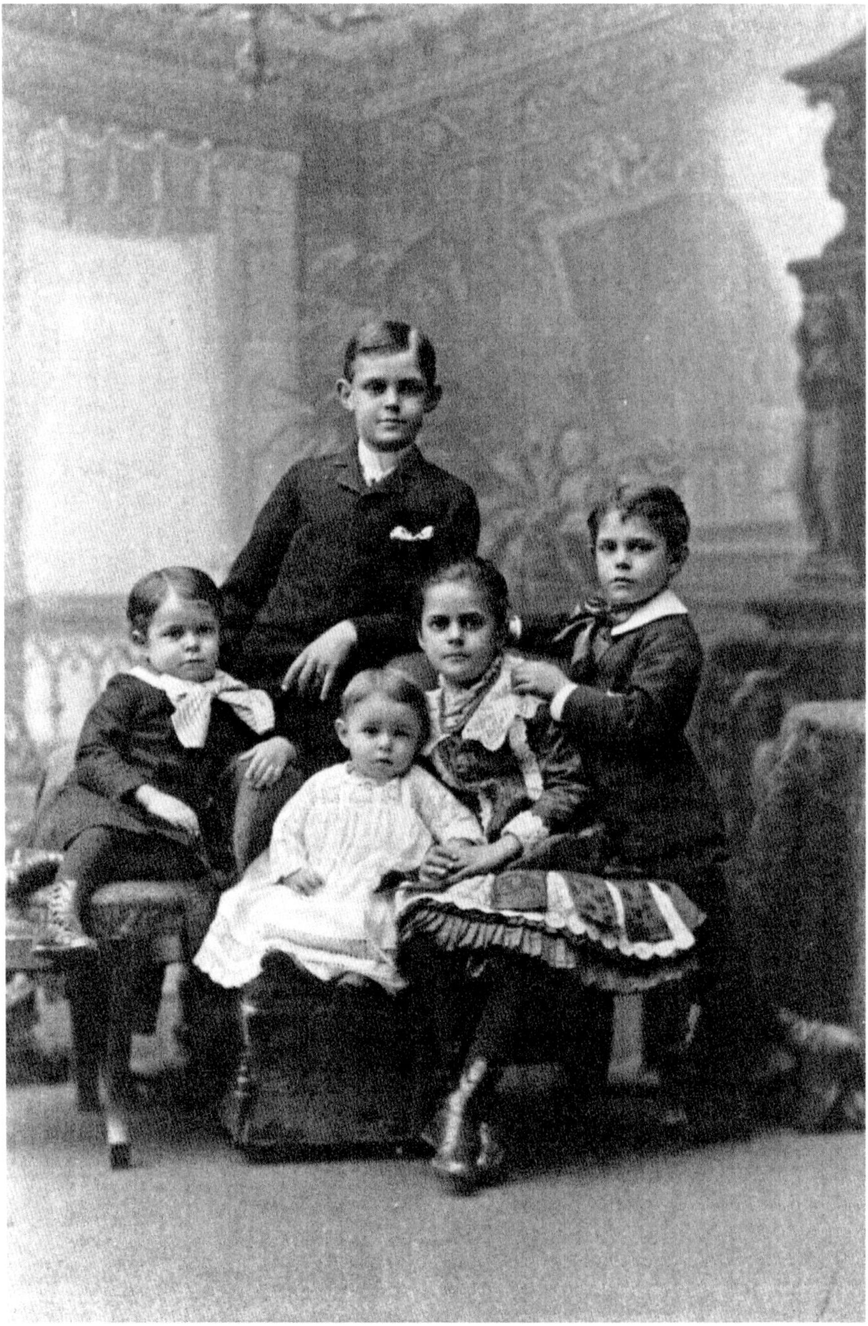

Conrad Born's children. The oldest, Conrad Jr., would become a brewer and marry Cincinnati brewer Christian Moerlein's daughter Lena. Anna (*center*) would marry George J. Hoster. *Courtesy Jay Hoster collection.*

The *Daily Capital City Fact* was a short-lived paper published in Columbus from 1851 to 1863. In a piece dated July 23, 1859, the paper praised Born's brewery, said to open later in the fall. Though it wouldn't open until early the next year, the paper called Born's cellar "incomparable, being of the lowest depth, the deepest, cool, dry and admirably ventilated." It went on to mention that the company had just taken delivery of a 2,500-gallon brew kettle (about seventy-five barrels), describing it as "a huge cauldron, which the 'three witches' would have much exercise in making 'boil and bubble.'" The article anticipated Born brewing ale, "beer" (likely "small beer," lighter in alcohol), porter and lager.

When it opened, Capital was the largest brewer in Columbus. It began by producing 6,000 barrels per year. After its introduction, production dropped to just 5,500 of its 6,000-barrel capacity in 1870. Still, the 1878 publication *Industries of Ohio, Columbus* says by that time, the brewery was doing $100,000 annually and employing between sixteen and twenty workers. Both Conrad Jr. and his assistant, Jacob Nagel, are praised for their management and bookkeeping skills. Born's brewery had begun improvements in 1873, with an addition and a huge new copper kettle weighing four thousand pounds and holding 100 barrels. The improvements included new icehouses. The output increased to 16,000 barrels.

Beginning with a rebuild in 1880 and continuing with a new stable, icehouse and cooper shop in the next two years, capacity grew. However, output lagged a bit through the 1880s. Production went from 25,000 barrels in the mid-1880s to 30,000 in 1889, then to about 50,000 in 1895 and 65,000 in 1902. Several factors contributed to the increases. The German native brewer Jacob Falter and Conrad Jr.'s brother Jacob had joined in the late 1860s. In 1877, Falter left and Jacob Born died. Charles Andre, a German native who brought with him experience in several American companies, took over in 1878, marshalling resources to introduce a period of huge expansion for the brewery. The plant added refrigeration to replace naturally sourced ice in 1889. Among other earlier innovations, a bottling works was added, boosting demand and, in turn, distribution.

The brewery's large horse barn burned in 1897, forcing Born to build a new one. Out of this misfortune, according to the *Columbus Evening Press*, Conrad Christian Born—grandson of Conrad Sr.—designed a new, considerably larger building, "one of the largest, best arranged and handsomest in the state, a beauty in architectural design and a credit to the enterprise and liberality of Mr. Born." Though the article didn't offer

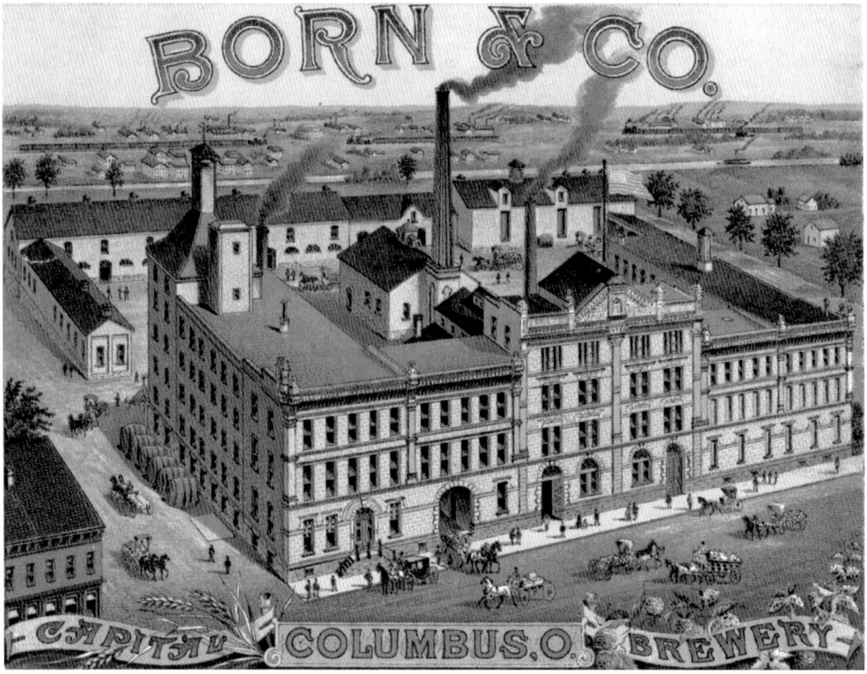

Born's Capital Brewery on the west side of Front Street a little south of the Hoster complex and Nicholas Schlee's home. Born's was the second-largest brewery in the city. *Jay Hoster collection.*

engineering details, it stated that the building was designed to retard the progress of a fire.

As with Hoster, a look at labels and ads from the time fill in some details and add character to the story. An ad from the very early 1860s, just a couple of years after the facility opened as the Capital Brewery, lists Born and Silbernagle as "proprietors" and touts its "Superior Lager Beer, for General and Family Use," while adding that the company also keeps "Constantly on Hand…All Varieties of Ales." An interesting detail in tiny print at the bottom of the ad promises—as do several other breweries of the time—"Ale and Beer delivered to any part of the City free of charge."

After the company began bottling around 1880, it expanded its capacity to service the added distribution and, by mid-decade, increased its production. An ad in the *Ohio State Journal* from 1879 focused on its bottled beer, advertising quart bottles delivered to any part of the city—it didn't say if delivery was now free—for one dollar per dozen. A note at the bottom,

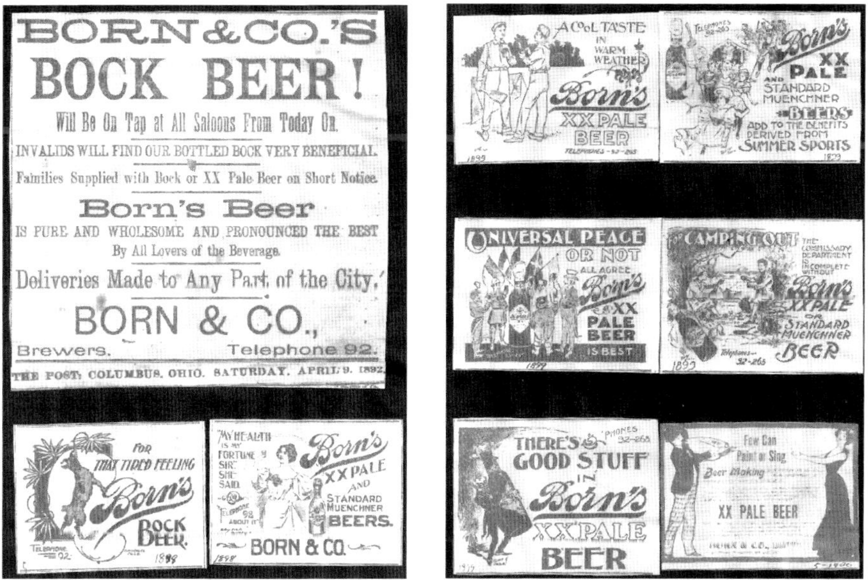

Born advertisements from the late 1800s. *Courtesy of David Foster collection.*

though, is something of a reminder of the times, as it promised "Prompt attention given to orders by Postal Card."

By the end of the century, the style of the breweries' products had grown more unique and the advertising had become far more colorful. An ad from 1899 containing the declaration "Words of Wisdom for Wise Heads" depicted a professor in robes reading a paper that contained a full-page description of the quality of Born's XX pale; another ad contained a lion with a full mane reclining next to a bottle of Born's and the headline "A Pair of Kings." Another quartet of headlines celebrated the benefits of and settings for drinking Born's: "After the Theater," "In Warm Weather," a drink "To Your Health" that is "Not Like Changeable April Weather, Always the Same High Quality." Children, elegant ladies, sportsmen and a count appeared in the ads.

As was the case with most of the successful brewers of the nineteenth century, the line of Borns originating with Conrad Sr. not only diversified their wealth and influence but also became civic leaders. Conrad Jr. was the president and the primary stockholder in the Columbus Baseball Club. His son Christian was a director in several local banks, including the Ohio National Bank, and insurance institutions and lived in a fabulous mansion at 671 South High Street, built in 1902. He was a member of

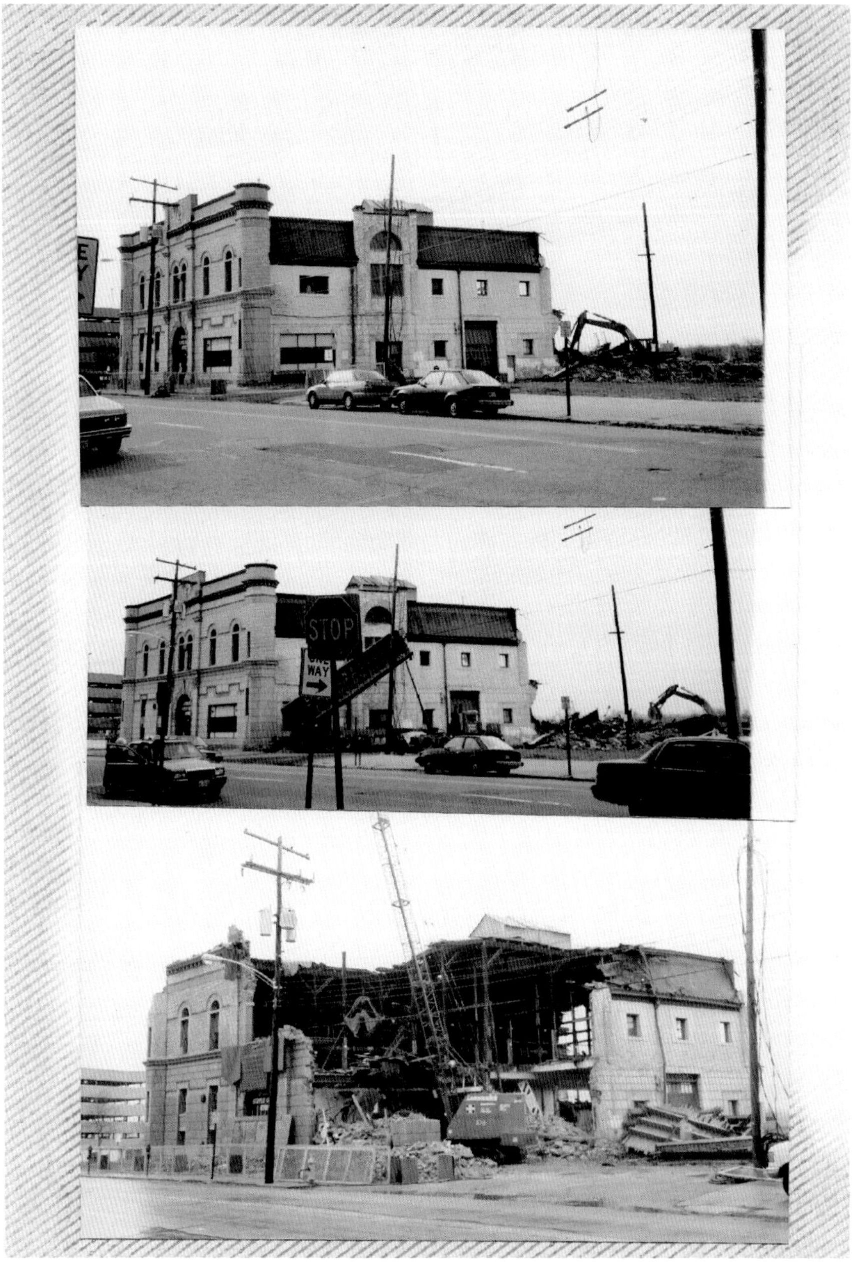

The Born stables, built in 1897 and demolished here, December 6, 1993. The original turrets had been removed in some earlier repurposing, as had the back half of the building. Still, a consortium made up of the Columbus Landmarks Foundation, Citizens for a Better Skyline and the German Village Society for two months fought the approval for demolition issued by the Brewery District Commission, failing in the eleventh hour. *Courtesy of David Foster collection.*

the Columbus Board of Trade and a member of the best social clubs in the city.

Conrad Born Sr. died in 1890 of diabetes. Though he was one of the wealthiest men in Columbus, he didn't live to see his brewery become the second-largest in the city, not to mention its decline, later merger and eventual fall just prior to Prohibition.

The Born name was nearly revived for the purpose of brewing in 2011, when a new company aimed to open a craft brewery at North Fourth Avenue and Fourth Street. After an obscure copyright connection to the brand was discovered, Collin Castore and Travis Spencer named their new brewery Seventh Son.

6

SCHLEGEL AND BLENKNER'S BAVARIAN BREWERY

(INCLUDING NICHOLAS SCHLEE AND BIEHL & SCHLEGEL)

John Blenkner and his daughter Margaret came from the Steigerwald in Bavaria in 1837, as did George Michael Schlegel, born in a village just four miles down the road. Blenkner's family settled in Rome, west of Columbus, and bought a farm. When the family moved to Columbus in 1846, Blenkner ran the Lafayette Hotel. Based on his experience at the establishment, Blenkner decided a brewery might be successful in the increasingly German mid-nineteenth-century Columbus. One estimate says that one-third of the city was German by midcentury. With Schlegel, a trained brewer who came to the States in 1849, Blenkner established the Bavarian Brewery, a three-man operation in a new two-story brick building, making four hundred barrels by the next spring. George married Blenkner's daughter, and the family lived in a part of the new brewery. An ad from 1850 not only includes a picture of the dapper, stately Schlegel but also indicates the nature of his product, at this time still ales. It would be another half decade before lagers became the stuff of German brewers in Columbus.

George bought out his father-in-law in 1856 but died soon thereafter, on December 18, of typhoid fever. The brewery was inherited by Schlegel's widow and the couple's four children, who were still young. Still, ownership of the brewery was left to the kids, who would presumably run it when they came of age. After a series of local management arrangements, Margaret went looking for a permanent brewmaster.

The Blenkners found a new brewmaster back home in Bavaria, George's nephew Nicholas Schlee. Born in Breiten Lohe, Nicholas was a skilled brewer who had studied under his father Georg, a respected professional brewer, and had visited the major German brewing centers. Nicholas's mother, Elisabetha (Schlegel) Schlee was George Schlegel's sister. Nicholas came to Columbus and became brewmaster in 1860; in April, he married his uncle's widow.

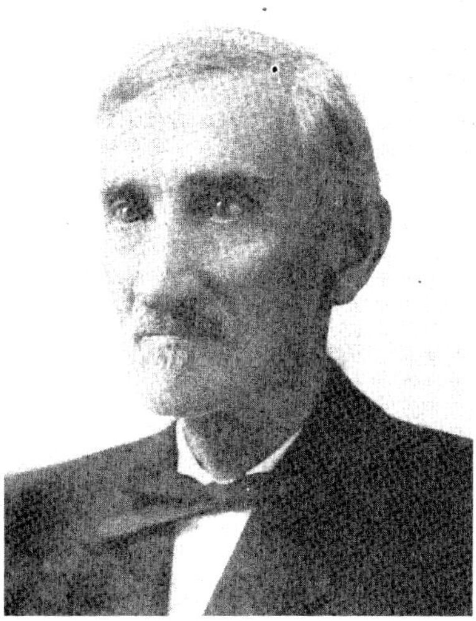

Nicholas Schlee, born on January 13, 1836, in the Bavarian Steigerwald. Schlee married into Schlegel's Bavarian Brewery in 1860 before turning it into the third powerhouse German brewery in Columbus. *Courtesy Columbus Metropolitan Library.*

Schlee not only had the ability and desire to make the best beer possible, but he also left his mark on Columbus architecture. He was responsible for steering the construction of the Southern Hotel, the steeple on Trinity Lutheran Church, the Schlee School and the First National Building at 33 North High Street. He owned the Lyceum Theater, the building occupied by the Columbus Blank Book company, the space housing the Bismarck café and other downtown structures. He was a director in the New First National Bank. His family lived in a fine home, today the Germania Society, across from his Front Street brewing complex.

Schlee bought a third of the business from Barbara, one of the three remaining Schlegel children who owned it. Through a complicated deal, he bought then transferred the original brewery building to George and Charles Schlegel. The 1858 introduction of lagers had boosted the business over nearly twenty years, when in 1875 Schlee built a grand addition to the Bavarian Brewery, fairly replacing the old facility, which became the Phoenix Brewery, thereafter operated by his stepsons, the Schlegel boys. The three-story, block-long complex likely sent a message to nearby competitors Born and Hoster, the latter of which continued to add substantial buildings until the end of the century. Phoenix became Schlegel Brothers, as evidenced in an advertisement from 1879. It is interesting to note in the ad that a twelve-pack is available for seventy-five cents, delivered to any part of the city.

In a few more years, though, the Phoenix/Schlegel brewery became part of Schlee's complex, now known as Schlee's Bavarian Brewery. Both Schlegel brothers were made officers in that company. The imposing malt house from Schlee's achievement remains today as the Buchsieb Building,

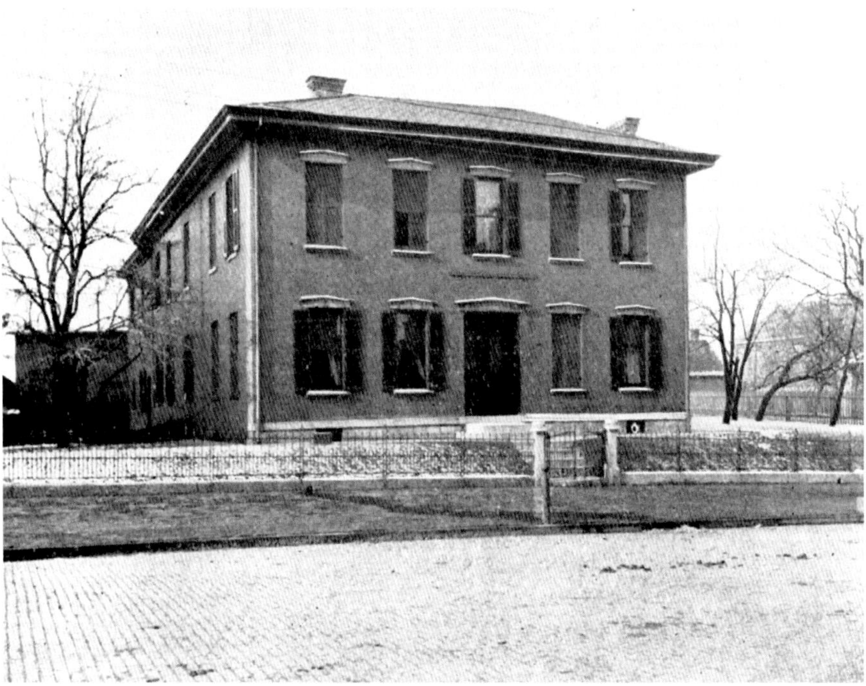

Nicholas Schlee's home at 543 South Front Street, today the Columbus Germania Society, was across from his brewery. *Courtesy Columbus Metropolitan Library.*

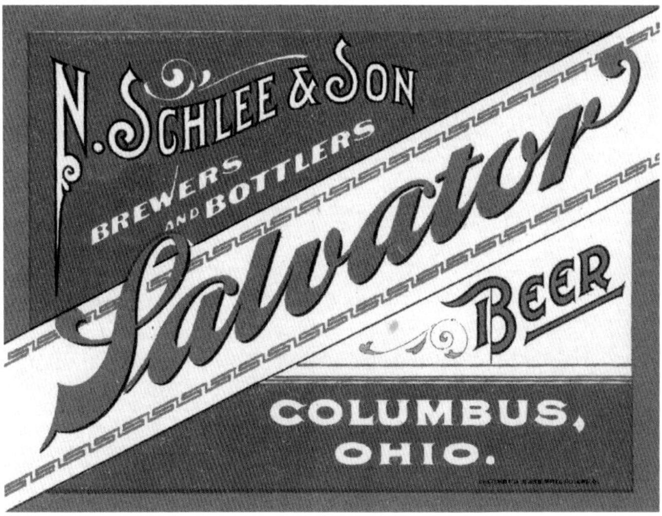

Beautifully designed label for Schlee's Salvator. In traditional German brewing, the "ator" suffix generally refers to a dopplebock, a late-winter, high-strength brew. *Jay Hoster collection.*

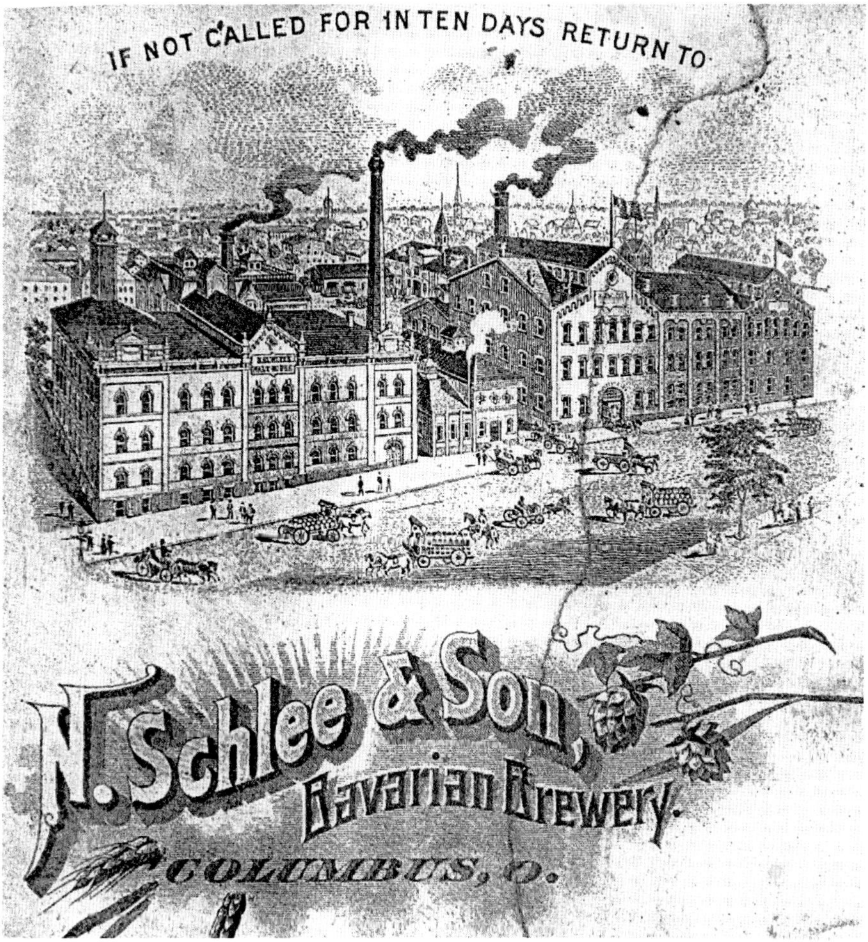

Schlee's new Bavarian Brewery, an impressive complex whose buildings remain today. The large one on the left is the E.G. Buchsieb Block; at far right is the Graystone Wine Cellar. Zimmerman's brewery between would be assimilated soon after this rendition. *Courtesy David Foster collection.*

the beer baron's head in stone relief over one of its doors, watching over his former domain.

Under Schlee and later with his son Theodore, the business—which was named progressively Schlegel & Blenkner, Nicholas Schlee, Schlee & Schlegel and, finally, Nicholas Schlee & Son—experienced exponential growth, according to a *Columbus Dispatch* article in 1892. The brewery's output began at two thousand barrels when Schlee took the reigns and increased to thirty-eight thousand in 1890.

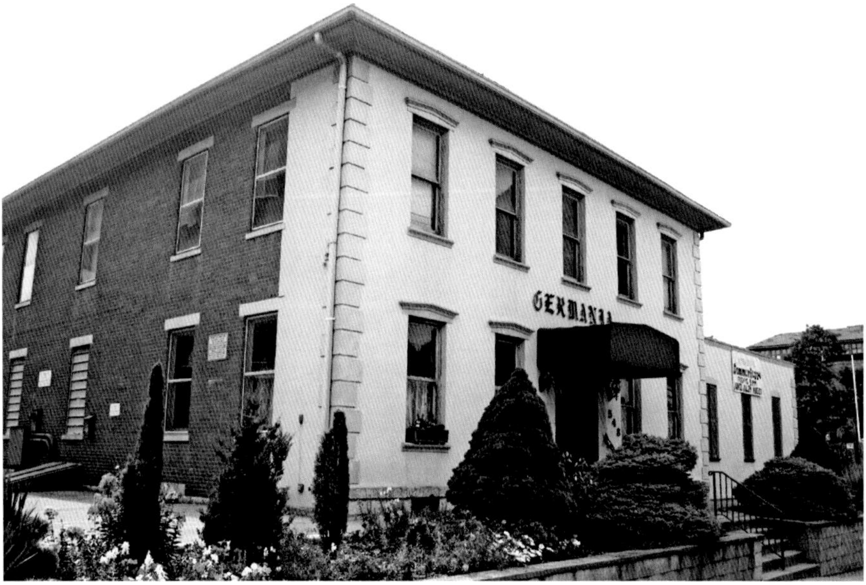

Germania Society, originally built by George M. Schlegel. Nicholas Schlee and Schlegel's widow raised their family in the mansion for years after. *Photo by the author.*

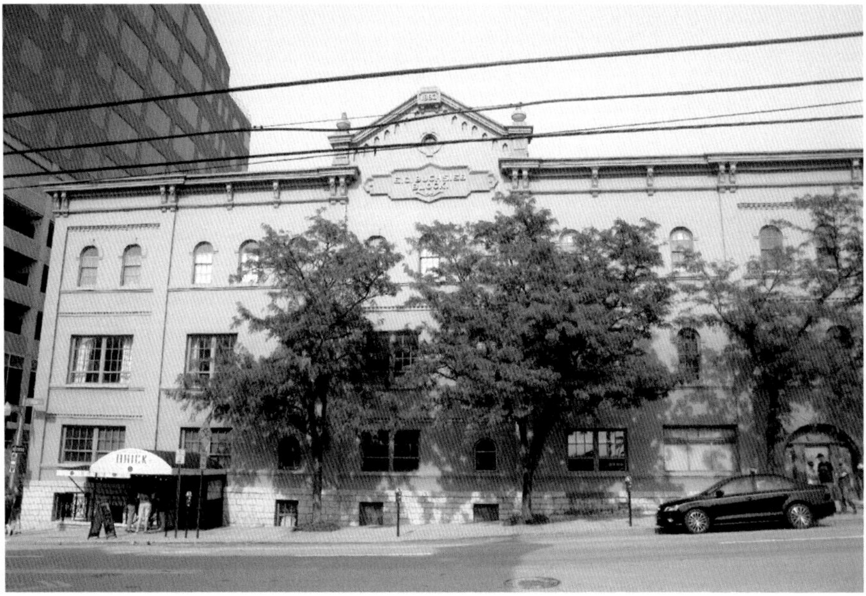

Buchsieb Building, seen here today, was long ago part of the N. Schlee and Son Bavarian Brewery. *Photo by the author.*

South of Schlee's new brewery was the Zimmerman ale brewery, built in 1862. The faltering business was absorbed by Schlee's complex in 1885. Still, at the turn of the century, Schlee was just the third-largest brewer in the city. Several more firms joined the fray in the first decade of the twentieth century.

Theodore Schlee, son of Nicholas and Margaret, was born in Columbus in 1861 and educated in our city schools. He was groomed to run a brewery from the start, though. His father sent him to Germany in 1880 at nineteen to study at the Worms' Brewing Academy. He returned home a year later and, by 1890, was made a partner in his father's business.

At its peak in the 1890s, Alexander Assmann was the brewmaster. A veteran of Born's brewery, not to mention having learned at a host of other regional breweries, including Cincinnati's important Christian Moerlein, Assmann's expert direction was credited for Schlee's biggest growth.

As the century turned, though, the rumblings of the Temperance movement were beginning to be felt, as was increasing competition from the outside. The railroads had not only made it possible for the local breweries, especially Hoster, to extend their reach, but, combined with pasteurization, had also allowed the national giants to infringe on their market.

There were other Bavarian immigrant brewers in Columbus during the time, as well as another branch named Schlegel. Paulus Schlegel was born in Bavaria and immigrated to Columbus in 1866. A trained cooper—the skilled builder of wooden kegs—and brewer, he went to work for Nicholas Schlee and his Bavarian Brewery, an establishment founded by his uncle George M. and subsequently taken over by Schlee. In Columbus, he married Christina Correll, herself a German immigrant born a little north of Bavaria, in the state of Hesse. After a stint in the City Brewery in Marysville, the couple returned to Columbus, where Paulus went to work at the City Park Brewery at the northwest corner of what was then known as Perry and Front Streets—today, Whittier and Front.

That brewery was founded by the grocer William Henkel and businessman Frederick Hanewald in the late 1860s. Schlegel and his cousin George J. Schlegel came into the business a couple of years after the brewery was founded, as it began to fail. Another immigrant from Hesse came into the fold. Henry Biehl had come to Columbus a little more than a decade before and had worked for the City Brewery and owned the Scioto. He put the money from his sale of the Scioto into City Park in 1873. Things didn't go well during several financial arrangements over the next eight years. In 1881, the brewery—an

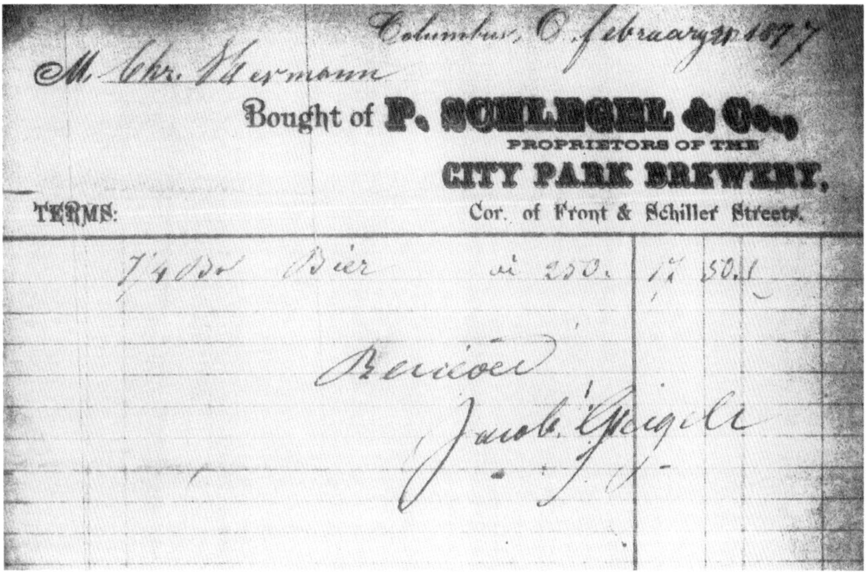
Bought of P. SCHLEGEL & Co.,
PROPRIETORS OF THE
CITY PARK BREWERY,
Cor. of Front & Schiller Streets.
TERMS:

Receipt from Paulus Schlegel's brief City Park Brewery located south on Front from the main action. *Courtesy David Foster collection.*

interesting but still emblematic side story about Columbus's early German brewers—stopped production forever.

George and Paulus went back and forth to Marysville, Paulus working at City until its closing and then moving back to Columbus. George remained in Marysville until his death in 1936. As Donald M. Schlegel observes in *Lager and Liberty*, a good recap of his family's time in the United States, George J. Schlegel was the only one of the German-born brewers to live through Prohibition into its repeal.

7

STOCK AND SALOON-OWNED BREWERIES

Though the three major breweries, Hoster, Schlee and Born, were producing 180,000 barrels in 1892, according to a *Columbus Dispatch* feature, there were others who came along after the turn of the century to add to the mix, making Columbus one of the most vibrant brewing centers in the Midwest at the time.

The second local brewery to bear its city's name was the Columbus Brewing Company, formed in November 1898 and jointly owned by about fifty taverns. It was the first but far from the last of the stockholder companies to shape the early twentieth-century brewing market. Henry Seibert was the first president of the new facility, located at Frankfort and Bank Streets and opened for business in spring of 1900. Though it was considerably smaller than the big three, it brought the city's brewing capacity to nearly half a million barrels early in the new century.

Seibert was born in 1851 in Hildesheim, Hanover, Germany. His parents immigrated to Columbus with their baby in the same year. Seibert was raised and schooled in Columbus, working as a blacksmith until 1893, when he opened a café on South High Street. He parlayed the success in that venture, joining with John Becker, Henry Weisbecker and Fred Zeigler to form the Columbus Brewing Company in 1898. He served as its president until 1900; Charles H. Engle was the vice-president. When Seibert left, Engle was replaced by vice-president Charles H. Frech, who became president in 1901.

The company's state-of-the-art brewery was not far from the epicenter of the Columbus brewing world. It included a three-story ice building with two

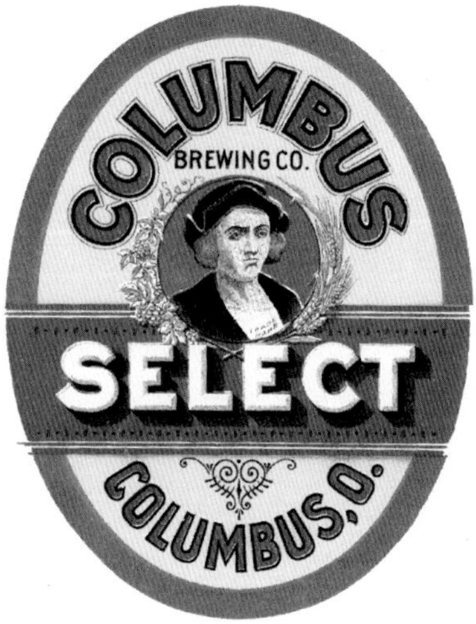

Columbus Brewing Co. label in the very early 1900s. The brewery, which would join the Hoster-Columbus Associated Breweries in 1905, would last barely more than a dozen years. *Courtesy Jay Hoster collection.*

thirty-ton machines and a 130-barrel copper kettle. Over the next several years, the brewery would distinguish itself with traditional styles such as its Select Pale and Columbus Pilsner and built anticipation each spring with its popular Bock. The company was capitalized with $100,000 and its property valued at $5,000.

As the brewery was owned by tavern owners (unlike the baron-led big three firms), the strike that gripped the Columbus brewing industry a couple years later left Columbus Brewery officials more receptive to the demands of workers. Perhaps, as a result, the strike's damage was lessened coming into the new century with the specter of abstinence. (The Anti-Saloon League moved to Westerville, just north of Columbus, in 1909.)

The brewery's more favorable emergence from the strike may also have been the reason that the Columbus Brewery was welcomed into a combine with the big three in 1905, called Hoster-Columbus Associated Breweries Company, and enabled it to survive longer before Prohibition in 1919. Columbus and Hoster, in fact, were the last two standing nearly to the beginning of Prohibition.

Three more stock companies would open before the looming specter of Prohibition all but extinguished Columbus breweries.

Henry Seibert, formerly president of the Columbus Brewing Company, jumped ship to head the new Franklin Brewing Company, incorporated with capital stock of $175,000 in 1903. Franklin's signature beers, especially the classic Ben Brew lager, came to represent this rich if brief period in Columbus brewing history. Its new $100,000 facility, situated on Cleveland Avenue near Fort Hayes, was an iconic brewery of the times, producing to a capacity of fifty thousand barrels when it opened in June 1904. The brewery's portfolio also featured the workaday staple New Life and seasonals such as its traditional bock beer. The company continued to grow, adding new investment as late as 1916 before facing off with

THE STRIKE OF 1903

Following nationwide trends, Columbus brewers began to unionize beginning in the 1880s. As in other markets, it started with a minority of brewery workers, as many—such as the firemen, engineers, wagon drivers, stable hands and others—had unions of their own, most affiliated with the American Federation of Labor (AFL). The United Brewery Workers union began to absorb the workers from other trades, though, giving it unprecedented clout in thousands of breweries nationwide. The last groups left out of the union were the engineers and firemen, which the AFL voted to keep under an independent jurisdiction.

When local brewers began to demand shorter working hours and higher pay, the biggest three companies were all too happy to support the national organization in order to separate them into camps, whose contracts were renewed at different times. The fourth largest, the Columbus Brewery, founded in 1899, acquiesced to the local brewers union's wish to keep the engineers and firemen among its ranks and granted raises. But it balked at shorter hours.

This was enough to keep the company out of the strike against the other three majors, which began late in the afternoon of March 31, 1903. Of the largest local newspapers, the *Columbus Citizen* gave the fifty-one-day lockout the most extensive coverage, placing the story on its front page every few days, beginning as negotiations were falling apart through to the settlement and its fallout. The *Columbus Dispatch*, however, began on strike day, covered it infrequently during its run and joined again for just a few articles at its conclusion, most of its stories buried on page seven.

Though the strike was relatively peaceful, there were altercations. A week into the work stoppage, a crowd attacked a loaded delivery truck; there were shots fired and stones hurled. There was tension for a great deal of the strike. Beer delivery stopped and started more than once.

The strike ended officially on May 21, 1903, with both sides satisfied with the outcome. The effect on everyone's futures, however, loomed on the horizon.

> There was one more strike, in July 1944—after Prohibition was lifted—against three of the four existing breweries: Franklin, Ohio and Wagner. The beef this time was a bit more complex, having to do with the return to a five-day work week—which the union did not oppose—and the continuing dual delivery of bottles and kegs—which it did oppose. In return for working a five-day week, the delivery workers wished to make their loads lighter and deliver both formats separately.
>
> This strike, which lasted seventeen days and involved 350 drivers and production workers, was settled without incident. The supply to taverns and retailers caught up in about a week.

Prohibition three years later. Its response, the Franko cereal beverage, met a tepid reception, and bottling soda and producing ice couldn't keep the firm in business. It closed in 1921, only to be reborn like a phoenix in a new incarnation on the other side of Prohibition.

When the new Franklin opened, in 1934, it moved closer to the action, brewery-wise, to a building at 119 North Sandusky Street in north Franklinton, operating for a very short time as the Riverside Brewing Company. Brewing just one style of beer with little success, the takeover allowed the new Franklin Brewing Company, incorporated in 1933 with a couple of the directors from before Prohibition, to brew the old brewery's signature Ben Brew. After some remodeling and the successful marketing of a beloved brand, the brewery's capacity grew to seventy-five thousand barrels. Capacity was doubled by 1948 with another big expansion.

Other improvements included a new garage of six thousand square feet, built in 1948 in the adjacent 117 North Sandusky. The company began canning some of its beer, an innovation pioneered just previously in Columbus by the Washington Brewery in 1940, continuing until metal rationing for the war effort curtailed the practice in 1942.

Perhaps its biggest nod to the future came in 1951, when the company changed Ben Brew to meet the increasing demand for a dry, lighter and fresher style of lager beer, a trend that has met its apotheosis in today's painfully pale, flavor-thin beer served at bouquet-killing frosty temperatures. An article in the *Ohio State News* early in the year put a speedy spin on the new recipe. New brewmaster James Russell Looman stated that the new Ben was born from extensive lab tests and built with choice malt and a crucial hops blend and "pin-point carbonation." The article adds that the brewery is a

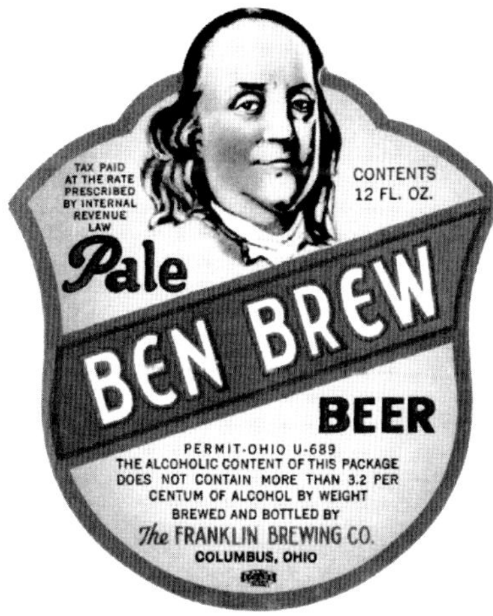

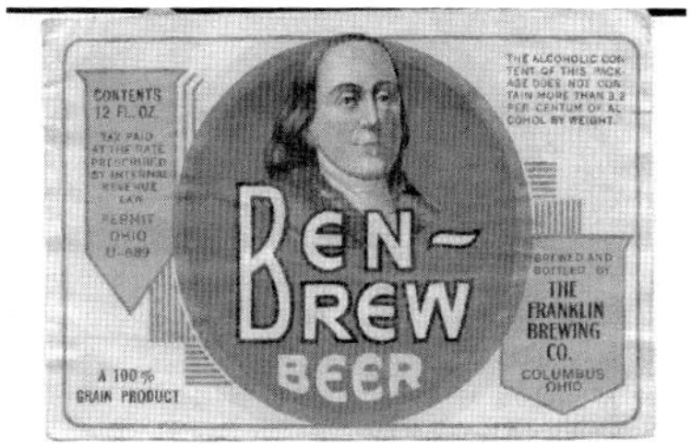

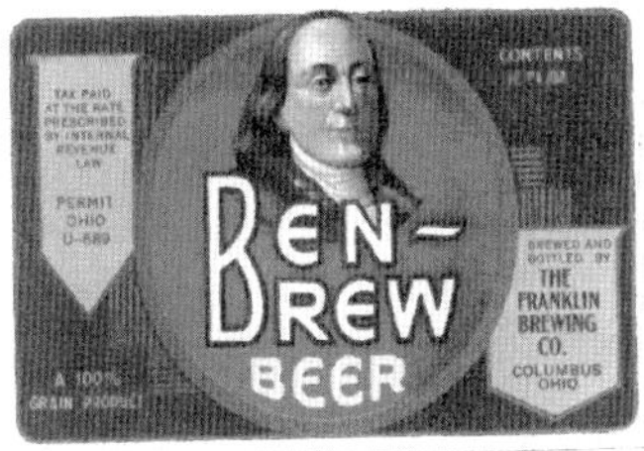

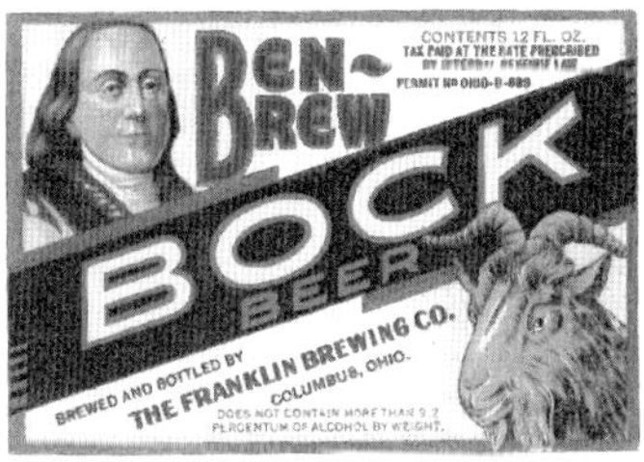

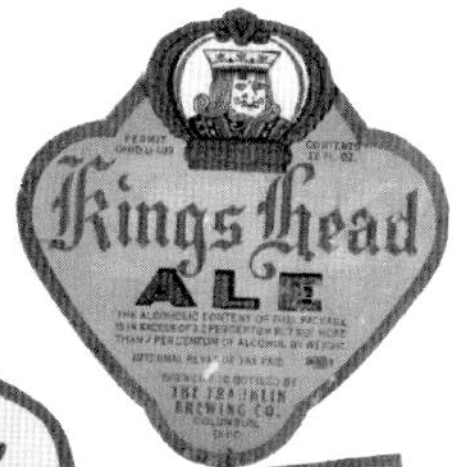

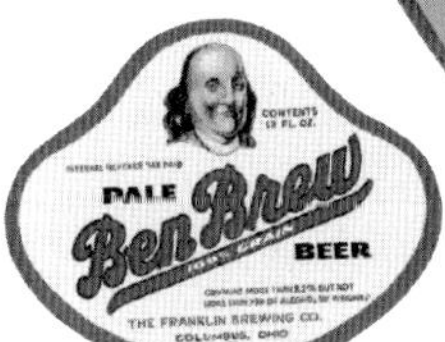

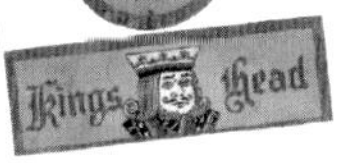

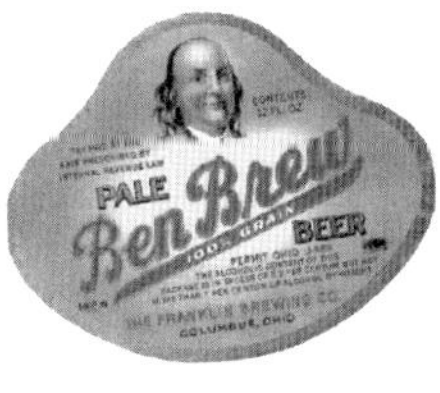

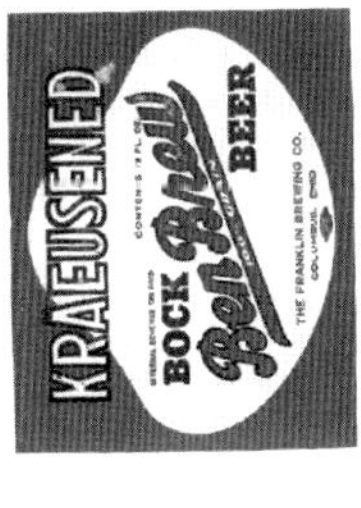

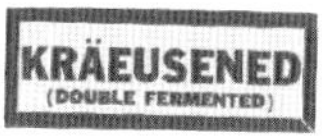

The top left image shows a Franklin Brewery signature Ben Brew label, soon after Prohibition. Note the 3.2 percent alcohol content. *Jay Hoster collection.*

The other images seen here are various Franklin Brewery Ben Brew labels, post-Prohibition. Ben Brew continued to be the brewery's main focus until its closing, after several re-alignments, in 1954. *Courtesy David Foster collection.*

"model small brewing plant by many authorities," pointing to its technical innovations. For all of that, though, Franklin, like most of the other local and regional brands, succumbed to the forces of conglomeration and big-business marketing. The company sold its brewery and assets to Chicago's City Products, which was looking for a place to increase its production for Pilsner Brewing's P.O.C. brand. It proved a temporary stopgap, and the facility was closed in 1954.

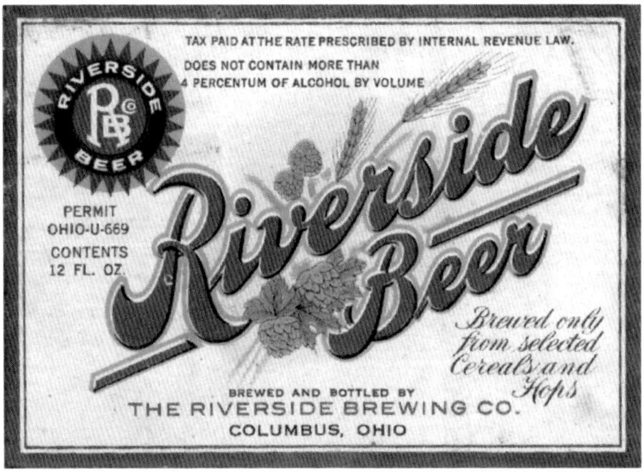

It was a short life for Riverside Brewery, post-Prohibition. Note the certified tax payment, permit number and approximate alcohol content. That last detail would come and go on packaging over the decades, culminating in the ABV (alcohol by volume) listings that appear on most current craft brews, often just to brag. *Courtesy Jay Hoster collection.*

The second of the saloon stock-driven breweries that opened after the turn of the century was the Washington Brewery, with a plant on West Second Avenue and Perry Street, a bit north of the brewing epicenter in what was to become Victorian Village. A piece in the *Columbus Dispatch* in January 1906 stated the company would "have 150 of the 700 saloons in Columbus to handle its product. The capacity of the plant will be 60,000 barrels annually. It will be so constructed, however, that the output can be doubled at comparatively small cost."

The four-story brewhouse contained a 225-barrel brew kettle and the most up-to-date equipment. News stories touted the plant's modern refrigeration system. Its signature brews included Old World traditional styles with the Washington Pilsner and Independence Dark Kulmbach. When Prohibition arrived in 1919, the company was renamed the Washington Company and made near beer and soda. When sales failed to keep it afloat, the company sold its copyrights to August Wagner's Prohibition-era soda and malt extract company. The factory, though, reopened as the Joy Products Company, making near beer and soda and getting the company through Prohibition to become phase two of the Washington Brewery, which began brewing real beer again immediately after legalization in 1933. The company soon began to brew Noch Eins, a brand previously brewed by the Ohio Brewery before Prohibition.

But Washington's biggest claim to Columbus brewing fame arrived in April 1940, when the company became the first in Columbus to market beer in crown-capped cans. An article in the *Columbus Dispatch* noted advantages such as less bulk, stackability and resistance to breakage, not to mention the elimination of the "return problem." The filling machine, the paper reported, processed 144 cans per minute. Soon, the war effort curtailed the

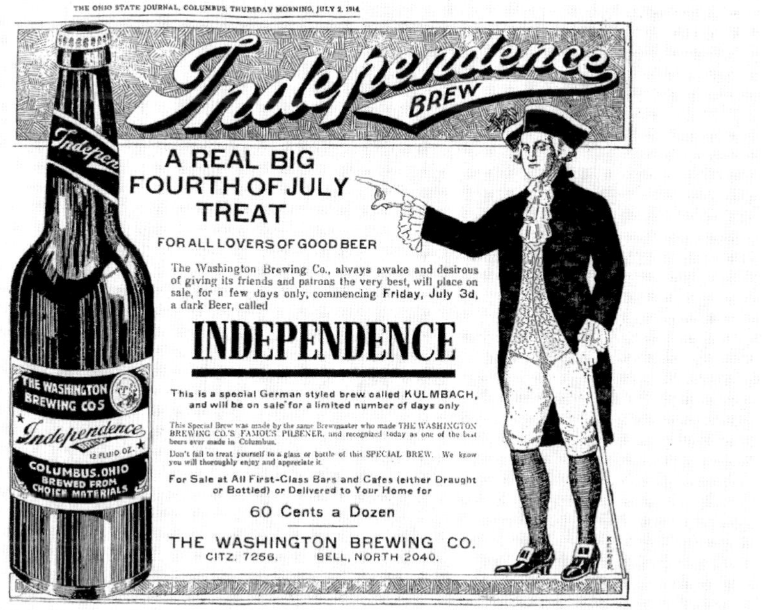

Washington Brewery's Kulmbach-style dark beer Independence was a limited edition, advertised in the *Ohio State Journal* in 1914. *Jay Hoster collection.*

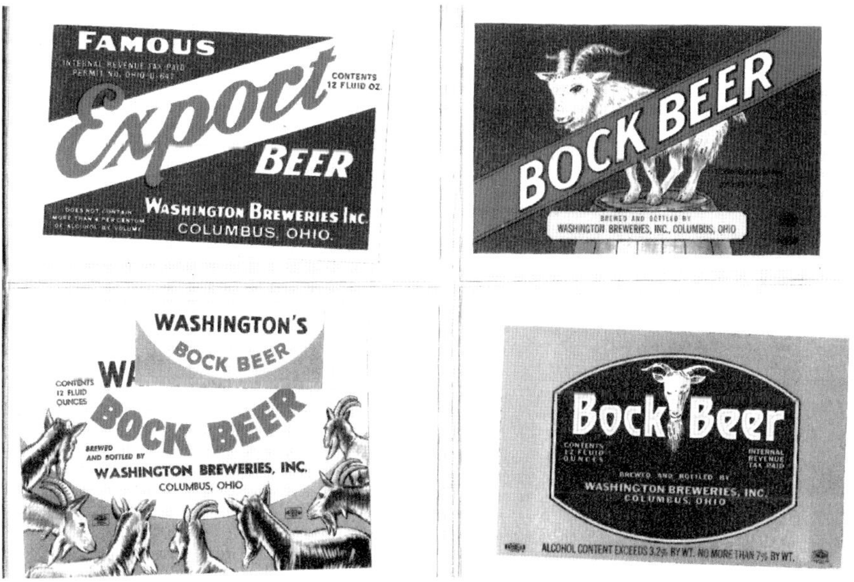

Another selection of great Washington labels, these date to the post-Prohibition era. *Courtesy David Foster collection.*

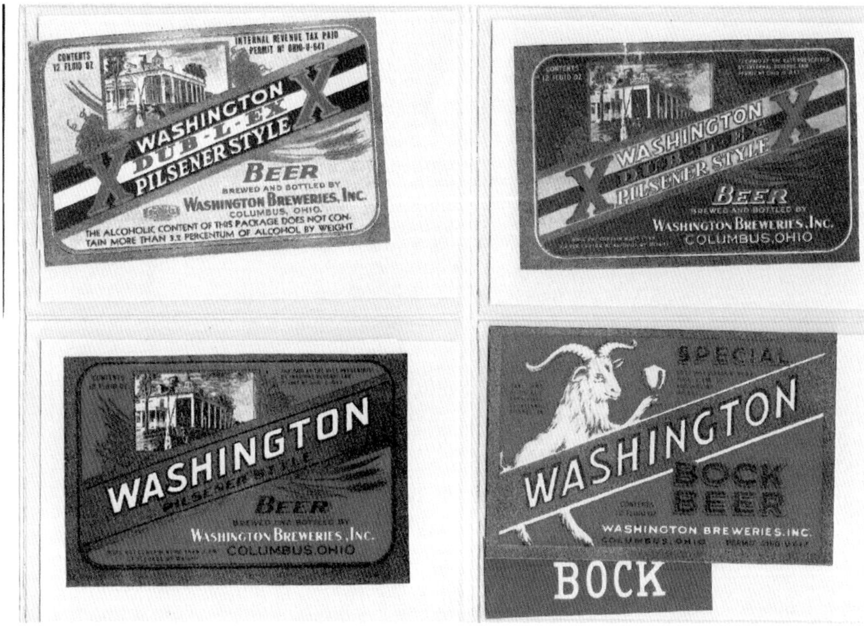

Another variety of Washington labels, also post-Prohibition. *Courtesy David Foster collection.*

use of metal for bottling, but the company continued with the strong sales of its XX Pale. The writing was on the wall, though, as national majors in the market provided crushing competition. Washington finally closed in 1952.

A *Columbus Dispatch* piece dated April 6, 1905, announced the Eagle Brewery, financed by stockholders, twenty-five of whom owned local saloons. The site was to be determined but most likely would be on the west or north side of town. The incorporation value was to be $500,000, and the plan was to include saloon owners and holders of real estate renting to bars in order to compete with the established majors. The brewery was listed in the *Columbus Directory* from that year, claiming the production of "English Ales, Porter and Stout Brewed Specially for Family Use, Delivered to any Part of the city in Kegs of Bottles. Orders Solicited by C.H. Trueman Prop., McDowell Street, S. Broad, W.C."

But the Eagle never flew.

Quite a lot of notice was given in the local press for one more stock-driven company, the Home Brewery, incorporated with $150,000 first in 1906. The ice plant was the first of its construction, begun at 1775 South High Street. As money became tighter, the five-story brewhouse didn't happen for another year. By the time it readied for brewing in 1909, the company began to fail. Late that year, the Ohio Brewing Company took over, run by veterans of other breweries from the region. An article in the *Columbus Citizen* of January 17, 1910, announced that a local company headed by Charles Andre and J. Kraemer had purchased the assets and would begin brewing within four months.

During this first phase of new-century brewing, the Ohio Brewery became known for its homage to vintage German beer, the Old German Lager, not to mention the pale Buckeye Brew and Almalz, a pale lager style fashioned after those native to Dortmund, Germany, and influenced by the great Czech pilsners.

The appearance of its Noch-Eins in 1915 gave the company a new standard bearer, one that led it until the beginning of Prohibition in 1919. When beer became illegal, the company reinvented itself as the Ohio Beverage Company and made ginger ale and cereal drinks, getting by until it went out of business in 1921.

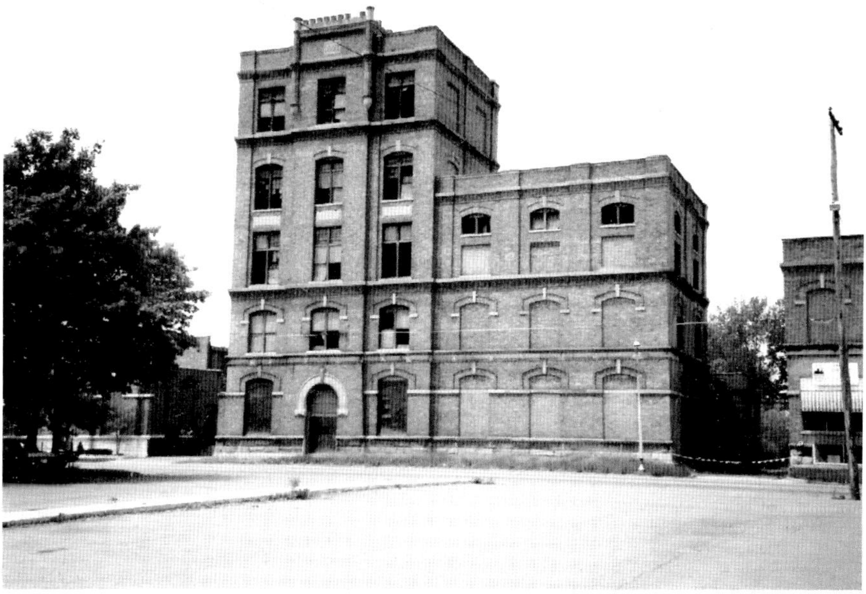

The remaining building for the Ohio Brewery, situated well out of the action in the Brewery District on South High Street, in the 1970s. *Courtesy David Foster collection.*

But the Ohio name had a few more colorful chapters to add to the state's brewing history. A couple of false starts and failed business ventures after Prohibition ended in 1933, when Ohio Brewery Incorporated put the beer's name back into business, incorporating on October 30, 1939, with Elmer E. Follmer president. It began circulation again in early 1941 under the direction of brewmaster John M. Schott, the last head brewer before the company had succumbed to Prohibition nearly fourteen years previous. A significant upgrade to the facility yielded a capacity of fifty thousand barrels. The renewed brewery began production with several trademark brands, including Edelbrau Pilsener and Home Town Ale, brewed, according to a news story in the *Columbus Dispatch*, "with pure spring water and...marketed in bottles." But the new business captured the attention of the public with an elaborate yarn about the source of its water, specifically for its Yotoc brand.

Beer memorabilia collector and brewer David Foster located the former source of the brand's water in the late 1980s. He found a small springhouse on a farm outside Amanda, Ohio, that had a leather pelt nailed inside its door with the legend of Yotoc detailed under a depiction of an Indian chief. It is the same portrait, by the way, that had appeared on the bottles of Yotoc beer four decades earlier.

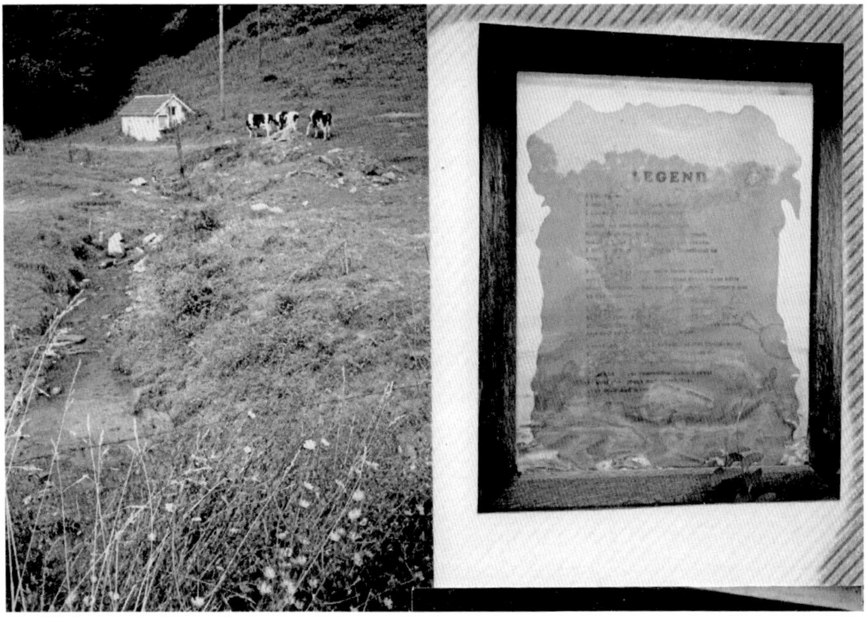

The springhouse on the farm, likely in Logan County, where the spring water was drawn for Ohio Brewery's Yotoc Beer, including a close-up of the plaque posted with Yotoc's legend. *Courtesy David Foster collection.*

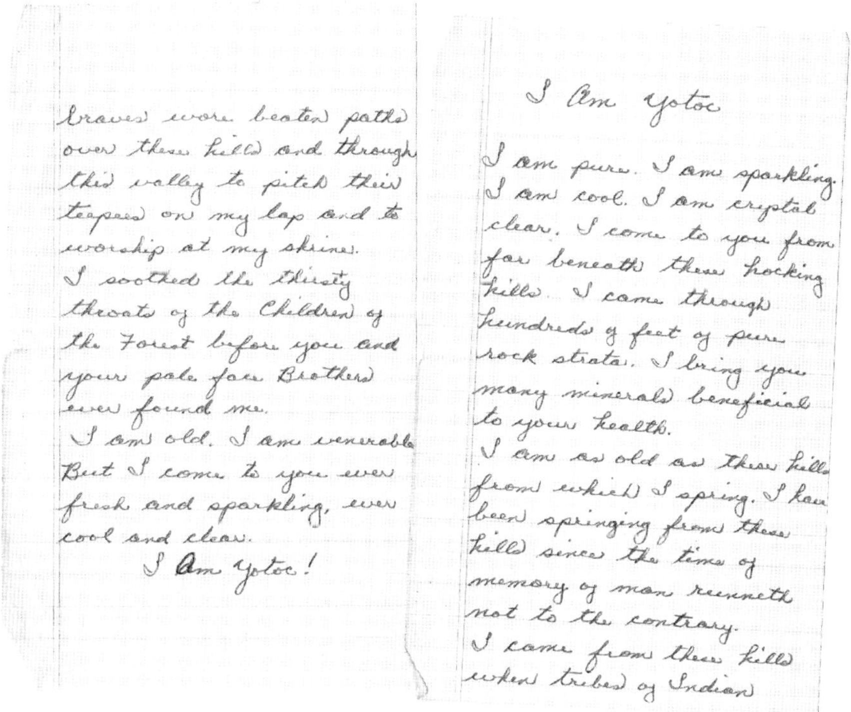

braves wore beaten paths over these hills and through this valley to pitch their teepees on my lap and to worship at my shrine.
I soothed the thirsty throats of the Children of the Forest before you and your pale face Brothers ever found me.
I am old. I am venerable But I come to you ever fresh and sparkling, ever cool and clear.
I Am Yotoc!

I Am Yotoc

I am pure. I am sparkling. I am cool. I am crystal clear. I come to you from far beneath these hocking hills. I came through hundreds of feet of pure rock strata. I bring you many minerals beneficial to your health.
I am as old as these hills from which I spring. I hav been springing from these hills since the time of memory of man runneth not to the contrary.
I came from these hills when tribes of Indian

The legend of Yotoc, as David Foster copied it from the plaque hanging in the springhouse supplying Yotoc Beer's water. *Courtesy David Foster collection.*

The legend seemed more about the spring itself, possibly the living incarnation of an Indian warrior spirit named Yotoc. The legend states: "I am pure. I am sparkling. I am cool. I am crystal clear. I come to you from far beneath these hocking hills. I came through hundreds of feet of pure rock strata. I bring you many minerals beneficial to your health."

At this point, the "legend" begins to suggest the pen of a white man, specifically one writing copy for a brewery. It continues by adding a little ancient history and then ends, closing the sale: "I am old. I am venerable. But I come to you ever fresh and sparkling, ever cool and clear. I am Yotoc!"

The owner of the farm told Foster that she remembered her father saying that a tanker from a brewery arrived intermittently to draw water from the well. Presumably, that was from the Ohio Brewery and at least some of the beer was, in fact, brewed from that water. The provenance of the legend is a bit dicier, likely created by the brewery, transferred to the pelt and posted in the springhouse in a playful game of authenticity.

Records of French campaigns in the Ohio Valley in the mid-eighteenth century mention both St. Yotoc and a tribe called the Scioto, perhaps a variation of St. Yotoc. The stories take place in the same general area as the Yotoc farm spring, so there is some historical foundation.

Advertisements and labels for several Ohio Brewery beers claim the spring as the water source. The company's Ohio Spring Water Beer and its Bock Beer both claimed spring water, presumably from Yotoc, as their source. Other brands included Red Book Ale and Blue Book Beer.

For all its colorful marketing, though, the Ohio Brewery never quite gained a significant part of the local market. Ohio, though it increased its capacity some and hired a new brewmaster, closed for good in 1948.

8

CONSOLIDATION

THE HOSTER-COLUMBUS ASSOCIATED BREWERIES

The rather brief brewery strike of 1903 (see sidebar in chapter 7) cost workers and bosses, nonetheless. Surely, it also caused the four largest breweries to examine how the new century might affect their industry in terms of costs, profits and production. Two other currents came into play, as well: the influx of major competing brands, a function of new pasteurization techniques and better transportation; and the ominous tone of the intensifying Temperance movement.

Still, after the strike, breweries flourished in Columbus, as evidenced by those added in the new century. Railroad tracks crisscrossed Front Street, giving Hoster especially a reach into several neighboring states, most significantly, West Virginia.

Unfortunately, it also brought national giants into our market from halfway across the country. Schlitz and Wiedemann appeared by 1896 and Pabst in 1898. Key in the breweries' continuing ownership of the market was growth, in capacity as well as in acquisition of the latest technology. Banding together to increase capital and reduce expenses was a growing trend in American business and industry of the time. Banks did it, manufacturers did it, the railroads did it. Why not brewers? It was a trend that put a few on top to remain there today, but it merely bought a little more time for a few others before larger conglomerates—and, more significantly, Prohibition—finished their day.

All of this must have in part inspired the big three—Hoster, Born and Schlee, plus newcomer Columbus—to sell their assets into a new, protective consortium called the Hoster-Columbus Associated Breweries Company beginning on December 30, 1904. As determined by Henry Boehmke, an officer in the Cleveland and Sandusky Brewing Company, a combine that already dominated brewing in northeastern Ohio, the big Columbus brewers were highly undercapitalized.

A newspaper article in November 1903 already reported the details that would take a year to finalize. Each of the four breweries was to sell its concern to the new company in return for cash, stocks and bonds. Each would continue to operate independently. The big benefits were to be felt in merging the four collective organizations into one and in the increased purchasing power leading to cheaper supplies. It was estimated that this would lead to a yearly savings of $300,000.

A piece in the *Columbus Citizen* of December 29, 1904, announced the final deal, with the new company being valued at $6 million. The office for the new company would be separate from those of the four, the article noted. Its location, though, was to be the southeast corner of Front and Livingston, right across the street from Hoster's megaplant.

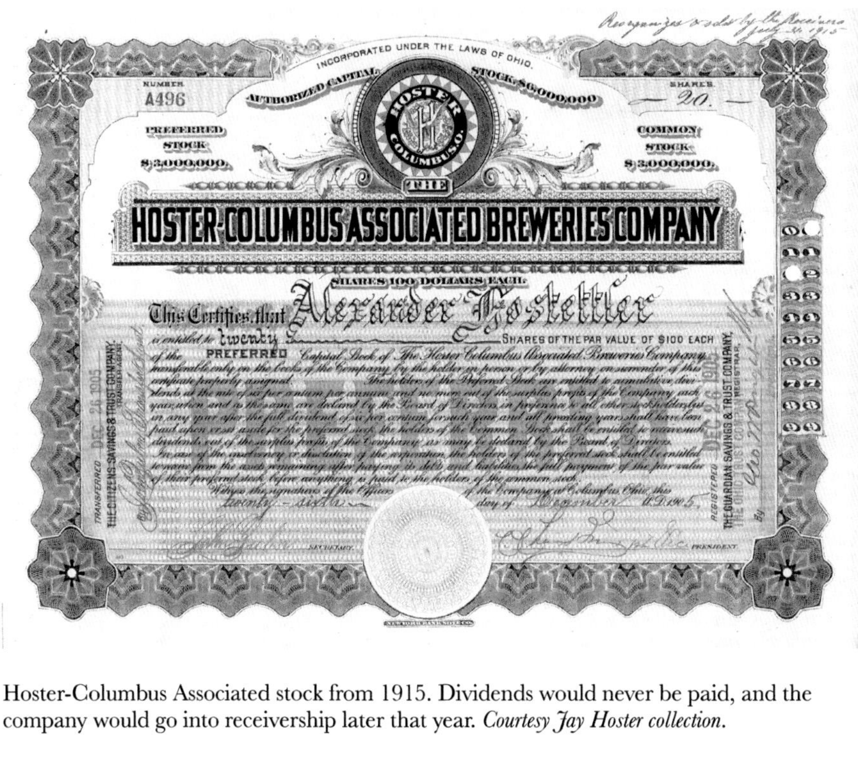

Hoster-Columbus Associated stock from 1915. Dividends would never be paid, and the company would go into receivership later that year. *Courtesy Jay Hoster collection.*

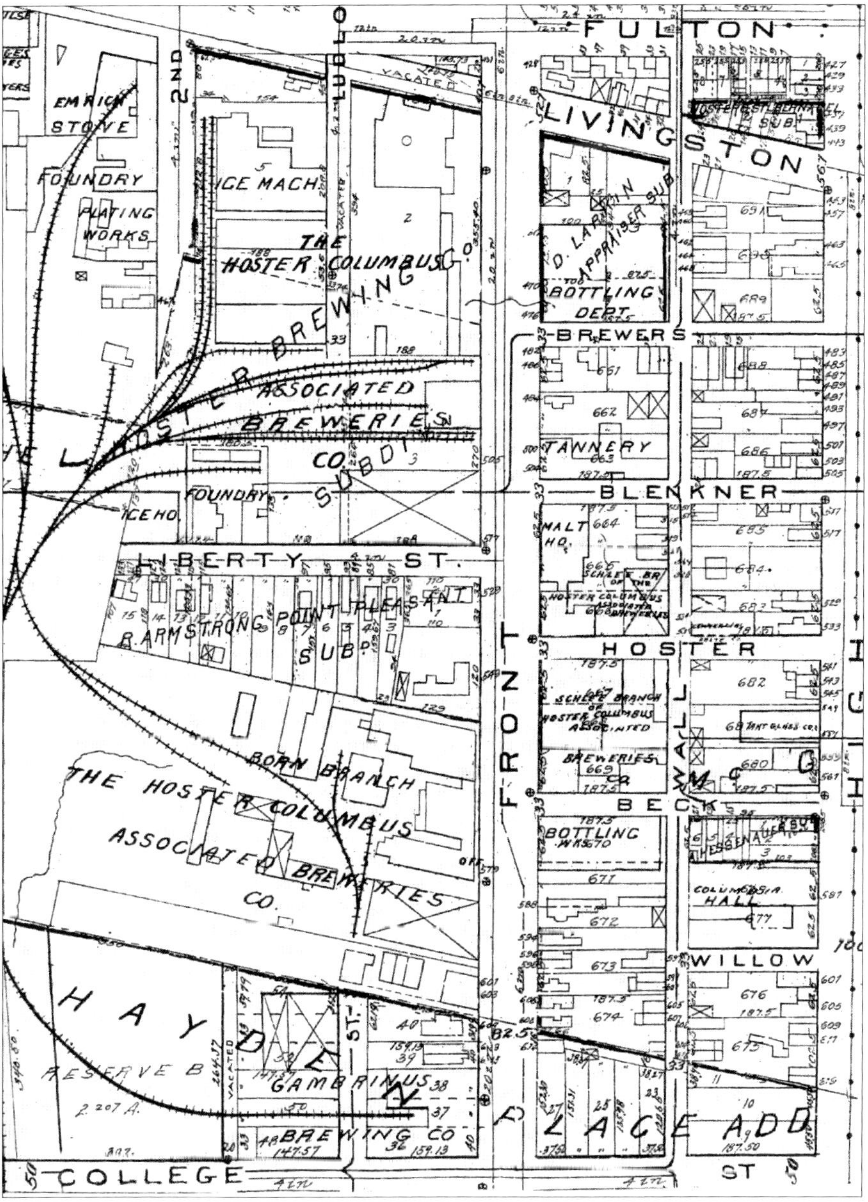

Map of the Brewery District around the time of the consolidation showing the various company branches. *Courtesy Jay Hoster collection.*

Though the new company drew from the largest three and Columbus was represented in the board of directors, president and manager Carl J. Hoster was clearly steering this new ship. Carl J. had done well in Columbus as the third generation of his family's brewers. He was also the director of the Columbus Railway and Light Company, vice-president of the Ohio Trust Company and director of the Hayden-Clinton National Bank. He was serious about auto racing, as well, owning several cars and especially known for his Pullman Pope-Toledo machine. He was president of the Columbus Driving Association.

The third-generation Borns had done well, too, especially Conrad Jr.'s son C. Christian Born. He was a director in several concerns, including the Ohio National Bank, Columbus Malleable Iron Company, Hayden-Clinton National Bank and Christian Moerlein Brewing Company in Cincinnati.

Officers for the new Hoster-Columbus Associated Breweries Company were Carl J. Hoster (president and general manager), C. Christian Born (first vice-president and assistant general manager), Theodore Schlee (second vice-president), John Zuber (secretary) and Louis Philip Hoster (general superintendent and purchasing agent). Directors included George J. Hoster, Carl L. Hoster, C. Edward Born and the wizard who brought it together, Henry Boehmke.

The new partnership put the four in a good position to rule the roost during the last golden era of brewing in Columbus, despite the opening of four more breweries in the first decade of the new century.

The consortium took advantage of marketing the larger brand, attributing all four of the breweries' individual brews with the virtues of high-quality ingredients, classic brewing tradition and—as the country began to inch toward temperance—health benefits. One ad featured a big portrait of George Washington with the headline "Of All the Good Ones These Are the Best." Below, it listed Hoster's Wiener, Born's XX Pale, Schlee's Elk Brew and Columbus Select. Another one, headlined "It's a Tonic That Makes for Health" and depicting two dowdy old folks toasting with a (small) beer, claimed, "When people approach the winter of life they feel the need of a tonic…we know of nothing that is at the same time so nourishing, so appetizing, that makes so for strength and vitality as does Associated Beer." This one, published after Born had gone out of business, cited Hoster's Famous, Schlee's Special Brew and Columbus Pilsner.

Each of the four successfully marketed its own flagship beers, as well, with Born scoring in an ad for its Eagle Brew, calling it "Korked Up Kuality for Konnoisseurs."

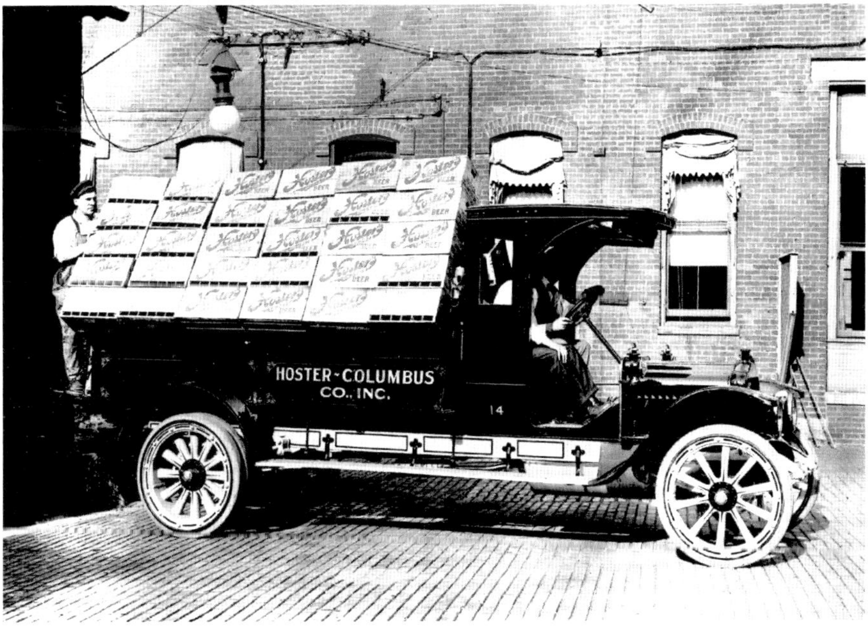

Post-consolidation and pre-Prohibition Hoster delivery truck. The Associated breweries enjoyed a measure of success until 1907–08, when sagging revenues began to predict the future. *Courtesy David Foster collection.*

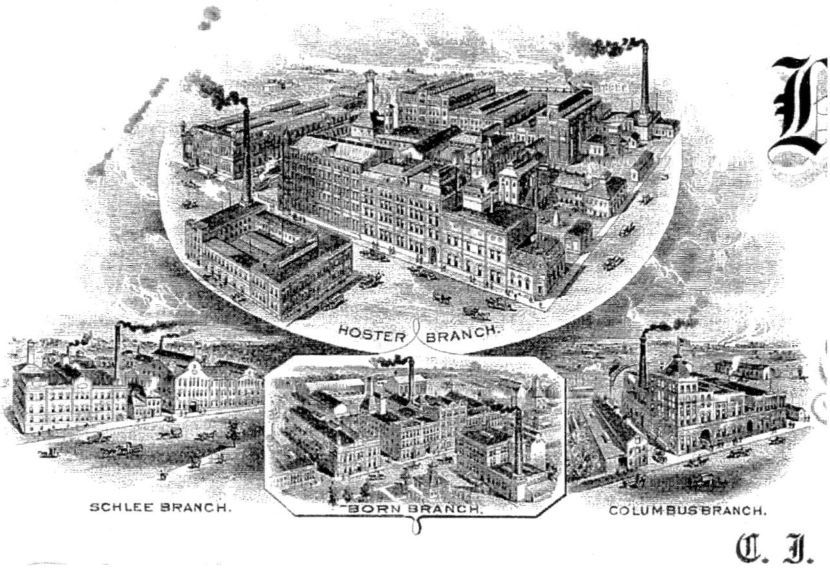

Letterhead from the fat years for Hoster-Columbus Associated, before Born closed in 1908 and the company went into receivership in 1915. *Courtesy David Foster collection.*

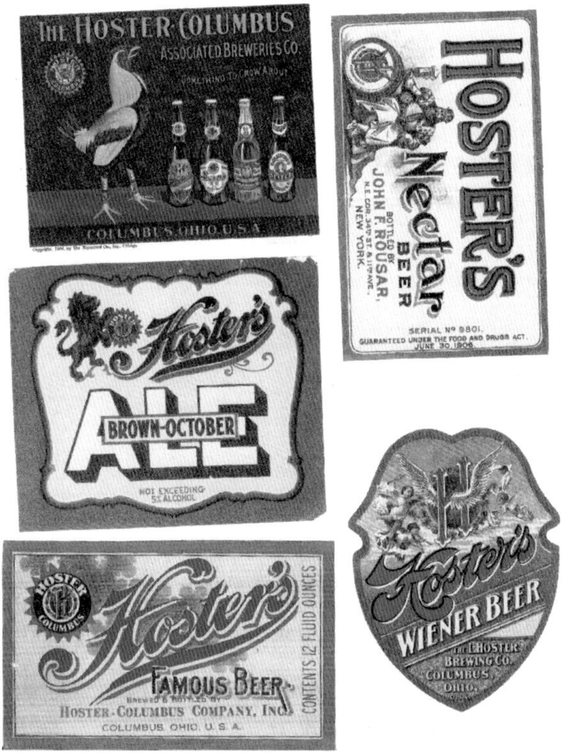

Left: Range of early 1900s labels, including Associated era and Hoster-Columbus period in bottom label, after Born was closed. *Courtesy David Foster collection.*

Below: Ad in race program. Carl J. Hoster was a big fan of auto racing. *Courtesy Jay Hoster collection.*

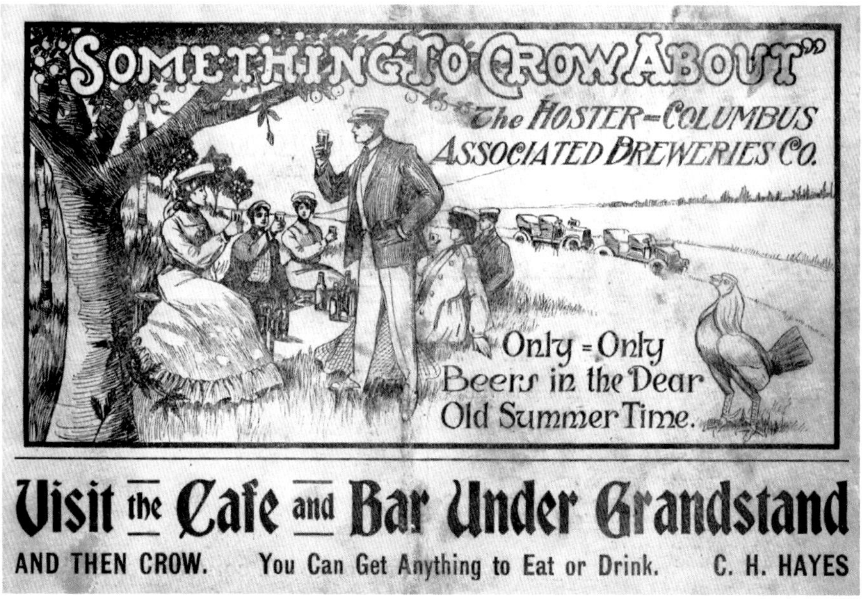

The king of them all, though, quickly became Hoster's Gold Top. The slogan "That's the Beer" became common parlance. The brand that bragged about being "light, clear and delicious"—perhaps predicting the move to lighter beer in future generations—was a beer so beloved that a song was written about it. By 1916, sheet music for "Gold Top for Mine," written by Saint Suttee and William S. Parks and dedicated to Bill Oldtop, was available from the brewery and all over town.

Eventually, though, the pressure from huge national breweries, the combined competition of newbies in the city and the shrinking market from graduated temperance laws in the region forced one after another of the Associated Breweries to close.

At the risk of spoiling the suspense, the company statement in a December 29, 1914 news article sums up the dynamics that would take the four largest breweries, united in a combine intended to guarantee their financial stability, one at a time right up to Prohibition's final nail in the coffin.

> *Ten years ago, the company was bonded and capitalized a basis of 440,000 barrels sales. These sales have been so curtailed by loss of territory and adverse legislation entirely beyond the control of any one to the point where the original sales were cut almost in two....*
>
> *In 1906 the Ohio legislature increased the liquor tax from $35 to $1000, closing over 20 per cent of the saloons in Columbus and nearly 25 per cent in the state. The loss in sales from this cause was over 17,000 barrels in the remaining nine months of that year. Two new breweries entered the Columbus market in 1907 and naturally got some of the trade. In the same year about 35 towns in Ohio in which we were doing business went dry.*
>
> *In 1908 the Ohio legislature passed the Rose County option law, which took from us annually over 81,000 barrels sales in Ohio.*
>
> *In 1909 the full effect of the Rose law was felt in the extent of reducing our sales in that year to about 274,000 barrels. In 1913 the new license law curtailed the number of saloons in Columbus 20 per cent and in the state of Ohio 33 per cent.*

The statement from the brewers continued, "In 1914 the crowning blow came in the loss of West Virginia, where we did a business of nearly half a million dollars last year, to say nothing of old Virginia going dry, which will go into effect in 1916."

The opinion piece went on to enumerate several other smaller causes, though at that point it became obvious that a perfect storm had formed to sink the ships of brewers everywhere and especially in Ohio.

The *Columbus Dispatch*, in a pointed piece on October 27, 1907, saw the issue differently. The article pointed out that the breweries were simply "Seekers of Political Power," as they owned 266 of the city's 493 saloons, remaining open Sundays even when local mores looked down on Sunday sales. The paper's undeclared opinion editorial posited that the local option law was simply the attempt of neighborhoods to regain control of their own values.

Hoster-Columbus pushed back, though, offering to sell beer to dry areas by mail with a properly completed coupon and introducing its own "non-intoxicating" near beer, Bruin.

They started to drop one by one, though. Born went first. The county option law of 1908 hit the larger company hard, with fifty-seven of the state's eighty-eight counties going dry by the end of the year. The company showed a loss of $218,000 that year, prompting it to cut losses and consolidate further. Born's famous brewery was closed, but its bottling plant and stables were absorbed into the larger operations.

The reorganization of 1914 left just two breweries, Hoster and Columbus, to carry the company, now named the Hoster-Columbus Company. Part of Schlee's operations continued until 1916; Columbus closed in 1918.

The final demise of the Old World German brewers in Columbus, reflecting national social trends, history and legislation, is outlined

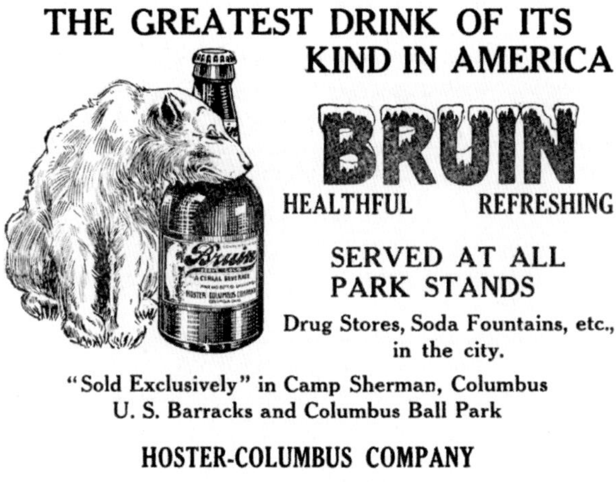

Bruin, Hoster-Columbus cereal beverage ad in theater program. *Courtesy Jay Hoster collection.*

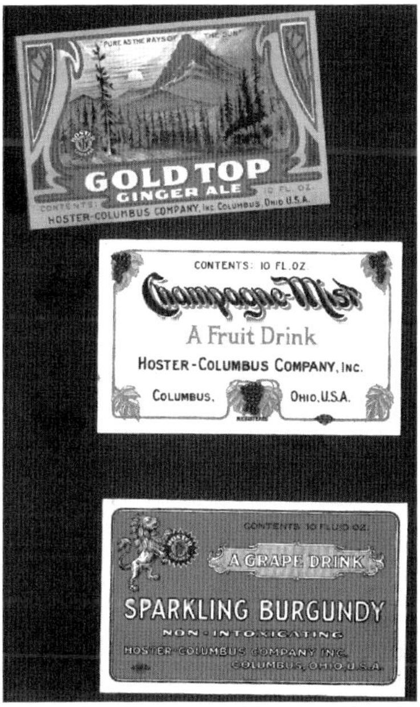

Hoster-Columbus Prohibition drinks, which didn't save the company any more than a year before closing. *German Village August Wagner collection.*

eloquently in Schlegel's *Lager and Liberty*. German Americans viewed the move toward Prohibition as an infringement on their lifestyle and culture, according to Schlegel. The organization most concerned with this challenge was the National German-American Alliance, which in the face of the prohibition push became the "chief lobbying arm of the United States Brewers' Association." Despite its pledge of loyalty with the United States entering the war against Germany in 1917, there was a backlash in Columbus, including a city ordinance in 1918 dictating the renaming of several city streets with German names. Schlegel suggests that the sentiment continued, affecting the vote for Prohibition cast in 1918.

Various parts of the Hoster company continued after Prohibition took effect on January 1, 1920, producing ice and bottling and manufacturing soft drinks. Hoster continued with nonalcoholic beverages until 1920, when all of its property, equipment and assets were liquidated. Interestingly, August Wagner, once Hoster's brewmaster who opened his own Gambrinus Brewery in 1905, bought the rights to Hoster's brands and logos, and after toughing out Prohibition making soft drinks and brewer's malt, returned after repeal in 1933 boasting a logo that replaced Hoster's flying "H" with a flying "W."

Jay Hoster, great-great-grandson of founder Louis Hoster, has said that the company locked the doors and walked away from the business, retaining none of the history, artwork or memorabilia from more than eighty years of brewing tradition.

9

PROHIBITION

"America had been awash in drink almost from the start," wrote Daniel Okrent, opening his fine *Last Call: The Rise and Fall of Prohibition*, "wading hip-deep in it, swimming in it at various times in its history, nearly drowning in it." By 1830, according to the website for the Ken Burns and Lynn Novick *Prohibition* documentary film, "the average American over fifteen years old consumed nearly seven gallons of pure alcohol a year… and alcohol abuse (primarily by men) was wreaking havoc on the lives of many, particularly in an age when women had few legal rights and were utterly dependent on their husbands for sustenance and support. The roots of Prohibition were thus sown near the beginning of the country, itself."

As early as 1826, Reverend Lyman Beecher sermonized about the evils of alcohol. The condemnation spread, and societies were formed, including something like Alcoholics Anonymous, called the Society of Reformed Drunkards. Though today that name might sound ironic, in those times, it signaled the redemption many began to find in giving up drink.

State legislatures began to get the message, too. Maine set the tone for localized legislation against alcohol, passing the first statewide prohibition in 1851. A dozen more states followed, enacting versions of what became known as "The Maine Law." As a result of unrest, resistance to enforcing the laws and in an effort to retain party unity in the face of the larger issue of slavery, before the Civil War all those states, including Maine, had repealed the legislation.

The Woman's Christian Temperance Union was founded in 1873 and gathered real steam with Frances Willard's ascension to director. Carrie Nation began smashing saloons in Kansas at the turn of the century. More important for our story, the Anti-Saloon League (ASL) was founded in Oberlin, Ohio, by Reverend Howard Hyde Russell in 1893 with a main office in Washington. When the league went looking for a location to establish its printing wing, the town of Westerville, located just north of Columbus and founded dry by its trustees in 1858, lobbied strongly. American Issue Publishing Company opened there in 1909 and soon became the epicenter of the ASL's national propaganda effort. A brochure today from the Westerville Public Library's Anti-Saloon League Museum states that the plant churned out forty tons of printed material every month. The library contains the recorded history of the league, research resources, tools of the crusaders and walls full of newspaper headlines, billboards and broadsheets, all devoted to temperance and its history. Many of the posters provide a fine study, not only of the mores of the day but also of its nascent propaganda arts.

Westerville's significant history in the movement is powerfully expressed in the library. It was the site of the "Whiskey Wars" in the late 1870s, when saloon owner Henry Corbin challenged the local statute twice, resulting in the bombing of his bar. Interestingly, and not accidentally, Temperance Row Brewery sits on State Street in downtown Westerville today, just a block from the historical violence. It produces the likes of Corbin's Revenge IPA and Hatchetation Pale Ale.

After repeal of Prohibition in 1933, the Anti-Saloon League devoted itself to education, changing its name in 1948 to the Temperance Education Foundation. The museum contains the largest temperance reference library in the world, according to its promotion.

Even before the Anti-Saloon League's presence in central Ohio, the drums of temperance had begun to sound, in the concerns of Americans reflected in the press. The tone of the 1892 *Dispatch* feature on the big three brewers sounded almost defensive, beginning with its third subtitle, "Influential Citizens Interested in This Enterprise—The Power of Lager Beer as a Temperance Medium."

In the twentieth century's first decade, the efforts of the league began to have an effect, as it targeted local, state and national politicians in "wet" vicinities, sometimes keeping Prohibition opponents from getting elected. If the presence of the ASL just a dozen miles north wasn't signal enough to Columbus brewers, the warnings of nationally mandated

Prohibition—signaled first by states going dry and, in Ohio, beginning with the county option law of September 1908—surely cast a chill.

The events caught the Hoster consortium in a period of shaky financial footing and ended the boomtown establishment of new breweries in Columbus by the end of the century's first decade. By the end of 1908, fifty-seven of the state's eighty-eight counties had voted themselves dry. Hoster-Columbus recovered a bit by adding distribution centers in surrounding states. But when West Virginia, where the company did half its business, went dry in 1914, it was a huge blow from which the company did not recover. That year, too, Nicholas Schlee, the last of the original German brewers, died, hastening the company's loss of self-determination, compounded by a significant reorganization in the same year.

Several other factors, national and local, contributed to the weakening of the brewery barons' position. With the establishment of a national income tax (the Sixteenth Amendment in 1913), the federal government had less reliance on the alcohol tax to make ends meet, decreasing its support for their financial well-being. Increasingly during the twenty years before Prohibition, as well, the brewers came to at least prop up and in many cases own the bar businesses, footing the bill for décor, free food for drinkers and considerable promotion. As the breweries forced themselves into communities that wanted to limit the number of saloons and their hours, the move to local determination began, according to a 1907 *Dispatch* article that counted brewery ownership of 266 of the city's 493 saloons.

When the United States joined World War I in 1917, Columbus Germans, especially the brewers, felt their lifestyles and traditions attacked even more strongly than may have been the case when the war broke out in Europe in 1914. The United States Brewers' Association, directed in large part by the German-born tycoons, came to control the German-American Alliance, a group founded to instill cultural pride. After the war began, however, the organization turned most of its attention to lobbying against Prohibition.

The fight was lost with the passage of the Eighteenth Amendment and its implementation beginning on January 17, 1920.

The struggle for some of the brewers to survive began that day. The Hoster-Columbus breweries, renamed with the loss of, first, Born and then Schlee, went into receivership in 1915, limped along into Prohibition selling ice and making soft drinks and closed for the thirteen years of the "noble experiment," in much the same way national giants did. The Volstead Act, which enforced the amendment, stated simply that the production, distribution and sale of alcoholic beverages should be outlawed, not the

Wasserstrom

The Wasserstrom Company, though founded by Jewish immigrants from Hungary late in the nineteenth century, nonetheless shared, with the German brewers who preceded them by seventy years, a belief in the opportunity to be found in the United States. There were other connections with the German brewers, as well. In fact, the company made its early living in the bar business, got through Prohibition marketing malt and hops and—about thirty years after it reinvented itself manufacturing and selling restaurant equipment—moved into the remains of the Hoster brewery at the southwest corner of Livingston and Front Streets.

Nathan Wasserstrom came to New York City in 1892 with his mother, Miriam, three brothers and a sister. During the time he worked in Gotham's sweatshops, he met Rebecca Rosenberg. They were married in 1897 and had twelve children in the coming years. With just three children, the couple moved to Columbus in 1902 and, after living at several addresses, bought a house 799 South Ohio Avenue, which was the family home for decades to come.

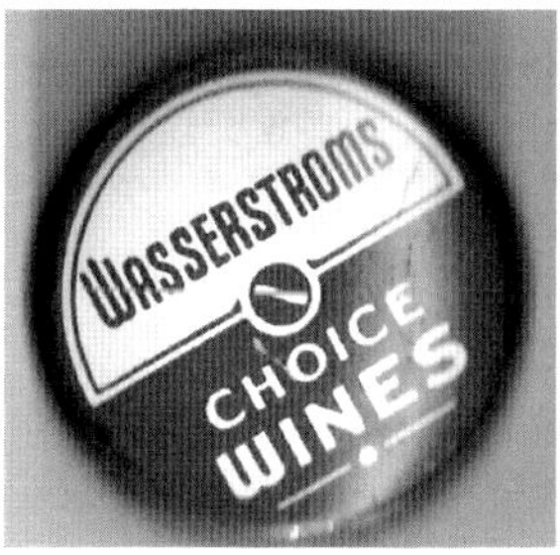

The Wasserstrom Company, which began owning a bar, got through Prohibition selling malt extract laced with hops. When repeal made that business obsolete, the company bottled wine and made restaurant equipment. *Object courtesy Wasserstrom Company.*

Nathan tended bar for his cousin when he first came to Columbus until the bar was sold, forcing the newcomer to improvise to provide for his family. He bought a horse and wagon and sold wares and sundries door to door. He also traded junk. Nathan bought a bar at 443 North High Street in 1916 and ran it until Prohibition put it in peril in 1920. He tried to survive on soft drinks and sandwiches but soon came up with another, career-changing plan—to sell malt syrup and hops for home brewing, taking advantage of a dodgy part of Prohibition law and its implementation. Soon, the family opened ten more stores around town, marketing ten different brands of malt—two likely local

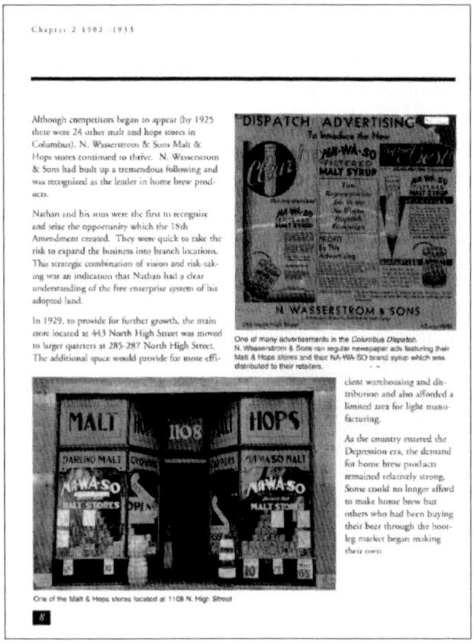

Chapter 2 1902 - 1935

Although competitors began to appear (by 1925 there were 24 other malt and hops stores in Columbus), N. Wasserstrom & Sons Malt & Hops stores continued to thrive. N. Wasserstrom & Sons had built up a tremendous following and was recognized as the leader in home brew products.

Nathan and his sons were the first to recognize and seize the opportunity which the 18th Amendment created. They were quick to take the risk to expand the business into branch locations. This strategic combination of vision and risk-taking was an indication that Nathan had a clear understanding of the free enterprise system of his adopted land.

In 1929, to provide for further growth, the main store located at 443 North High Street was moved to larger quarters at 285-287 North High Street. The additional space would provide for more efficient warehousing and distribution and also afforded a limited area for light manufacturing.

As the country entered the Depression era, the demand for home brew products remained relatively strong. Some could no longer afford to make home brew but others who had been buying their beer through the bootleg market began making their own.

One of many advertisements in the *Columbus Dispatch*. N. Wasserstrom & Sons ran regular newspaper ads featuring their Malt & Hops stores and their NA-WA-SO brand syrup which was distributed to their retailers.

One of the Malt & Hops stores located at 1108 N. High Street

8

Photo of Wasserstrom's hops and malt shop at 1108 N. High St. during Prohibition. *Scan of image in the company's in-house publication,* The Wasserstrom Company: 1902–1997, the First 95 Years, *courtesy Columbus Metropolitan Library.*

producers were August Wagner and Alex Hostettler. Wasserstrom carried two proprietary brands, NA-WA-SO and Darling.

There was plenty of extract available, much of it laced with hops. National brewers such as Budweiser, Schlitz, Miller, Pabst and Blatz toughed out Prohibition producing malt syrup. Prohibition enforcement was hugely inconsistent—controlling a substance was, in and of itself, not illegal, but it was instrumental in producing one that was. The answer to one legal challenge stated that, by a strict measure, cornmeal, sugar and grains, which could be used to produce intoxicants, could not be deemed illegal. Though the purported use of malt extract was in baking, the presence of hops went unexplained. So did the huge rise in sales of a commodity that before Prohibition was largely nonexistent.

Its sale made Wasserstrom a success story during Prohibition but put the company in jeopardy in 1933, when repeal made home brewing unnecessary.

In the meantime, Wasserstrom was forced to reinvent itself once again. It began with what it knew: bars and beer. By the time repeal was implemented, Wasserstrom had designed, built and marketed a system of beer delivery for saloons called the "Novelty Box," which stored, preserved and tapped kegs of beer. That led

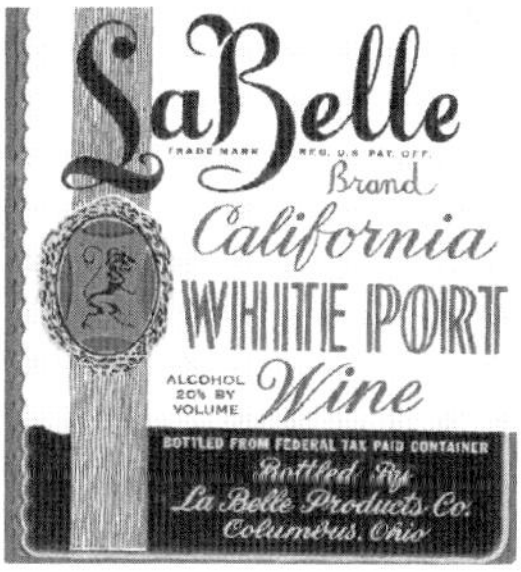

Wasserstrom also bottled for wineries, retaining their own names. *Label courtesy Wasserstrom Company.*

to a variety of products designed for bars and, more significant, for food service in general.

The company also began bottling and marketing its own brand of wines, as well as bottling and distributing under contract from wineries across the country. Wasserstrom not only had successfully weathered Prohibition and its repeal, it also became a key support for restaurants, bars and food services nationwide, as well as a wine distributor. In 2016, it was the third-largest supplier of foundation equipment for new restaurants in the nation, according to *Foodservice Equipment & Supplies* magazine.

In 1962, the company bought a large portion of the Hoster brewery buildings, leveled the part closest to Front Street and built a modern home office. It gradually came to inhabit about a third of the other buildings, built nearly a century ago and joined by tunnels, lifts, chutes and staircases. While much of it has been gutted and turned into office space for 220 or so Wasserstrom employees, a tour of the buildings fairly oozes with history.

In late 2016, the company announced it would sell the complex for mixed-use and move to East Broad Street.

ingredients used in its manufacture. In that interpretation, which was upheld by state supreme courts despite busts from liquor-control agents, malt extract was fair game. National brands, including Budweiser, Schlitz, Miller Pabst and Blatz, began producing malt officially for use in "baking bread" but, in reality, almost exclusively employed in home brewing. One challenge to the new law noted that "brewing" was deemed illegal but not "home brewing." According to one estimate, 500 malt shops popped up and another 100,000 businesses sold malt extract.

Locally, August Wagner's Gambrinus Brewery became August Wagner and Sons Products Company, producing Wagners Malt Tonic, Select, Gold Top ginger ale and Bruin cereal beverage. He also produced and marketed malt extract.

Former Hoster brewmaster Alex Hostettler, the first in a lineage of brewers who would populate the local companies, broke off and produced and marketed his own extract. Both Hostettler's and Wagner's malts were likely distributed in the Malt and Hop shops owned by the Wasserstrom family, whose company had formerly manufactured kettles and equipment for brewers across the country.

Wagner survived Prohibition with the help of his other businesses, including real estate and an auto dealership. Plus, the brewery, which was founded in 1905, had done good enough business to have paid off its $200,000 of start-up bonds in seven years. With the election of Franklin Roosevelt in 1932 and the mounting pressure to repeal the law, Wagner rebuilt his factory and hired Hostettler to head up the brewing, in anticipation. When the Eighteenth Amendment was repealed by the Twenty-First and sale became legal once again, he had stockpiled a supply of beer for the magic midnight of April 6, 1933. Sale was restricted to 3.2 percent beer until the fall, when the limit was raised to 6 percent.

The *Ohio State Journal* of April 7 called it "New Beer's Eve" but noted that many were disappointed, as the supplies ran out quickly. The *Columbus Citizen* blamed the lag in authorizing permits. Still, the newspaper described a merry scene at Wagner's brewery, where trucks full of beer were lined up until the plant's whistle blew at 12:15, when they rushed off to restaurants, hotels and nightclubs, with some dispatched to other cities. The piece's headline hailed, "Beer King Reigns, Throngs Herald Return of Brew."

(Interestingly, even with the legal sale and manufacture of alcohol beginning again, home brewing was not legalized federally until 1978, though some states kept the ban into the new century. Good ingredients for home production only began to replace hopped malt extract with the national law in 1978.)

10

AUGUST WAGNER

The future of the city's breweries, through Prohibition and beyond, was defined by a German immigrant cut from more colorful cloth. Born in Munich in 1871 into generations of brewers and butchers, August Wagner would become the rogue brewer who sprang from the great German brewing tradition, toughed out Prohibition and became the last man standing when independent Columbus breweries disappeared in 1974.

In 1878, his father immigrated to America; August came to the States at sixteen, working at unloading grain at a brewery. Like many Midwest German brewers, he apprenticed in Cincinnati's famed Moerlein Brewery. He married Frieda Marie Volz and worked up to superintendent of the Queen City Brewing Company in that city. From there, he moved to Chillicothe, where he became brewmaster at the Knecht Brewing Company and then back to Cincinnati's Foss-Schneider Brewing Company before moving to Columbus in 1897, eventually becoming brewmaster at Hoster.

Then, amid considerable buzz, Wagner, accompanied by two other Hoster execs, Charles C. Janes and Edward Prior, left the company to pursue their own interests. Initially, the new partners negotiated with the proposed Washington Brewing Company, slated to be built north and west of the traditional German brewing district. Dr. S.B. Hartman became interested in investing but favored a brewery located at the south end of the district. He wished to throw $150,000 into the project, but the Washington organizers wanted to restrict all stock investments to $5,000. According to a newspaper article from the time reporting these details, the former Hoster trio decided to form its own company, with at least $165,000 in investments and not to exceed $200,000. This would have made Hartman, who owned a huge dairy distribution on the south side, the largest partner.

Thus, Wagner and his partners founded their own brewery, a state-of-the-art facility down from Hoster at 605 Front Street, at the corner of Sycamore, in 1906. The new brewery hit the ground running, with a brand-new brewery, a solid investment and a brewmaster with a peerless German pedigree and the ambition to make the finest beer in the city.

He chose the name Gambrinus after the mythological god of beer, a legend that had circulated for centuries. The Bavarian historian Aventinus first referred to Gambrinus in 1554, according to John P. Arnold's 1911 work *Origins and History of Beer and Brewing*, saying that the King lived about 1730 BC and invented beer. This larger-than-life figure, according to Aventinus, consorted with the Egyptian goddess Isis. Later images of Gambrinus portray him as a Flemish knight, wearing a crown and sporting a goblet of beer.

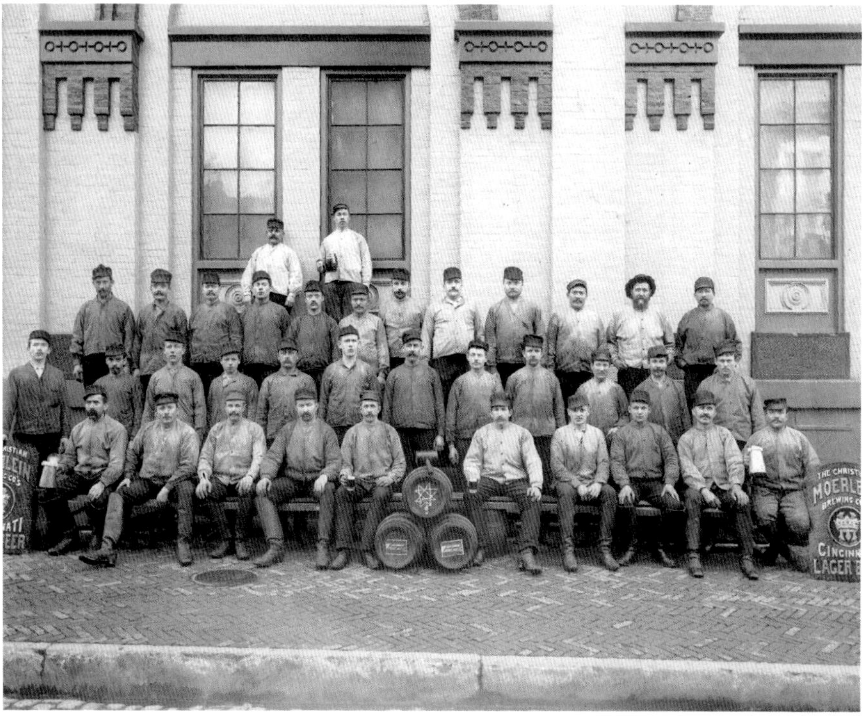

August Wagner apprenticing at Christian Moerlein in Cincinnati. He's in the second row, second from left of center. *German Village Society August Wagner collection.*

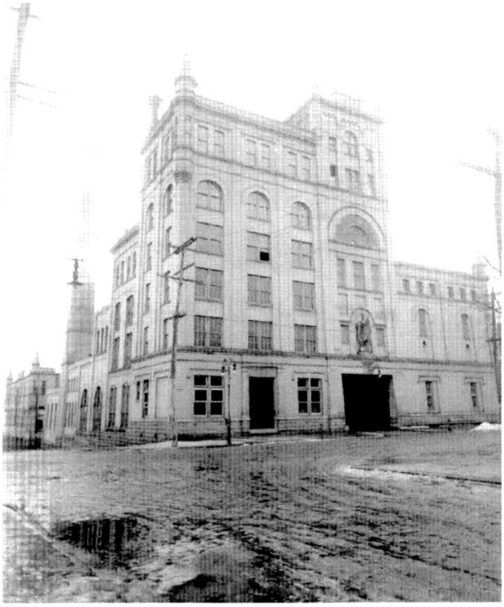

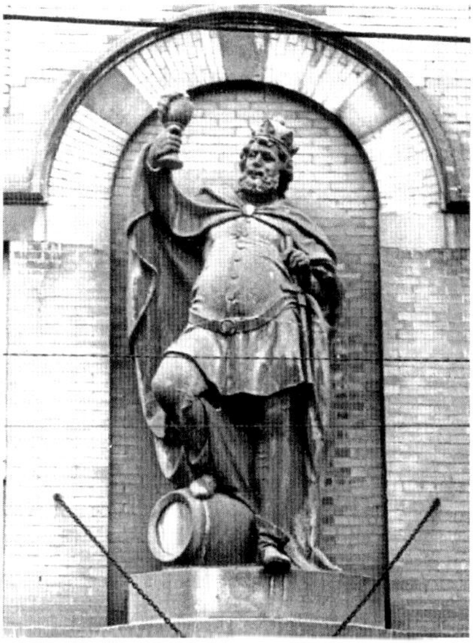

Left: Wagner's new Gambrinus Brewery, which began production in 1907, was an impressive sight at Sycamore and Front. *German Village Society August Wagner collection.*

Right: The statue of the mythical King Gambrinus, which oversaw comings and goings at the brewery. Wagner's daughter Helen said August, himself, posed for the sculpture. *German Village Society August Wagner collection.*

There are several other historical descriptions of Gambrinus, not to mention theories about the invention of beer. The fact is, though, that the deity—admittedly something of a Falstaff character—was tailor-made to be the mascot of Wagner's new effort.

Wagner himself would prove to be a colorful and headline-grabbing character in Columbus cultural history. At six feet, four inches tall, he was imposing, sporting a long, wizard-like beard in his older years. In fact, Wagner posed for the famous sculpture of the king that lorded over the entrance of his brewery. After the brewery's demolition, the statue was moved to a tiny green spot in front of the Kroger grocery store on Front Street, where he laments over his fallen kingdom today. Wagner was known to dress up as the king at times; in a photograph from years later, he dons the garb and rides a horse.

The quality of his beer, though, came to advance his reputation. Within a few years, Gambrinus Brewery brands began winning awards at international brewing expositions, with its Augustiner Beer topping German and Austrian brands for the highest prizes in France and Belgium in 1912. According to one news report, Wagner represented the "old school," taking "extreme care in having conditions just right," exercising "close personal attention to the details of all the processes" and insisting that "beer must be seasoned—lagered—before it is a wholesome drink."

A huge ad in the Sunday *Columbus Dispatch* of July 21, 1912, states that Augustiner won "the *Highest Awards: Cross of Honor, Medal and Diploma* at the Pure Food Exhibition at Paris, France and Antwerp, Belgium. The awards were for wholesomeness, purity and ingredients used in the manufacture of this beer." The extended text below the headline goes to lengths to explain the health benefits of drinking beer and the role of beer in the German family, from the oldest to the youngest.

Catchphrases in other print ads of the time included, "The Elixir of Youth THE KING OF BEERS," "There's nothing richer—clearer—keener than a glass of Augustiner" and "The Premium Is in the Brewing Not the Price."

About that time, Wagner began using trucks in addition to horse-drawn carts to deliver beer. (Interestingly, the trucks were manufactured by the Kinnear Manufacturing Company of Columbus, the same outfit that made

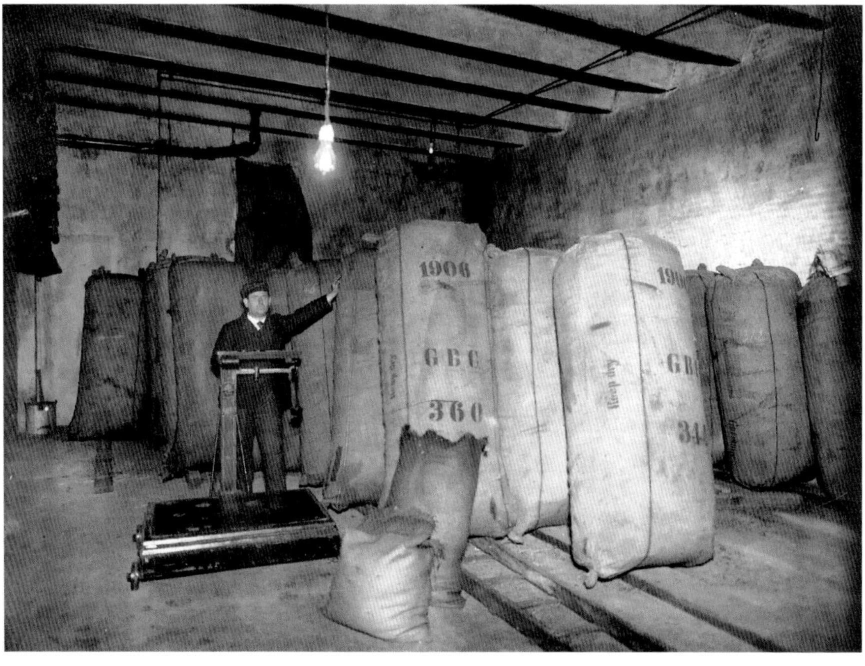

Wagner weighing hops in the storage of the Gambrinus Brewery. *German Village Society August Wagner collection.*

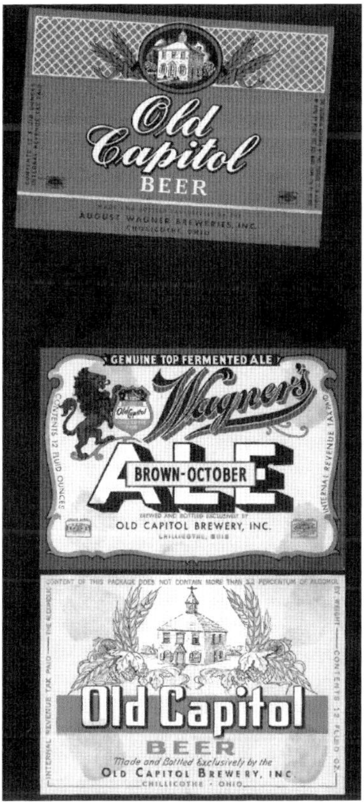

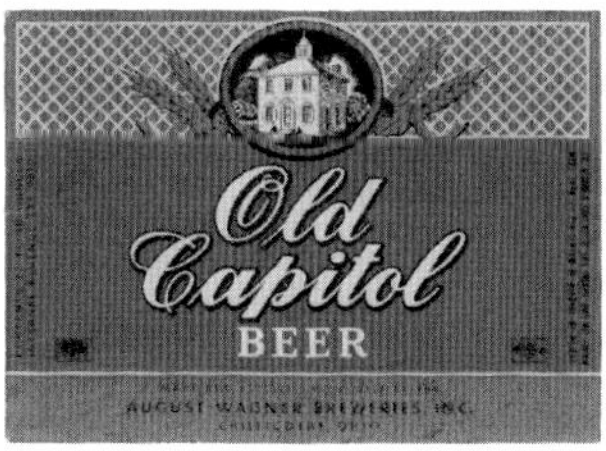

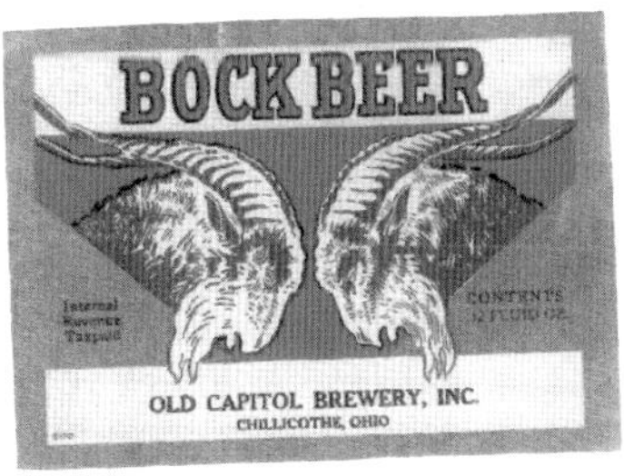

Harry C. Knight's Rovan Special race car. Knight had a significant role in the result of the first Indianapolis 500, on May 30, 1911, running near the front of the race to the finish, crashing and briefly calling into question the results. Knight died during a two-hundred-mile race in Columbus in the Columbus Driving Park in July 2013 in his Rovan Special racer.)

In the fifteen years between Gambrinus's founding and the start of Prohibition, Wagner's company not only had established itself with a superb, award-winning product, but it also had considerable financial success. It paid off its founding bonds, totaling $200,000, and increased its capital stock by half that amount. While Hoster-Columbus Associated Breweries dealt with reorganization and then the closing of the Born and Schlee breweries leading up to Prohibition, Gambrinus was busy battening down the hatches for the coming storm.

Like other breweries in the nation, August Wagner's found its way to the repeal of Prohibition, when the Twenty-First Amendment passed on December 5, 1933. During thirteen dry years, Wagner's Gambrinus was known as August Wagner Products Company.

This page: Bottle labels from Wagner's Chillicothe brewery Old Capitol. *German Village Society August Wagner collection.*

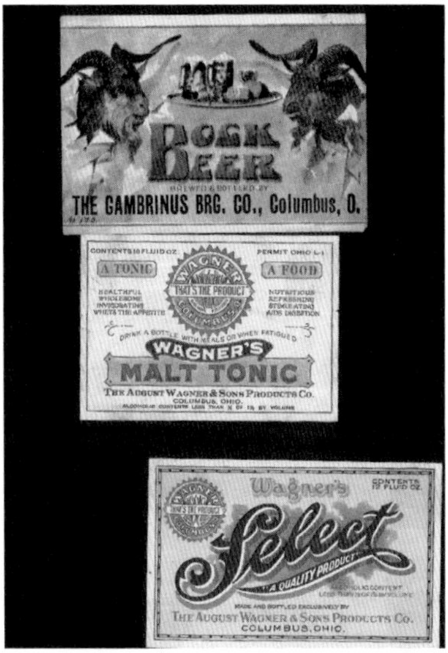

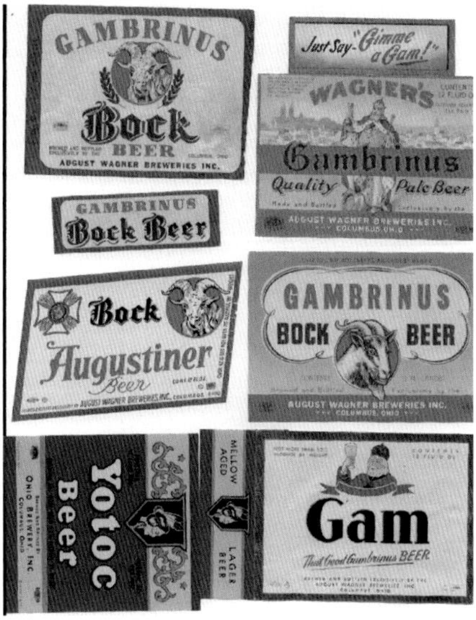

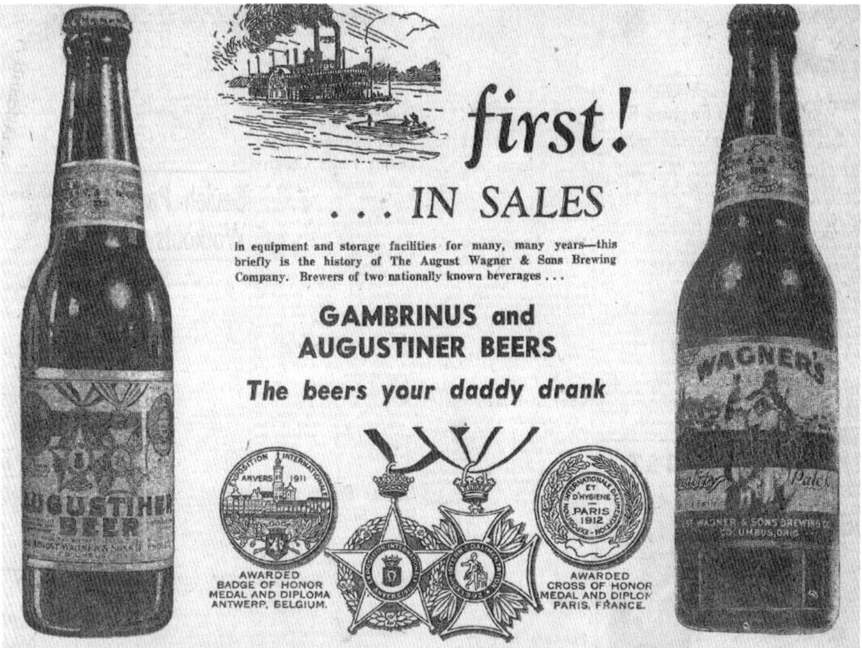

Top, left: One Wagner beer and two nonalcoholic beverage labels. *German Village Society August Wagner collection.*

Top, right: Five Gambrinus and one Ohio Brewery label, the Yotoc of legend. *David Foster collection.*

Bottom: Newspaper ad for Wagner's award-winning Gambrinus and Augustiner beers pre-Prohibition. *German Village Society August Wagner collection.*

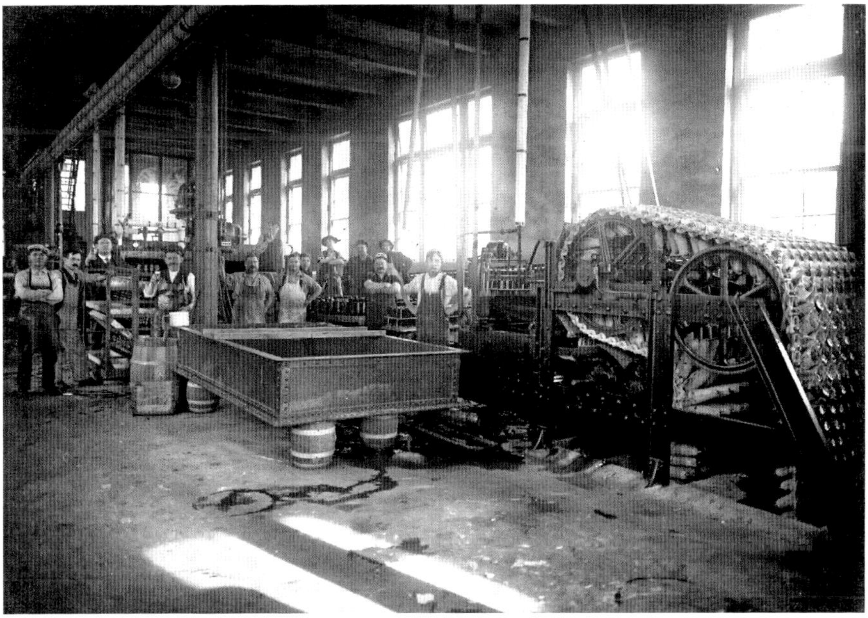

Gambrinus Brewery bottling line, pre-Prohibition. *German Village Society August Wagner collection.*

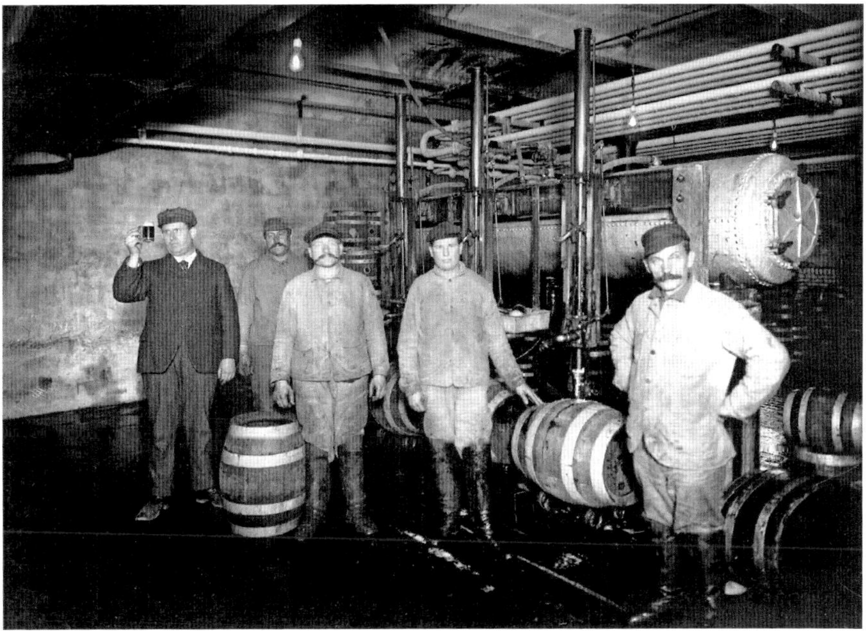

Gambrinus kegging line with August Wagner checking the quality of his beer. *German Village Society August Wagner collection.*

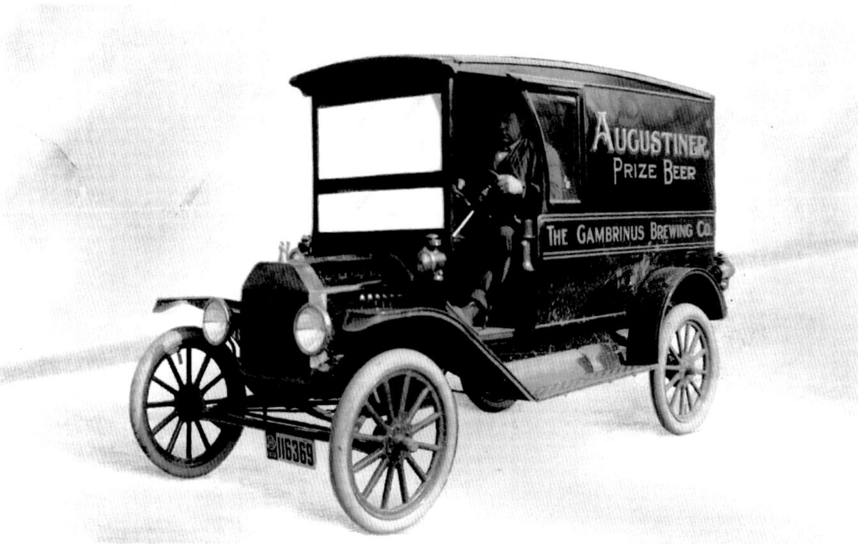

Gambrinus delivery truck, pre-Prohibition. *German Village Society August Wagner collection.*

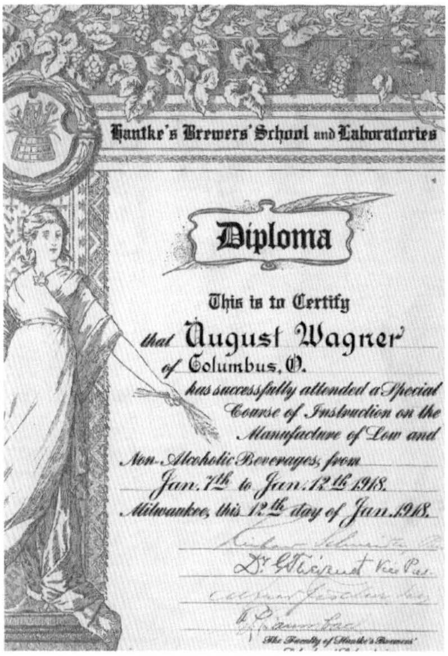

Hantke's Brewers' School and Laboratories

Diploma

This is to Certify

that August Wagner
of Columbus, O.
has successfully attended a Special Course of Instruction on the Manufacture of Low and Non-Alcoholic Beverages, from Jan. 7th to Jan. 12th 1918.

Milwaukee, this 12th day of Jan. 1918.

Dr. G. Tiepert Vice Pres.

The Faculty of Hantke's Brewers'

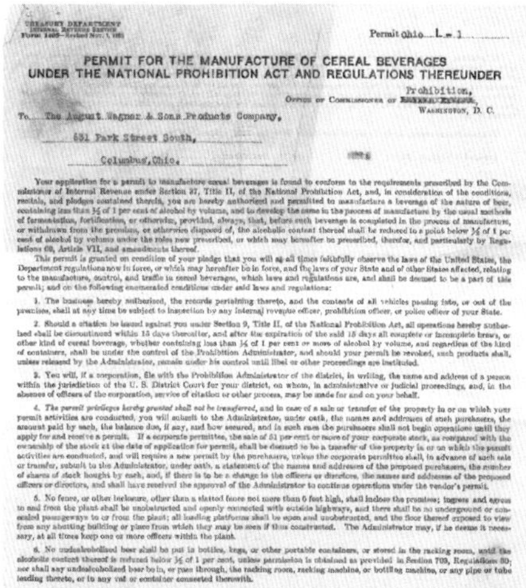

TREASURY DEPARTMENT
INTERNAL REVENUE SERVICE

Permit Ohio L-1

PERMIT FOR THE MANUFACTURE OF CEREAL BEVERAGES UNDER THE NATIONAL PROHIBITION ACT AND REGULATIONS THEREUNDER

OFFICE OF COMMISSIONER OF Prohibition,
WASHINGTON, D. C.

To The August Wagner & Sons Products Company,
631 Park Street South,
Columbus, Ohio.

Your application for a permit to manufacture cereal beverages is found to conform to the requirements prescribed by the Commissioner of Internal Revenue under Section 37, Title II, of the National Prohibition Act, and, in consideration of the conditions, recitals, and pledges contained therein, you are hereby authorized and permitted to manufacture a beverage of the nature of beer, containing less than ½ of 1 per cent of alcohol by volume, and to develop the same in the process of manufacture by the usual methods of fermentation, fortification, or otherwise, provided, always, that, before such beverage is completed in the process of manufacture, or withdrawn from the premises, or otherwise disposed of, the alcoholic content thereof shall be reduced to a point below ½ of 1 per cent of alcohol by volume under the rules now prescribed, or which may hereafter be prescribed, therefor, and particularly by Regulations 60, Article VII, and amendments thereof.

This permit is granted on condition of your pledge that you will at all times faithfully observe the laws of the United States, the Department regulations now in force, or which may hereafter be in force, and the laws of your State and of other States affected, relating to the manufacture, control, and traffic in cereal beverages, which laws and regulations are, and shall be deemed to be a part of this permit; and on the following enumerated conditions under said laws and regulations:

1. The business hereby authorized, the records pertaining thereto, and the contents of all vehicles passing into, or out of the premises, shall at any time be subject to inspection by any internal revenue officer, prohibition officer, or police officer of your State.

2. Should a citation be issued against you under Section 9, Title II, of the National Prohibition Act, all operations hereby authorized shall be discontinued within 15 days thereafter, and after the expiration of the said 15 days all complete or incomplete brews, or other kind of cereal beverage, whether containing less than ½ of 1 per cent or more of alcohol by volume, and regardless of the kind of containers, shall be under the control of the Prohibition Administrator, and should your permit be revoked, such products shall, unless released by the Administrator, remain under his control until libel or other proceedings are instituted.

3. You will, if a corporation, file with the Prohibition Administrator of the district, in writing, the name and address of a person within the jurisdiction of the U. S. District Court for your district, on whom, in administrative or judicial proceedings, and, in the absence of officers of the corporation, service of citation or other process, may be made for and on your behalf.

4. *The permit privileges hereby granted shall not be transferred*, and in case of a sale or transfer of the property in or on which your permit activities are conducted, you will submit to the Administrator, under oath, the names and addresses of such purchasers, the amount paid by each, the balance due, if any, and how secured, and in such case the purchasers shall not begin operations until they apply for and receive a permit. If a corporate permittee, the sale of 51 per cent or more of your corporate stock, as compared with the ownership of the stock at the date of application for permit, shall be deemed to be a transfer of the property in or on which the permit activities are conducted, and will require a new permit by the purchasers, unless the corporate permittee shall, in advance of such sale or transfer, submit to the Administrator, under oath, a statement of the names and addresses of the proposed purchasers, the number of shares of stock bought by each, and, if there is to be a change in the officers or directors, the names and addresses of the proposed officers or directors, and shall have received the approval of the Administrator to continue operations under the vendor's permit.

5. No fence, or other inclosure, other than a slatted fence not more than 6 feet high, shall inclose the premises; ingress and egress to and from the plant shall be unobstructed and openly connected with outside highways, and there shall be no underground or concealed passageways to or from the plant; all loading platforms shall be open and unobstructed, and the floor thereof exposed to view from any abutting building or place from which they may be seen if thus constructed. The Administrator may, if he deems it necessary, at all times keep one or more officers within the plant.

6. No undealcoholized beer shall be put in bottles, kegs, or other portable containers, or stored in the racking room, until the alcoholic content thereof is reduced below ½ of 1 per cent, unless permission is obtained as provided in Section 709, Regulations 60; nor shall any undealcoholized beer be in, or pass through, the racking room, racking machine, or bottling machine, or any pipe or tube leading thereto, or to any vat or container connected therewith.

7. Reports on Form 1418 of the production and disposition of cereal beverages each month shall be submitted to the Administrator on or before the 10th day of the following month.

8. No wort shall be manufactured or sold by you; and no malt syrups, malt extracts, or like preparations shall be manufactured or sold for brewing or distilling, and if manufactured and sold for legitimate purposes it shall be under the most rigid supervision, and sale thereof for brewing or distilling, or without careful inquiry and assurance as to the intended use, or sale or removal under circumstances from which an unlawful use may be inferred, will be held grounds for the revocation of this permit; and you will, when called upon by the Administrator, furnish full and complete information in writing as to the date, amount, and purpose of such sales.

9. This permit is issued with the understanding that you will be held responsible, as to civil liability and as affects this permit, for any violation of Section 37, Title II, of the National Prohibition Act, or regulations made thereunder, by any employee of yours, whether or not such violation was with your knowledge or consent.

(OVER)

Left: August Wagner, always a guy to look ahead at the curve, earned his non-alcohol brewing diploma in 1918, nearly two years before Prohibition. *German Village Society's August Wagner collection.*

Right: August Wagner's permit to manufacture low and nonalcoholic products. With these and malt extract, Wagner's Gambrinus survived Prohibition. *German Village Society's August Wagner collection.*

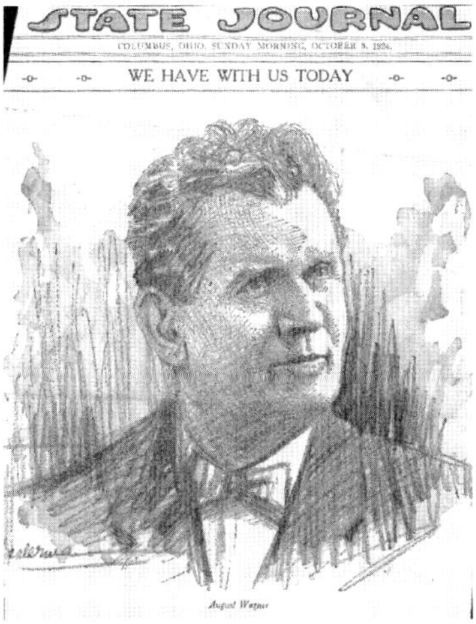

Cover story on August Wagner in the *Ohio State Journal* in 1924. *Courtesy of the* Columbus Dispatch.

The tag "That's the Beer"—which the shrewd, forward-thinking brewer bought from the failed Hoster—became "That's the Product." Hoster, under receivership since 1914 and dealt a fatal blow with prime market West Virginia's statewide dry vote in 1914, struggled through the onset of Prohibition but sold its copyrights to Wagner. Hoster descendant Esther Hoster Dawson wrote in her self-published *History of the L. Hoster Brewery of Columbus, Ohio*, "George J. Hoster, the only remaining son, felt there was no chance to beat Prohibition. He sold all rights to the name and trademark to the August Wagner Brewery. Today its 'W' with the wing emblem reflects the original 'Flying H' design of the Hoster Brewery."

The products in Wagner's new name were soda, ice, near beer and cereal beverages. A diploma dated January 1918 from Hantke's Brewer's School and Laboratories in Milwaukee marked the veteran brewer's mastery of producing low- and nonalcoholic beverages. A permit from a couple of years later, granted by the Treasury Department and issued by the Office of the Commissioner of Prohibition, allowed Wagner to manufacture cereal beverages under the National Prohibition Act. The news piece that extolled the fine skills of his brewing tradition insisted that, under his father's direction, brewer Philip Wagner's versions of the famed Augustiner and Select, with the alcohol extracted by "mechanical means," had "the same taste exactly, the old-time flavor that won the prizes at Munich, Paris and Antwerp." Gambrinus even produced its own Gold Top Ginger Ale, a brand name bought from Hoster and derived from the former company's best-known beer.

An ad from the time touted a range of products, including malt tonic; pale dry ginger ale; root beer, chocolate and burgundy soda; and malt extract. Pabst, Busch and others nationally distributed malt extract, presumably for bread making and the like. It was rarely used for that purpose but, rather, in the making of home brew. Frequently it was laced with hops, hardly an ingredient in bread making. As the authorities generally looked the other way, on account of its alcohol-free natural state, malt and hops

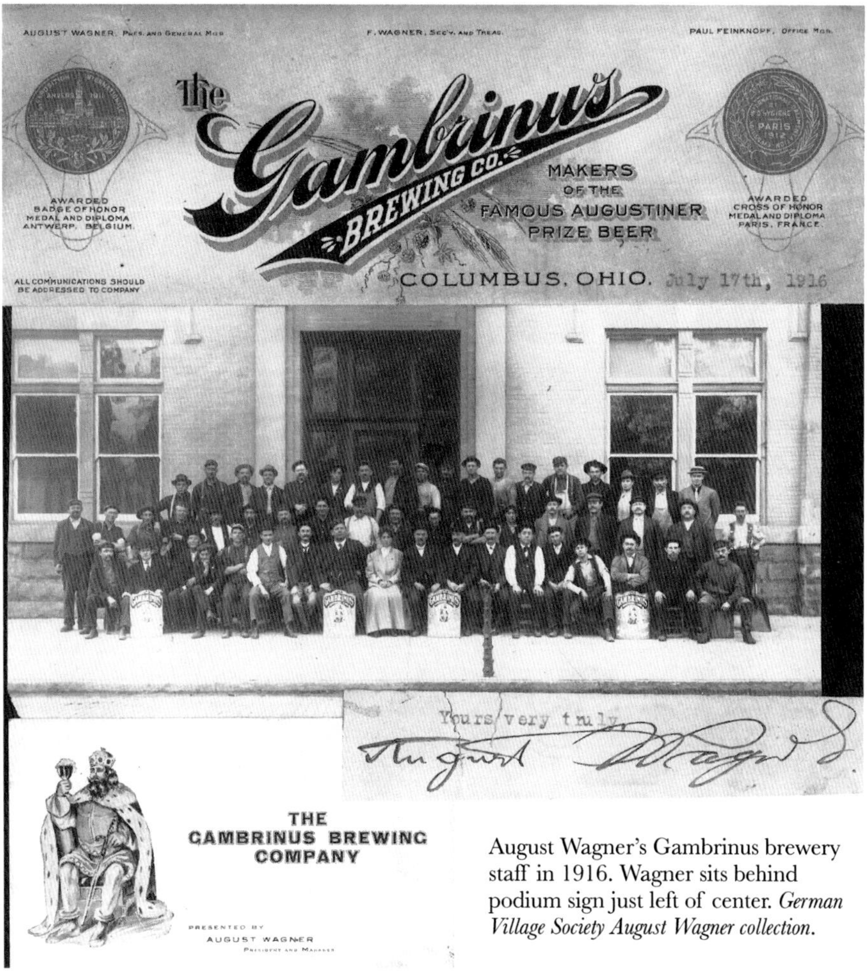

August Wagner's Gambrinus brewery staff in 1916. Wagner sits behind podium sign just left of center. *German Village Society August Wagner collection.*

shops sprang up all over the country, and former brewers supplied extract. Wagner not only propped up his brewing business with his growing real estate company, he also employed family whenever possible in tough years. He also owned the Greater Columbus Hardware Company.

Wagner sensed that repeal was right around the corner when Franklin Roosevelt was elected in 1932. He began preparations for the deluge of business that would result. He updated his plant, hired more workers and, as soon as the last vote was cast, started brewing 3.2 percent beer, the legal limit for the first six months of the new alcohol law. When repeal kicked in, the shrewd brewer was ready to pounce. Newspaper articles of the time described the scene at Wagner's brewery, the trucks lined up just inside its

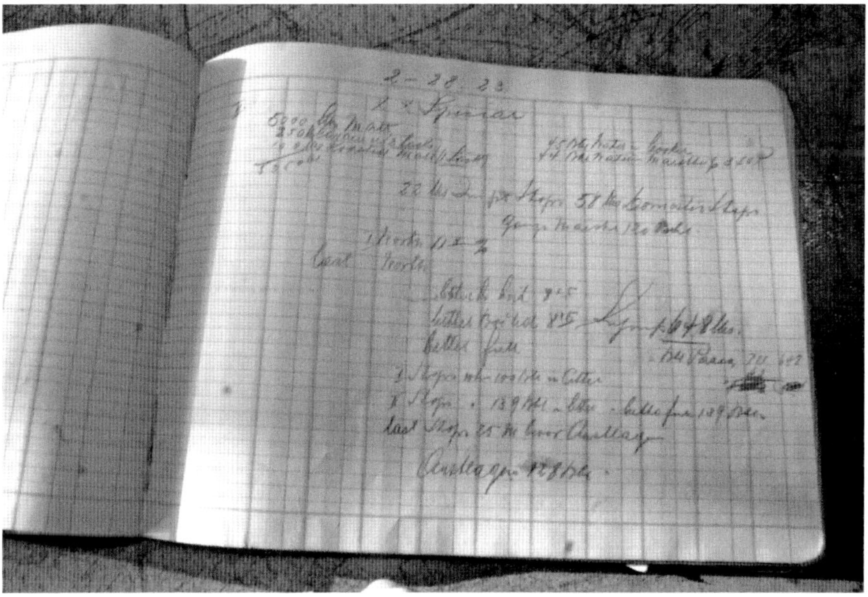

August Wagner's brewing log from 1923 for a batch of XX Special. Two years into Prohibition, this would be a brew that was subsequently de-alcoholized. *Photo by the author of an object in the David Foster collection.*

gates, loaded and ready to run to eagerly awaiting taverns all over town. The plant's whistle blew at 12:15 a.m. on Friday, April 7, 1933, officially marking the end of thirteen years of drinking alcohol furtively and of brewing terrible imitations of the real thing at home. Those years had witnessed a national habit of lawbreaking that ranged from home brewing, bathtub gin and speakeasies to the violent, big business of organized crime.

That was all behind, as Wagner's trucks raced to both out-of-town accounts and downtown restaurants and hotels. One of the first restaurants in Columbus was the Clock, at 161 North High Street and today the site of the Elevator Brewery and Draught Haus, an early participant in the city's craft brew revolution, established sixty-seven years later. The scene all over town at restaurants and, later, hotels, was one of celebration. One paper noted that the state had collected $142,000 in licensing fees. In fact, jubilation over the return was only limited by Gambrinus's capacity and the slow authorization of permits. Delivery to homes lagged slightly behind, as well.

Gambrinus was off to a grand restart, impeded only slightly by the opening of a couple of new breweries over the next few years. Wagner's reborn brewery had hit its stride.

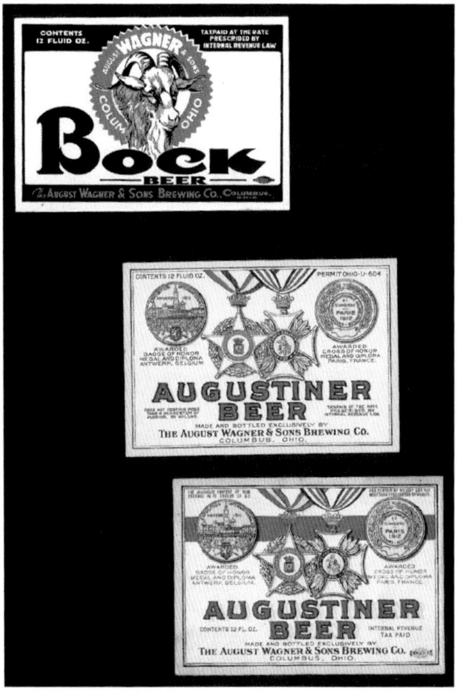

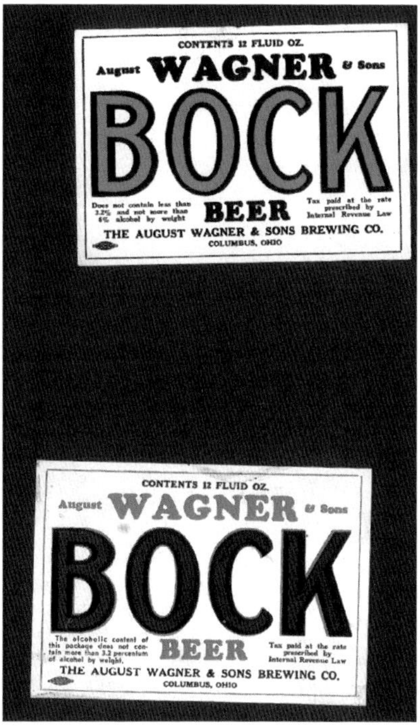

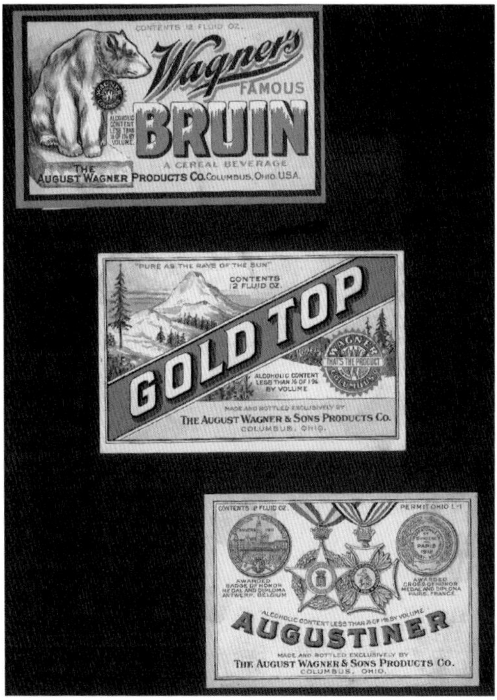

This page: A range of Wagner/Gambrinus labels spanning several decades. The colorful, fanciful design is constant. Many of Wagner's labels also had an iconic storytelling quality. *German Village Society August Wagner collection.*

HOSTETTLER

What's in a name? When German brewers came to Columbus in the mid-1800s, they brought not only their cultural traditions but also professional histories. In the case of Alex Hostettler, brewmaster for Hoster and, later, August Wagner's Gambrinus Brewery, the family business stretched back to Switzerland in the mid-1800s and forward to Gambrinus's closing in 1974.

According to his grandson, Alex O., Alex was born in Murten, Switzerland, in 1870 and came to the States likely in 1890. His father, Rudolf, was a brewer in Basil, Switzerland, and Alex continued the craft in America, beginning in Cincinnati's Schneider then coming to join Columbus Brewery in 1902. Interestingly, August Wagner, Hoster's brewmaster at the time, also had apprenticed in Cincinnati, with Moerlein. When Columbus, Hoster, Born and Schlee merged in 1905, the Hoster-Columbus Associated Breweries honored Hostettler's contract with Columbus. Alex became Hoster's brewmaster when Wagner abruptly left in 1905 to found his own Gambrinus Brewery. He remained with Hoster until the start of Prohibition, according to his grandson.

Hostettler got through Prohibition making malt extract and selling it primarily to the German community on the south side of town. He also patented a heating element that burned off alcohol in the production of near beer (.5 percent alcohol.)

After Prohibition was lifted in 1933, a consortium of investors attempted to rebuild Hoster, putting together a business plan and capital enough to offer the senior Hostettler shares in the new

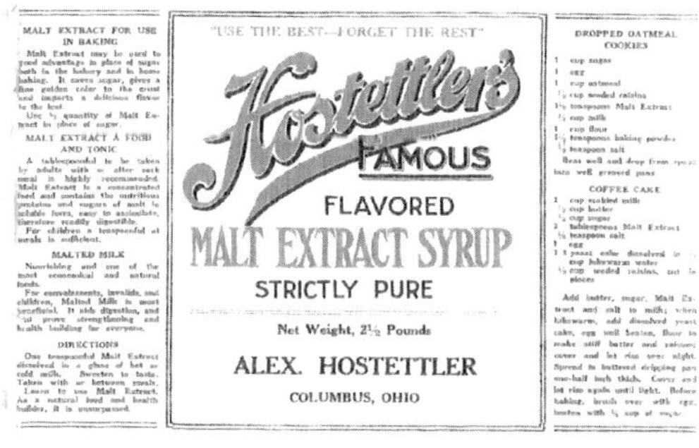

Label for Hostettler's malt, Prohibition era. *Courtesy David Foster collection.*

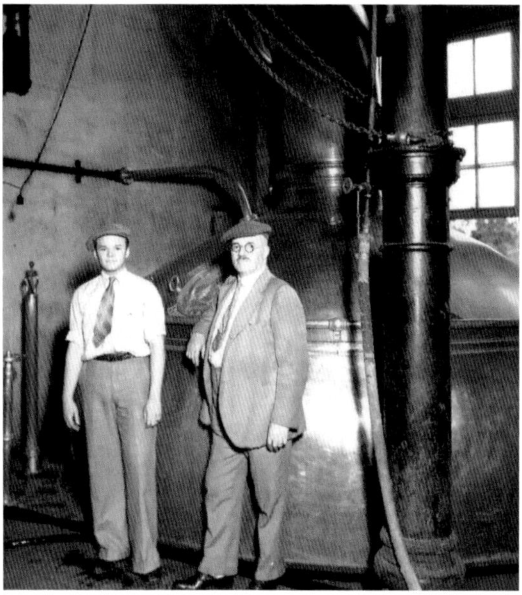

Alexander H. Hostettler (with his dad, Alexander Hostettler) in Wagner's Gambrinus brewery soon after repeal of Prohibition. *Courtesy Chris Hostettler collection.*

company and the titles brewmaster and one of five directors. The brewery was to be situated in a new building, with Stephen Stepanian acting as president and Theodore G. Hoster as vice-president. A letter from the company dated February 20, 1934, threatening Hostettler with legal action if he didn't honor his contract with the new company seems to indicate he may have initially signed on but decided to go with the renewed Wagner/Gambrinus instead. According to his grandson, he remained at Gambrinus from then until 1936. From there, he joined Gold in Florida until 1939. He died in 1943.

While at Hoster, the eldest American Hostettler lived on the brewery grounds, where his son Alex H. Hostettler was born in 1913. When his dad went to Wagner's Gambrinus after Prohibition, the youngster soaked up all he could, hanging out in the brewery. Then he studied brewing in New York's United States Brewer's Academy and went to work for several breweries, including Pabst in the Midwest and the South. For a brief time, he was the brewmaster at the Ohio Brewery before entering the service. In the army during World War II, he became a colonel, managing the army's brewing operations in the European theater, where he

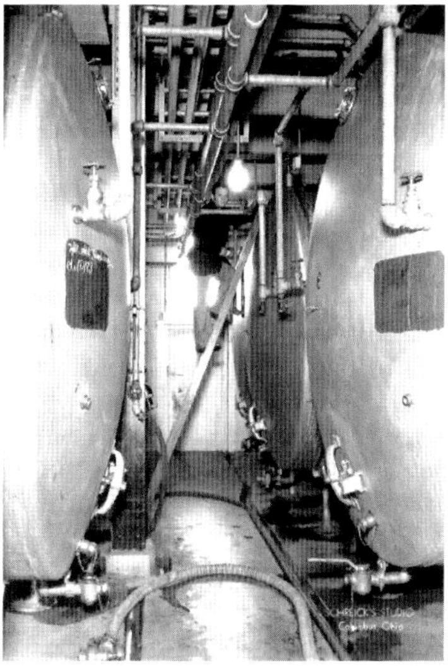

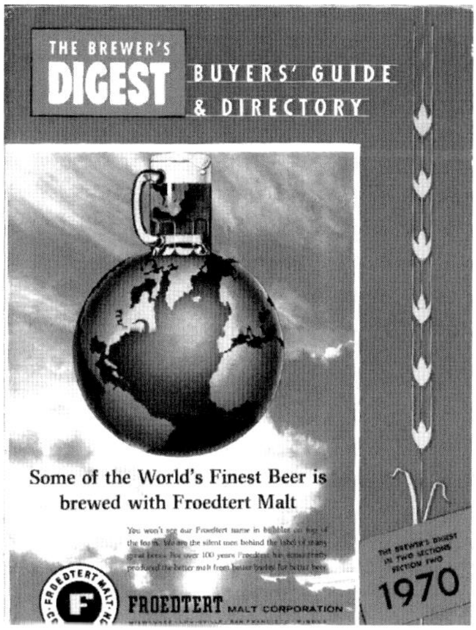

Left: Alexander H. Hostettler at Wagner after the war. *Courtesy Chris Hostettler collection.*

Right: *Brewer's Digest* magazine, 1970, with Wagner listing inside. *Courtesy Chris Hostettler collection.*

oversaw fifty-four breweries in six countries. While in Europe, he got to know many of the local brewers in an open exchange of information and technique. When he returned home, he became Wagner's brewmaster, remaining for more than twenty years and becoming executive vice-president toward the end.

During the 1950s and '60s, Hostettler led Gambrinus through its golden era. The veteran brewer not only maintained the high standards founded by Wagner, who won international awards for his beer before Prohibition, but he also made creative innovations. Potentially, the most groundbreaking was the development of a process to brew light beer. Beginning in 1967, Gambrinus produced its Mark V Slim Line, a low-calorie beer that scooped the majors by at least five years. Hostettler had found an enzyme imported from Switzerland that would reduce the residual carbohydrates in beer. Mark V—like Chicago's Meister Brau Lite, also developed in 1967—never received the national attention or commercial success that Miller Lite received beginning with its introduction in 1973.

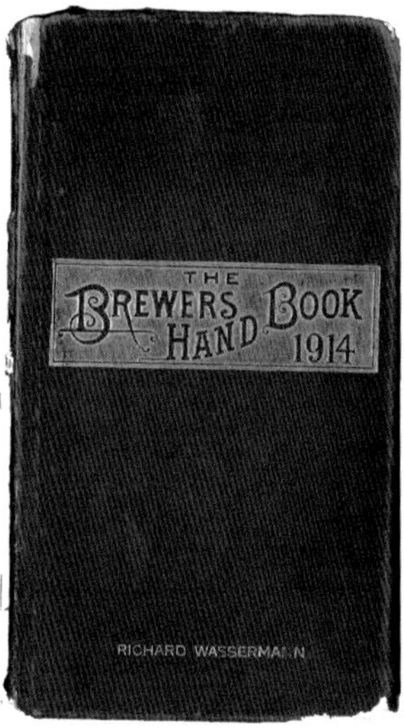

Left: 1914 Brewers Handbook listing Alex Hostettler as brewmaster for Hoster. *Courtesy Chris Hostettler collection.*

Below: *Brewer's Digest*, page 28, with Wagner listings, including "Exec. Vice-Pres. & Master Brewer—Alex H. Hostettler. *Courtesy Chris Hostettler collection.*

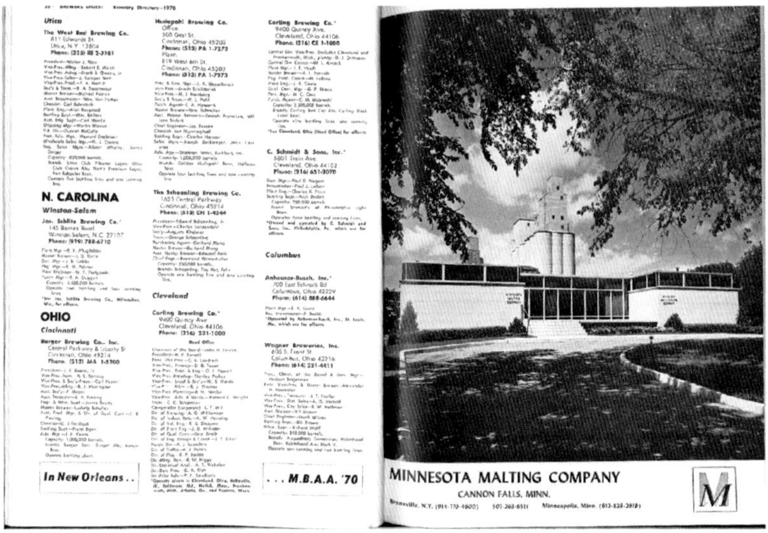

Alex H.'s son Alex O., like his father, grew up around brewing. The Hostettlers lived in an old Victorian mansion on South High Street, where the youngster could hear the Gambrinus whistle at the end of the day. He loved accompanying his dad to work on the weekends and riding the train that brought malt into the brewery. The youngster apprenticed for Wagner in 1968–71, after which he studied brewing in two different programs in New York. From there, he joined Schlitz and worked in Brooklyn, Milwaukee and Memphis. He finished up with Anheuser-Busch beginning in 1991 and retired in 2008. Going through his father's archives, he found a recipe for Budweiser, which likely influenced his dad's style of brewing for American troops.

Though not a brewer, brother Chris mysteriously ended up in the aged haunts of a brewery. When he took a job with landscape architecture firm MKSK as it moved into its new offices, he had no idea where his office would be until the day he reported for work. Finding the address, he quickly realized the new offices were in the old Hoster Brewery icehouse, a stone's throw from where his grandfather had worked and his father was born.

Toward the end of Prohibition, Wagner had taken sons Carl J. and Philip L. into the business. When beer became legal again, the name went from August Wagner & Sons Products Company to the August Wagner & Sons Brewing Company. The success of the revived, remodeled and recrowned brewery, though, was tainted by the death of Wagner's sons, in 1934 and 1938, respectively. Previously, his wife, Frieda, had died in 1933 and his son Edward had passed in 1931.

The company prospered, nonetheless. A modernization program was launched in 1947, with new beer coolers installed and the brewhouse updated. A new electric transformer room was built in 1948 as well as a garage to house the expanding delivery fleet. A completely automatic power plant was installed in 1949, and the bottling line was completely modernized the next year. A news article from the time depicted just part of the brewery's new trucks, announcing that the fleet had swollen to fifty, as the daily sales of Gambrinus reached the thousands. The article also noted innovations at the plant, including a malt grinding mill "of the newest style." For the cleanest, most consistent brew, Wagner had acquired an "apparatus" to assure that its yeast culture remained pure. By 1954, capacity had grown to 250,000 barrels, the company employed two hundred workers and distribution had grown to West Virginia and parts of Indiana.

Wagner also diversified his business interests. In addition to the August Wagner Realty Company and the Greater Columbus Hardware Company, he owned six farms in Ohio, Michigan and California. He was the president of the Old Capitol Brewery in Chillicothe.

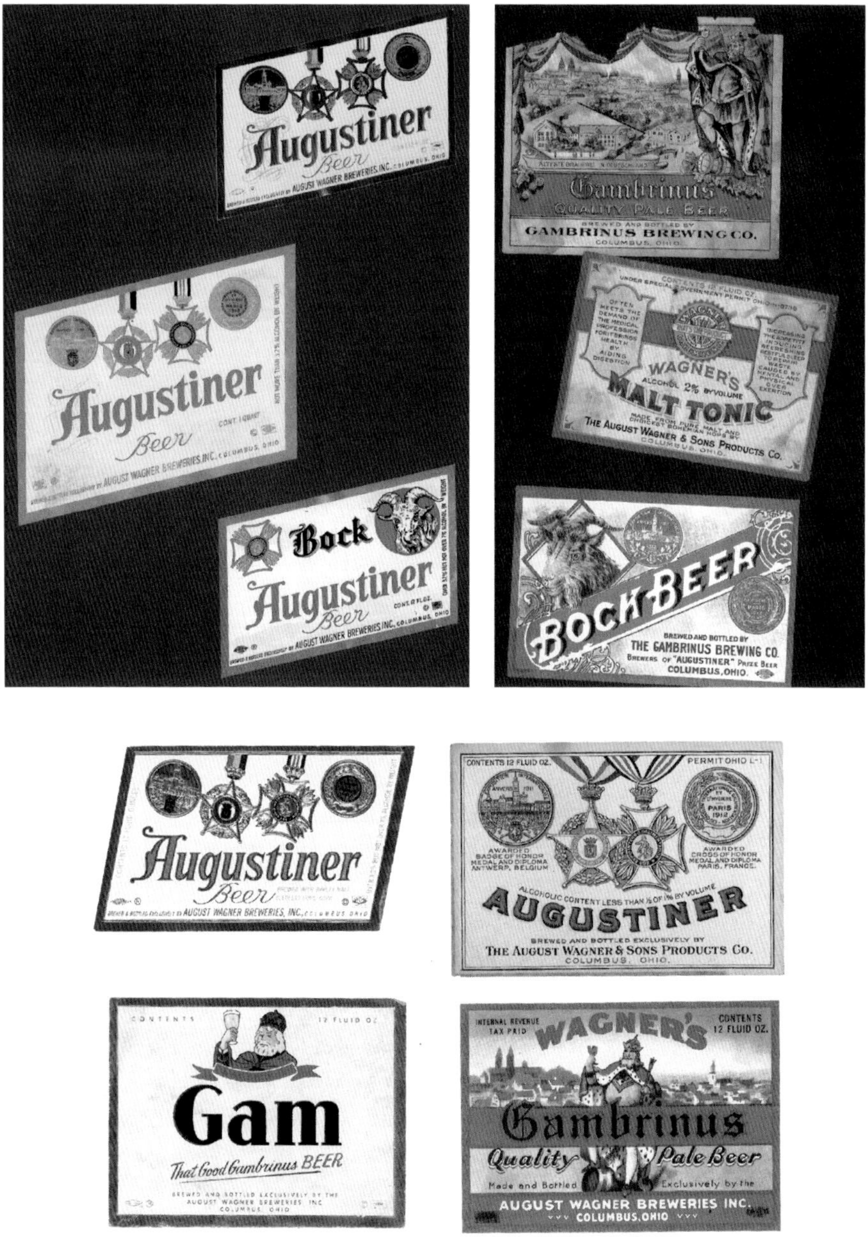

This page: Another range of Wagner/Gambrinus labels spanning several decades. *German Village Society August Wagner collection*.

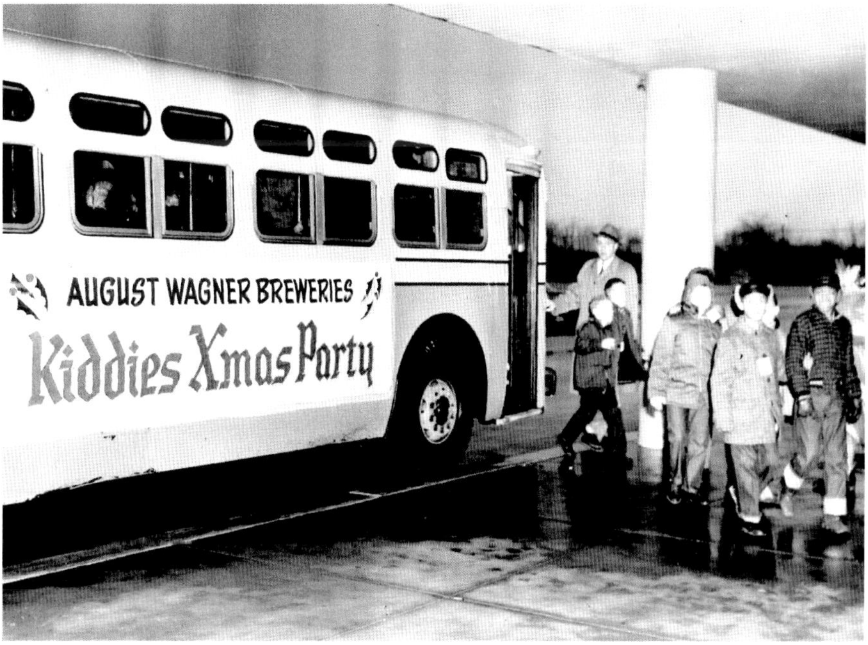

Wagner's Christmas parties for kids were one of the brewery's several charity and community programs. *German Village Society August Wagner collection.*

Wagner began to make his mark in Columbus society and philanthropy, as well. Diversifying his interests in real estate and elsewhere, he became a highly respected businessman in addition to an award-winning, expert brewer. His generous devotion to the community and personal interests were profiled in a 1939 article in the *Columbus Citizen*, announcing that he would donate $10,000 to the Columbus Municipal Zoo for an elephant house that would contain hippos, rhinoceros and giraffes, as well. Throughout his life, Wagner gave to hospitals, churches and programs for children. Though he described work as his favorite hobby, the newspaper announcement of his donation noted that he continued an interest in boxing and music. He confessed to being a "good zither player," but that he was out of practice.

Wagner also became known for his sense of humor, recalled in a retrospective for the *Columbus Dispatch*. Asked to testify for the defense of a prominent son at his drunk-driving trial, Wagner put numbers to his typical daily consumption of beer. He said he drank two for breakfast, a dozen with clients at the brewery in the morning, two more at lunch and maybe a dozen more at the brewery during the rest of the day. The judge asked the brewer

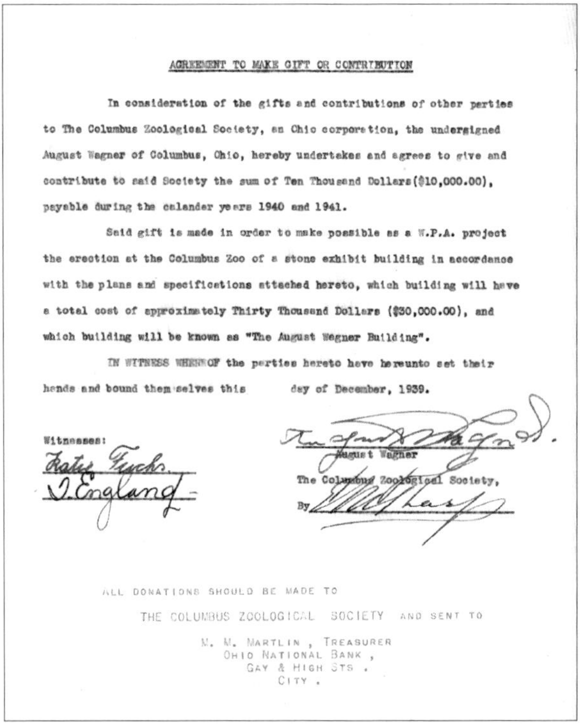

AGREEMENT TO MAKE GIFT OR CONTRIBUTION

In consideration of the gifts and contributions of other parties to The Columbus Zoological Society, an Ohio corporation, the undersigned August Wagner of Columbus, Ohio, hereby undertakes and agrees to give and contribute to said Society the sum of Ten Thousand Dollars($10,000.00), payable during the calender years 1940 and 1941.

Said gift is made in order to make possible as a W.P.A. project the erection at the Columbus Zoo of a stone exhibit building in accordance with the plans and specifications attached hereto, which building will have a total cost of approximately Thirty Thousand Dollars ($30,000.00), and which building will be known as "The August Wagner Building".

IN WITNESS WHEREOF the parties hereto have hereunto set their hands and bound them selves this day of December, 1939.

Witnesses:

August Wagner

The Columbus Zoological Society,

By

ALL DONATIONS SHOULD BE MADE TO

THE COLUMBUS ZOOLOGICAL SOCIETY AND SENT TO

M. M. MARTLIN, TREASURER
OHIO NATIONAL BANK,
GAY & HIGH STS.
CITY.

Left: Wagner donated $10,000, or a third of the cost, to the Columbus Zoo for its new elephant home, built in conjunction with the WPA. *German Village Society August Wagner collection.*

Below: Wagner dressed as King Gambrinus early after Prohibition. He posed for the statue of the king that graced the entrance to his brewery. *German Village Society August Wagner collection.*

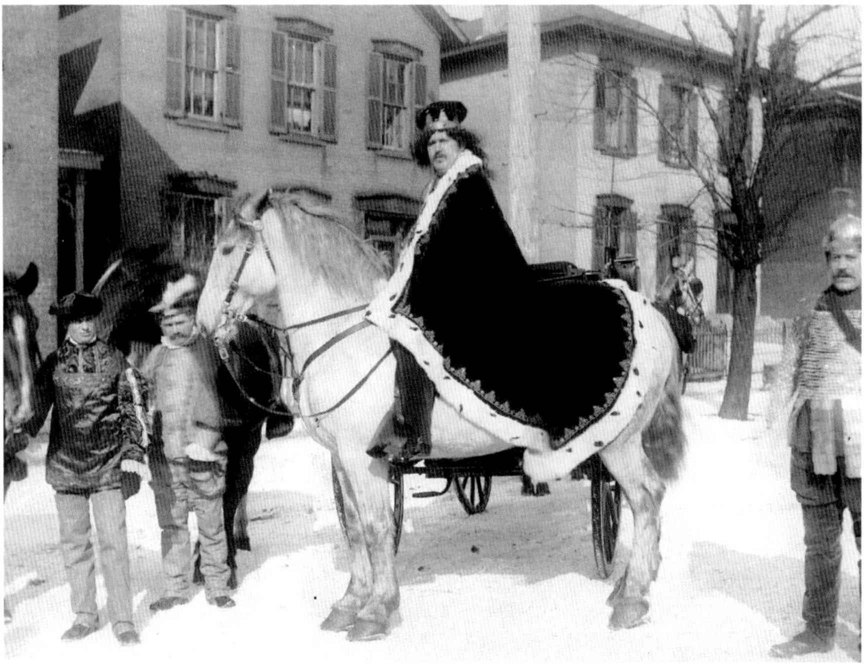

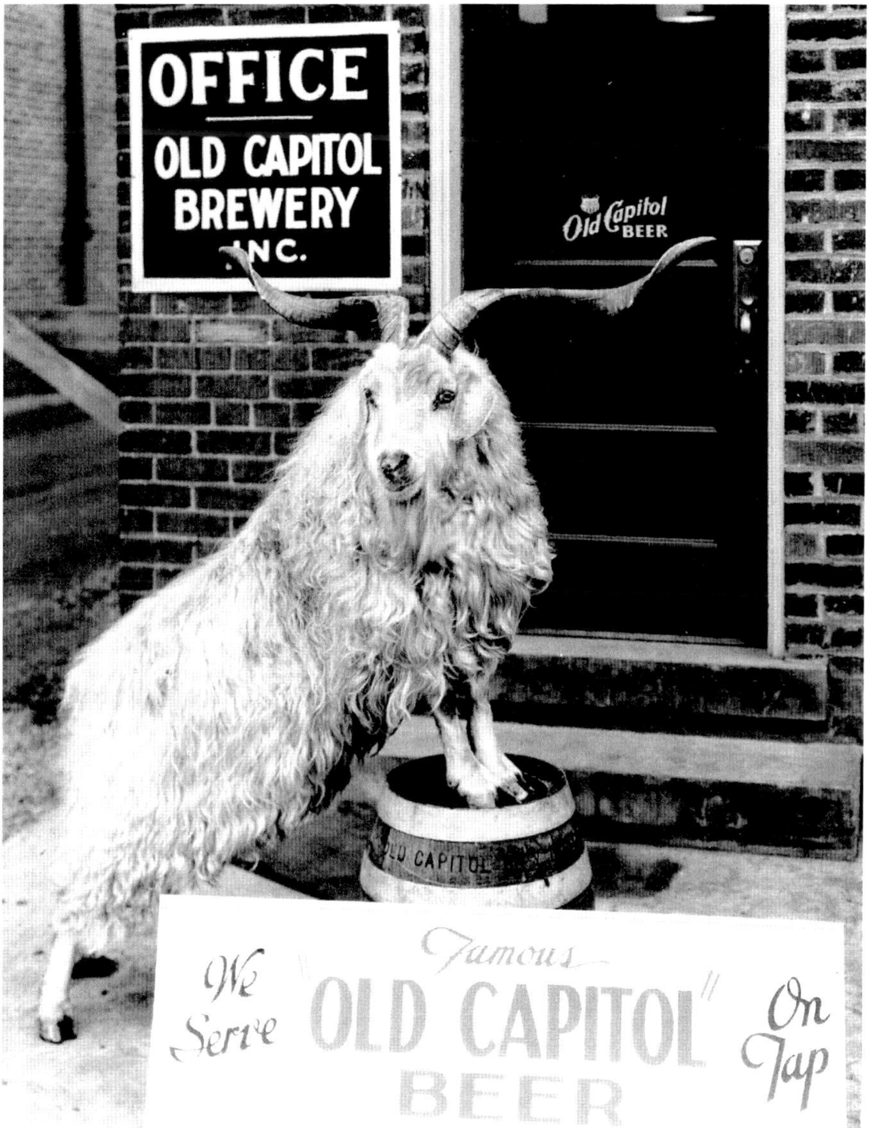

Publicity stunt for Chillicothe's Old Capitol Brewery's bock beer. *German Village Society August Wagner collection.*

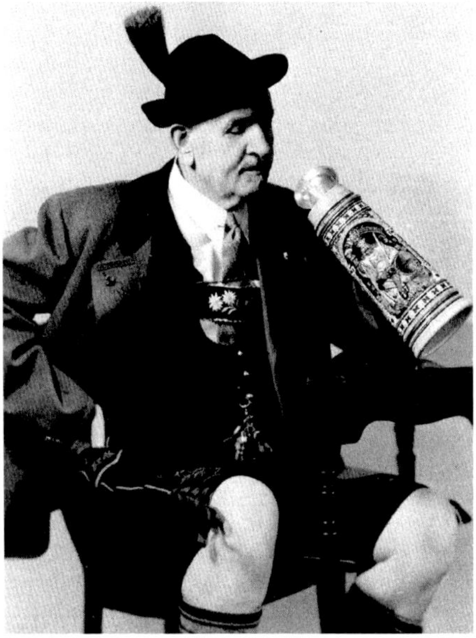

August Wagner donning traditional German Octoberfest gear. *German Village Society August Wagner collection.*

if he thought it was possible to become intoxicated from drinking beer, to which Wagner famously replied, "Well maybe, that is, if a man makes a big hog of himself."

Always one to sing praises to the brewery business, he noted in an interview in the *Dispatch* that brewing was an $11 billion industry, employing one million people in production and distribution and in the one hundred trades that served the industry.

Still, the industry felt blips and setbacks in Columbus with the closing of breweries such as the Ohio (1948), Washington (1952) and Franklin/P.O.C. (1954), all of which had begun around the turn of the century and had come back in some form or another after Prohibition.

There was a hiccup, too, with a strike—mild in comparison to the one in 1903—that began on July 10, 1944, with Brewery Workers Local 47 union shutting down three of the four operating breweries. The beef was from delivery drivers, who, having recently returned to a five-day week, didn't want to continue doing keg and bottle deliveries separately, as they had during the just-ended four-day work compromise. Rather, they found it easier to do both simultaneously. Eighteen days into the work stoppage, an agreement was reached with only a week's worth of shortages in stores and taverns.

The war effort started to kick in a few years after the attack on Pearl Harbor brought the country into World War II. The conflict's demand for steel in 1942 interrupted the new packaging of beer in cans—pioneered locally by the Washington Brewery in 1940. Beginning on February 29, 1945, grains began to be rationed, with a 12 percent reduction passed on to breweries—this despite a record-setting consumption that year.

Wagner wouldn't witness the shortages or the end of the war, though. He had a cerebral hemorrhage during a vacation at his northern Michigan retreat on Mackinac Island in the summer of 1944 and died in Little Traverse Hospital in Petoskey, Michigan, on August 21.

The directions his business took after his passing were as unique and newsworthy as the career that had brought his uncompromising brewery into existence, guided it through Prohibition and colorfully directed it into the modern world. Wagner's faithful assistant Nellie D. Lenahan took the reins of the business on his death. Lenahan started as a stenographer at the company in 1912, was made secretary in 1934 and became vice-president in 1937. After his death, she became president, treasurer and chairperson of the board. Known nationwide as one of the few women heading a brewery, Lenahan was also the acting president of the Ohio Brewery Association in 1941 and '42 and a member of the United States Brewers Foundation.

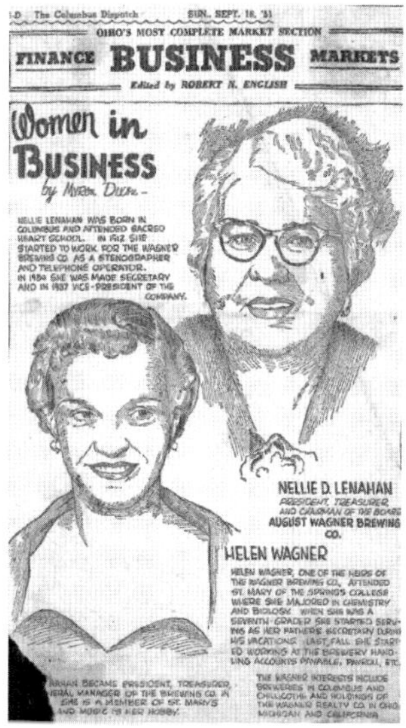

The Columbus Dispatch SUN., SEPT. 16, '51

OHIO'S MOST COMPLETE MARKET SECTION

FINANCE BUSINESS MARKETS

Edited by ROBERT N. ENGLISH

Women in Business

by Myron Dick -

NELLIE LENAHAN WAS BORN IN COLUMBUS AND ATTENDED SACRED HEART SCHOOL. IN 1912 SHE STARTED TO WORK FOR THE WAGNER BREWING CO. AS A STENOGRAPHER AND TELEPHONE OPERATOR. IN 1934 SHE WAS MADE SECRETARY AND IN 1937 VICE-PRESIDENT OF THE COMPANY.

NELLIE D. LENAHAN
PRESIDENT, TREASURER AND CHAIRMAN OF THE BOARD
AUGUST WAGNER BREWING CO.

HELEN WAGNER

HELEN WAGNER, ONE OF THE HEIRS OF THE WAGNER BREWING CO., ATTENDED ST. MARY OF THE SPRINGS COLLEGE WHERE SHE MAJORED IN CHEMISTRY AND BIOLOGY. WHEN SHE WAS A SEVENTH-GRADER SHE STARTED SERVING AS HER FATHER'S SECRETARY DURING HIS VACATIONS. LAST FALL SHE STARTED WORKING AT THE BREWERY HANDLING ACCOUNTS PAYABLE, PAYROLL, ETC.

THE WAGNER INTERESTS INCLUDE BREWERIES IN COLUMBUS AND CHILLICOTHE AND HOLDINGS OF THE WAGNER REALTY CO. IN OHIO, MICHIGAN AND CALIFORNIA.

A *Dispatch* article from September 1951, when two women ran the August Wagner Brewing Company. Nellie D. Lenahan was president and chairman of the board, while August's daughter Helen was in charge of much of the operation of the business. *Courtesy of the* Columbus Dispatch.

At Lenahan's death in 1953, James Amento became president, Max Gumble was vice-president and Wagner's adopted daughter Helen became second vice-president. She continued to grow her role in the business, taking brewing instruction and managing production, though not officially a brewer. For a company to be led by two women in succession in the 1950s was truly an anomaly, one that gained Helen and Nellie a cover story in the September 16, 1951 Sunday *Columbus Dispatch*.

Between the two, they helped Gambrinus bounce back during the postwar prosperity of the 1950s. That included solidifying the brewery's favor in the city. Not only did the company sponsor community Christmas events for children, it also staged more unusual events that earned it stories in the local press. A particularly frivolous piece in the *Ohio State Journal* touted the benefit of washing hair with beer; another lightweight blurb from 1951 announced a new metallic label for the company's beer, now referred to as "Gam."

At 10:00 p.m. on June 29, 1951, though, Gambrinus reset the local bar for beer promotions. Television cameras filmed and radio broadcast the dedication and lighting of a huge new sign at the northeast corner of Broad and High Streets over the Roy's Jewelry shop. Gambrinus had a presence at

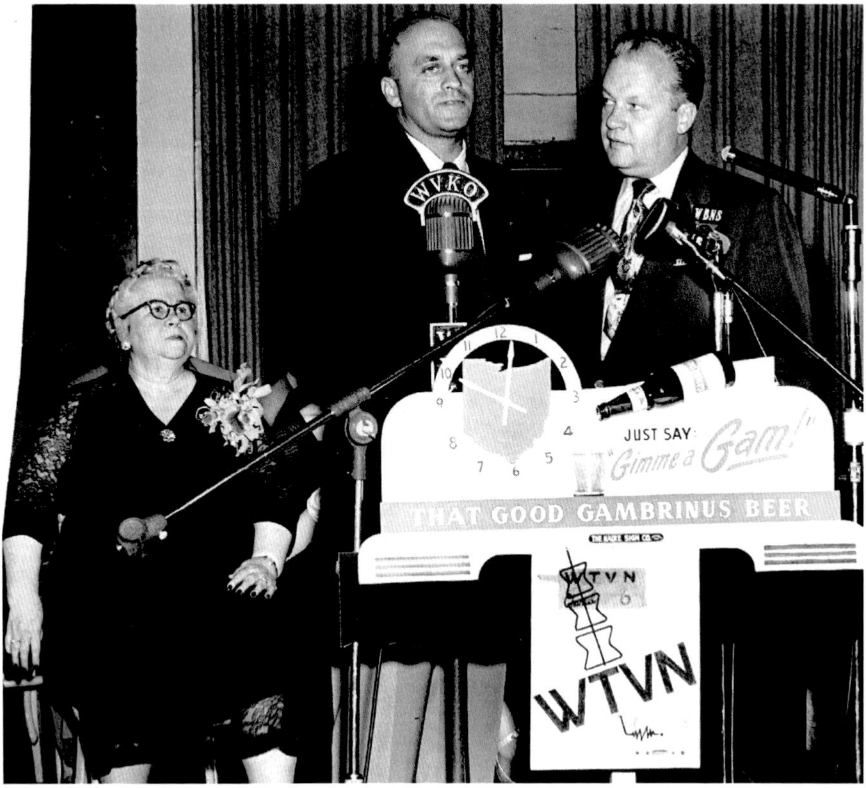

Unveiling the model for the gigantic pouring bottle billboard at the corner of Broad and High Streets in 1951. The lighting ceremony was broadcast on WTVN. *German Village Society August Wagner collection.*

that location for some time, promoting the beer with the phrase "Give Me a Gam." The new sign was something else, though. According to an article in the *Columbus Citizen*, it was "the largest activated display sign in the country." Photographs showed a model sitting atop a foaming, ten-foot pint glass, which, mounted on the sign, would receive liquid poured continuously from a seventeen-foot beer bottle next to the slogan "Just Say Gimme a Gam!" A gigantic Ohio-shaped clock was mounted alongside.

For its fiftieth anniversary, Gambrinus added a little more glitz, hiring notable actor Adolphe Menjou to bring a bit of exotic elegance to town in tribute to King Gambrinus's fifty-year reign over Columbus brewing. The company that still held on to its German brewing heritage—a huge ad for its fiftieth celebrated its use of classic Hallertau hops in its headline—employed a cosmopolitan flair and modern marketing savvy with the American-born,

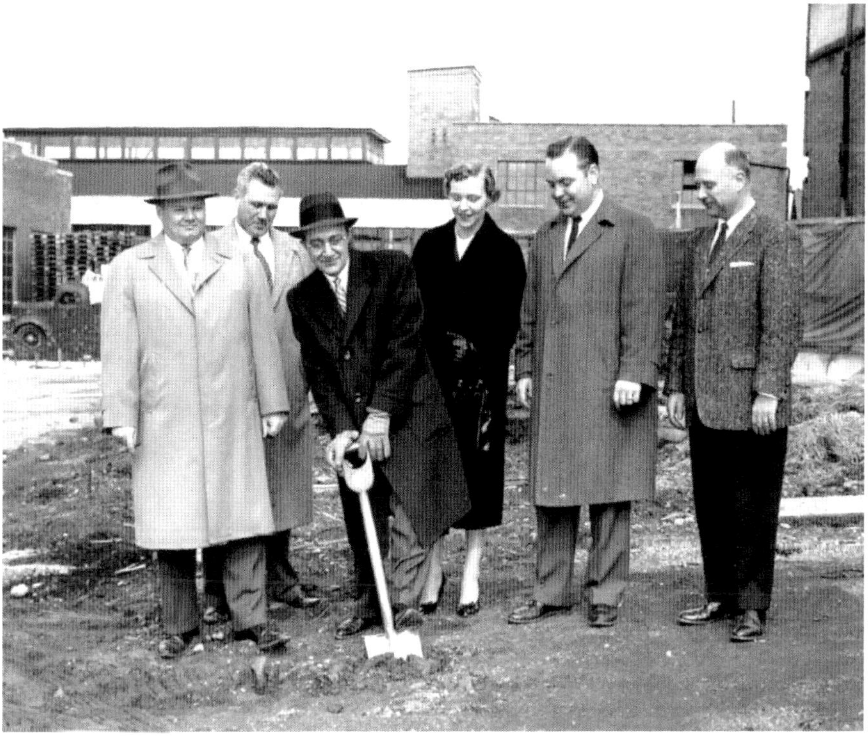

Above: Wagner bottling plant expansion, 1959. Alex H. Hostettler (*far left*), president James Amento (*with shovel*) and Helen Wagner on his left. *Courtesy Chris Hostettler collection*

Right: Giant, kinetic Gambrinus sign at the northeast corner of Broad and High Streets, 1951. The giant bottle poured liquid continuously into the huge pint glass. *German Village Society August Wagner collection.*

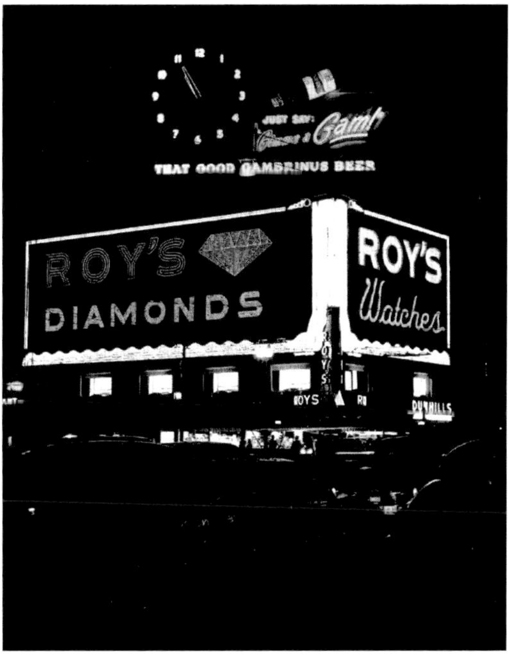

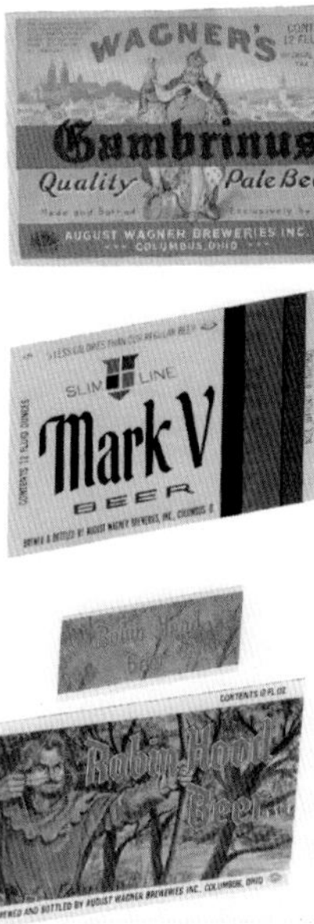

More Wagner-branded labels. Mark V was the brewery's groundbreaking light beer. Robin Hood was made in the 1960s. *David Foster collection.*

French Irish actor. Menjou was in town for three days, attending parties, civic events and any other opportunity to be seen.

The company embraced television and radio promotion early on, sponsoring broadcasts of Cleveland Indians games and weekly TV shows. Jonathan Winters, who appeared on WBNS early in his career as "Johnny Winters," was one of several famous actors to pitch Gambrinus over the air.

Gambrinus truly broke new ground, though, when Helen Wagner appeared on an episode of the popular television game show *What's My Line* in June 1962. In the program, a panel of celebrities asked a series of questions in an attempt to guess the special guest's occupation. (A tape of the show can be accessed today on YouTube.) Her secret occupation, "brewmaster," wasn't entirely accurate, though. According to a document from the United States Brewers' Academy in Mount Vernon, New York, she attended a two-week executive Seminar in Brewing in 1953. The seminar included instruction in basic malting, brewing and bottling; biochemistry; and the fundamental engineering of brewing operations. Nonetheless, her position of power as the vice-president and general manager of a very successful brewery made Wagner's appearance on the show significant. That it echoed the career of the company's unique, passionate founder was to become a fitting epilogue for a storied brewery that would go dark a dozen years later.

Beginning after World War II, consolidation of breweries and the growing homogenization of American beer taste led small, family-owned companies to drop away. By the late 1960s, when the mammoth Anheuser-Busch satellite plant was built in the northeast corner of Columbus, they were dropping like flies. Helen Wagner relinquished control of her father's company, selling her stock in 1968. A Detroit corporation bought her majority early in January, retaining James Amento as chairman of the board. The company continued with its current management, producing the brands it had previously made. Ms. Wagner remained as vice-president and handled public relations duties.

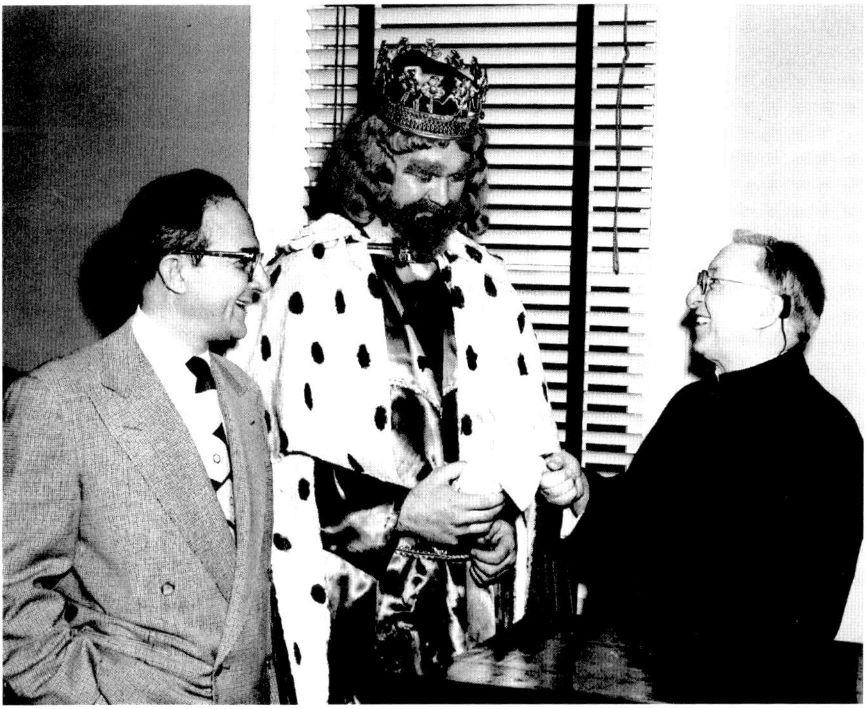

James Amento, anonymous King Gambrinus imposter and Father Burkley of St. Mary's. *German Village Society August Wagner collection.*

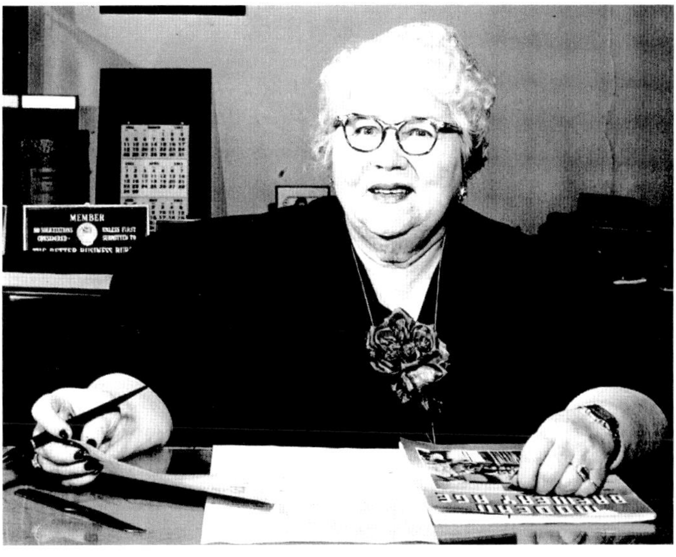

Nellie Lenahan, who became president with Wagner's death in 1944. *German Village Society August Wagner collection.*

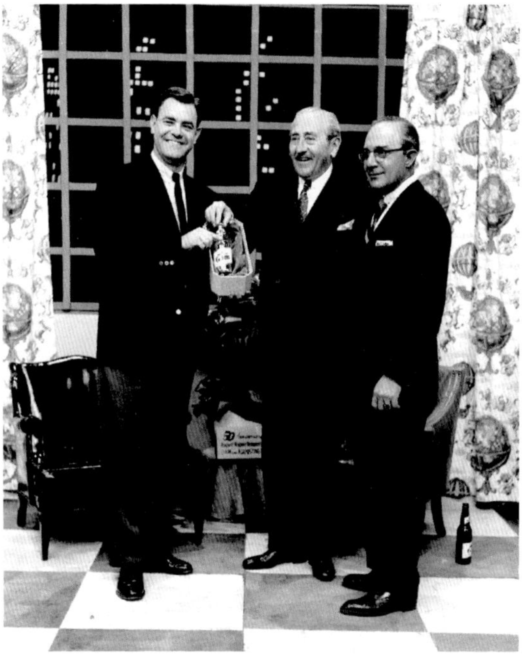

Left: Actor Adolphe Menjou came to town for several days to celebrate Wagner's fiftieth anniversary in 1955. *German Village Society August Wagner collection.*

Below: Helen's appearance as a contestant on TV's *What's My Line* was Gambrinus's best promotional scheme. She's flanked by Buddy Hackett and Arlene Francis to her right and Dorothy Kilgallen and Bennett Cerf on her left. *German Village Society August Wagner collection.*

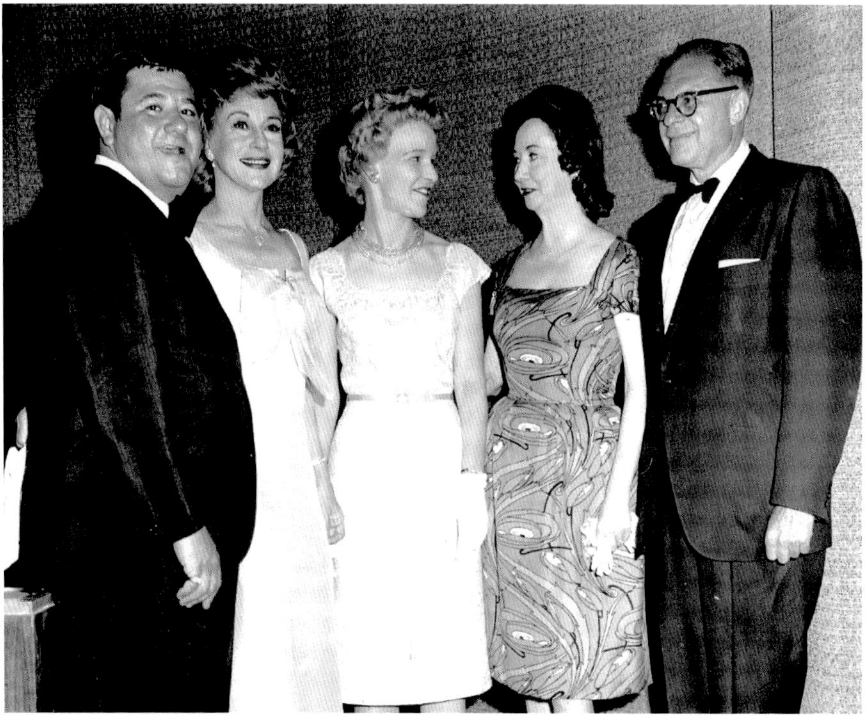

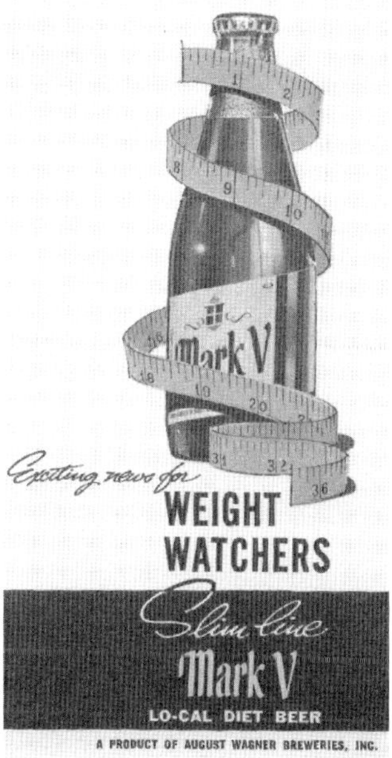

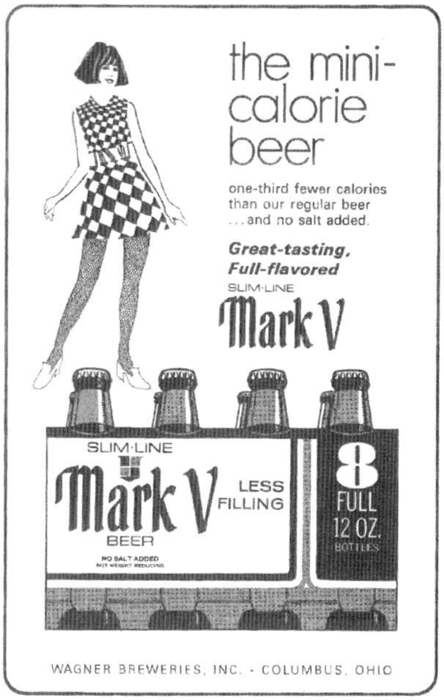

Left: Handbill for Mark V with its diet qualities hard to ignore. *Courtesy Chris Hostettler collection.*

Right: Alex H. Hostettler, at Gambrinus, developed and marketed its Mark V light beer in 1967, before Miller took the brewing world by storm with its light beer in 1973. *Courtesy Chris Hostettler collection.*

By late 1969, one of the corporation's chief investors, Herbert Singerman, became president, board chairman and sole owner, while Alexander H. Hostettler remained as brewmaster. The company had big plans for 1970, including better distribution, marketing and community visibility, according to a *Dispatch* article. It was particularly enthusiastic about its Mark V low-calorie brew, developed with a secret process by Hostettler.

Beginning in 1967, Gambrinus produced its Mark V Slim Line beer, a low-calorie beer that scooped the majors by at least five years. The difference that made the big guys successful with it, of course, was marketing muscle, just then beginning the lopsided domination of a few brewing giants. In fact, Miller Lite, the first hugely successful low-cal beer, introduced in 1973, was a reworked recipe bought from Chicago's Meister Brau Lite. Biochemist Joseph L. Owades developed the process, which also employed a unique enzyme, for New York's Rheingold Brewery and its Gablinger's Diet Beer, produced in 1967. The beer, which failed to sell at both Rheingold and Meister Brau, was a home run for Miller and its marketing machine just a couple of years later.

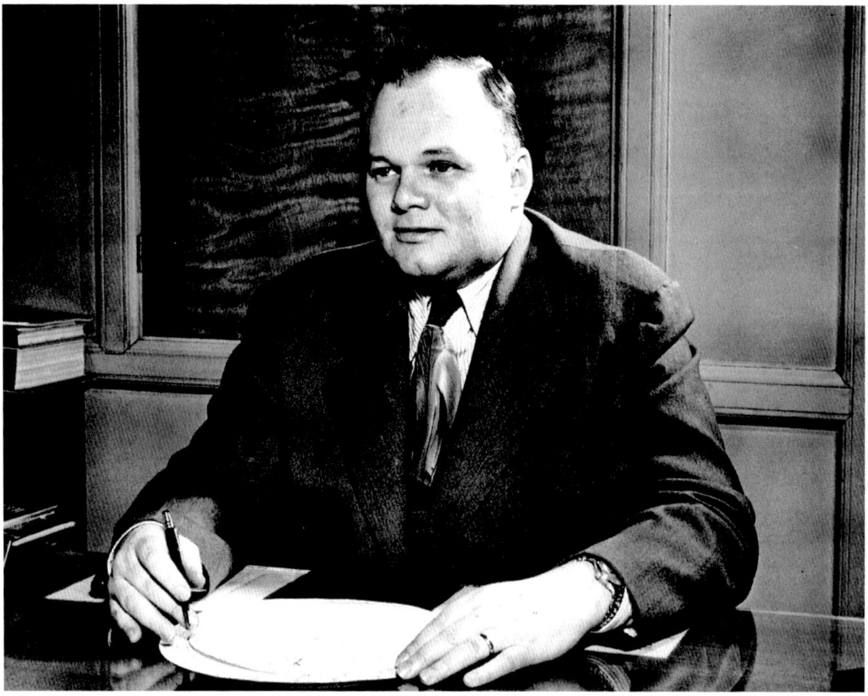

Alex H. Hostettler in the early 1960s. *German Village Society August Wagner collection.*

The revolutionary new beer didn't save the company from the eventual downturn in business. Singerman cleaned house in early 1970, putting Richard Navarre in charge of the brewery, its marketing and distribution. Navarre improved relations with the labor force while making the factory more efficient. He opened distribution in Detroit, adding another $1 million in revenue. He sought to raise local awareness about the brand on television with ads and by becoming the public spokesman. Then he injected some marketing innovation into that effort, first opening the Bottle House restaurant in the old bottling area. He bought the Columbus Bucks semiprofessional football team to help spread the word about Gambrinus and its continuing quality product. None of it worked so well, though, because in April 1973, Navarre became sole stockholder, and the company went into receivership early in 1974. A.C. Strip, the lawyer in charge of the receivership, told the *Dispatch* that much of the problem had to do with rising costs and the legal restriction on passing the expense to the consumer on a timely basis. He also cited ageing equipment and the drain on the business from the Barons football team, likely an evolution of the Bucks.

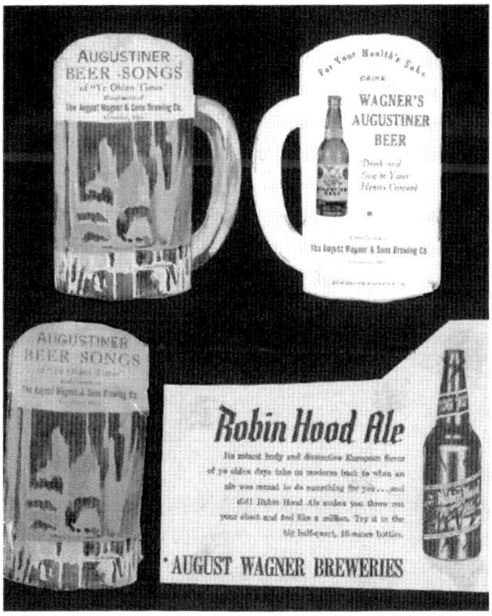

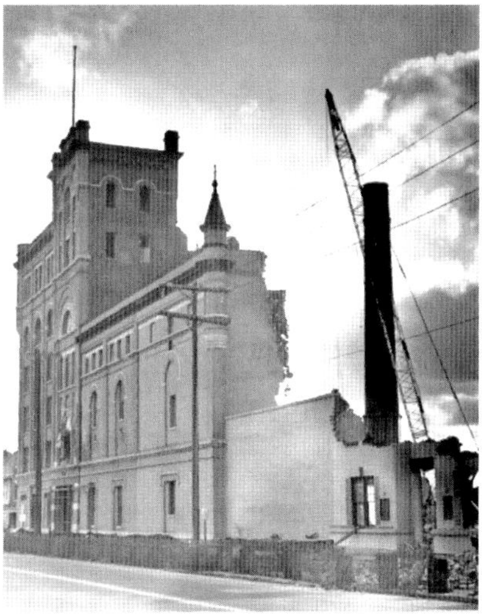

Left: An ad for Robin Hood Ale and several booklets that were distributed in bars and restaurants with the lyrics for well-known German drinking songs. *German Village Society August Wagner collection.*

Right: The wrecking ball takes the Gambrinus Brewery in 1974, wiping away a 68-year run and 138 years of continuous German brewing history in Columbus. *German Village Society August Wagner collection.*

More likely, though, Gambrinus was just outflanked by the big national brands that had come to dominate all but the most stubborn local markets. The forces of conglomeration that had been gathering for decades became especially ominous in Columbus with the August 15, 1968 opening of Anheuser-Busch's 1.7-million-barrel-capacity brewery on the north side of town.

Gambrinus limped along for another couple of months until the end of 1974, when King Gambrinus watched as the business inside his domain went dark and his kingdom came under the wrecking ball.

Sixty-nine colorful years of history turned to dust as August Wagner surely spun in his grave. One hundred and sixty years of traditional brewing in Columbus came to an end, succumbing to bland, corporate-produced lagers that were a mere shadow of the German tradition from which they were derived.

It would be fifteen years before locally based brewing would return to Columbus, riding the rising tide of home brewing and falling in step with the craft brew movement that had begun on the West Coast about the time King Gambrinus shed his last tear.

The *Columbus Dispatch* bought the property on which Wagner's brewery stood, deciding to demolish the structure. Responding to sentiment, perhaps, it had the limestone king planted at street level in a little park at Sycamore and Front Streets.

He was permanently installed some time later on a pedestal planted in a tiny piece of real estate immediately north of the old brewery, in front of a new Kroger grocery store, all eleven feet of him proudly lifting a goblet to his turf and, more important, to the deep history he'd represented in Columbus.

11

EPILOGUE

CRAFT BREW SETTLES IN, 2011–PRESENT

The beer business is really the American dream. It's something cool, it's something fun, and beside a little government intervention, you get to do what you want to do every day.
—Eric Bean, owner and brewmaster, Columbus Brewing Company

It might be said that King Gambrinus exacted revenge decades after his perch atop the Gambrinus brewery crumbled and his domain became a grassy patch in front of the Kroger grocery on Front Street just north of the brewery's historic site. The craft brewery movement took hold in Columbus two blocks north on Front Street with the establishment of the Columbus Brewing Company in 1989. The national rebirth posed little threat to the corporate brewers, however. The craft breweries' paltry national market share resounded every time CBC's Scott Francis, Hoster's Allen Young, Barley's Angelo Signorino and Elevator's Vince Falcone tried to wean local drinkers off bland corporate brew. As Francis remembered, it was tough to give away this new, flavorful beer, which in some ways echoed the product of the city's long-ago, independent German and English breweries.

Depending on how the numbers are read, craft breweries accounted for roughly 1 percent of the American beer market when CBC opened. There were 247 breweries in the United States at that time, including microbreweries, brewpubs and majors. That number marked an upswing, though, having bottomed out in 1978, with the total count of all breweries at 89. The afterburners were lit in the second decade of the twenty-first century, though. In 2015 alone, there were 620 new breweries, according to the Brewers Association, bringing the total in 2016 to 4,269, the highest number in U.S. history and representing 12 percent of the beer market in the United States. Surely, *this* made the King feel redeemed.

It was convenient—and sentimental—to view the boom as a rebirth of the localized, European-inspired brewing tradition of the previous era. The care and pride that marked the classic German and English brewers seemed to be echoed by the new ones. In Columbus, that notion was reinforced by the fact that the first two, Columbus Brewing Company and Hoster Brewing Company, revived names from the bygone era and were located in the center of the city's historic brewing neighborhood. That CBC—and Barley's in 1992—focused on traditional English and Hoster, German beers like the earliest Columbus breweries, only reinforced the notion.

David Foster's revival of the Gambrinus name and its signature beers in 1993 was even more literal, an attempt to recreate a brand and its traditional German styles popular in mid-twentieth-century Columbus. The last of the new craft breweries, Elevator, founded in 1999, tapped both traditions with a mild spirit of stylistic experimentation that would predict the larger current in craft brewing as it began to take off. There were few new breweries established during the dawn of the millennium, though, perhaps in response to the dip in sales witnessed by CBC in the late 1990s and reflected in the business difficulties at Hoster, which closed its restaurant/brewpub in 2001.

Perhaps, too, the hesitation had to do with the city's growing pains, as Columbus caught up with its visionary brewers. The city went through a huge transformation in the last three decades of the century, first, in terms of business and investment, second, in the arts, and finally, the forward-thinking cultural climate that comes with the combination of the two. The lifestyle changes were marked during the first decade of the new century. Columbus became a city of foodies and, soon, a youth mecca, in part because its hip amenities were combined with an uncommonly affordable economy. Brooklyn on the cheap.

During the brief lull, the breweries that opened, including Gordon Biersch, Mulholland, Neil House and Hops, tended to build on the initial brewing revival, one in which the skills, styles and traditions of European brewing generally continued to hold sway. Brewing in Columbus was about to become more freewheeling and creative with the next boom, though. And the differences between the old-time local brewers and the small new craft breweries would become considerably more pronounced.

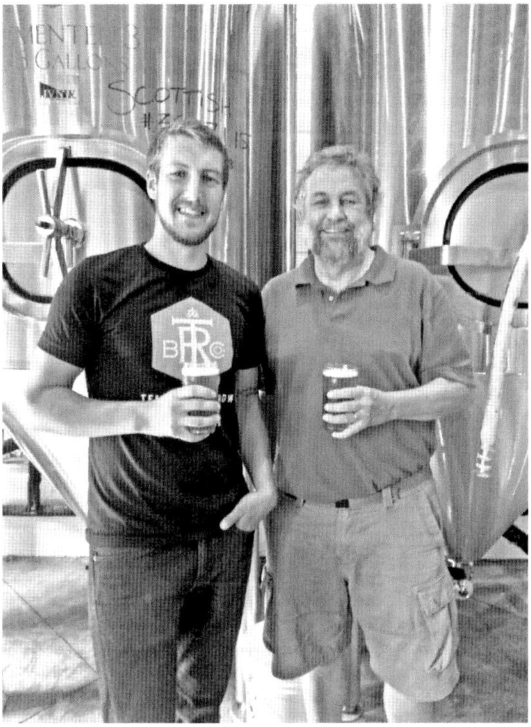

Left: Scott and Alex Francis in the brewery at Temperance Row, 41 North State Street in Westerville. Alex is evidence that the tradition carries on. *Photo by Evan J. Schieber.*

Below: Allen Young today in Atlanta. Young is retired from brewing, but he sells brewing ingredients for Brewers Supply Group. *Photo by Allen Young.*

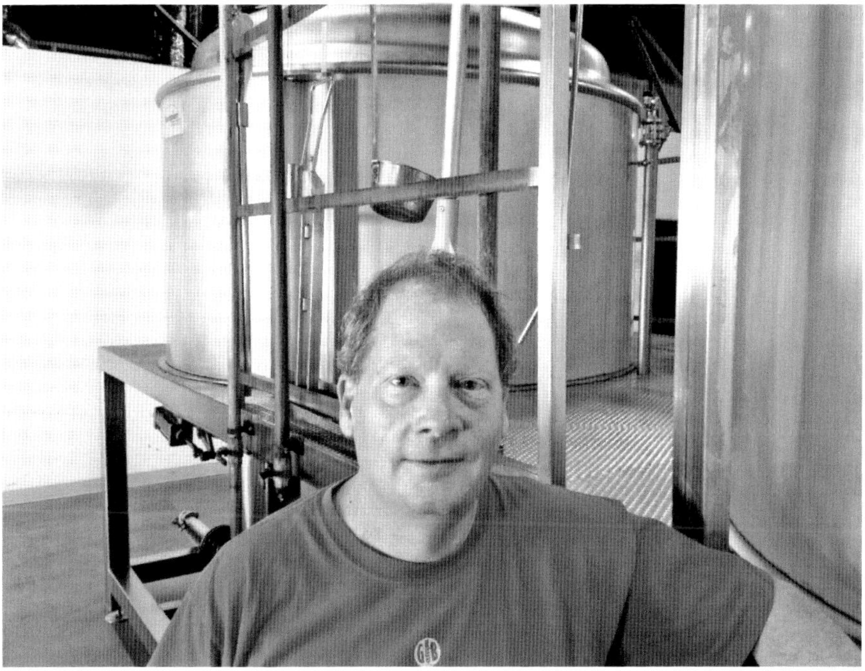

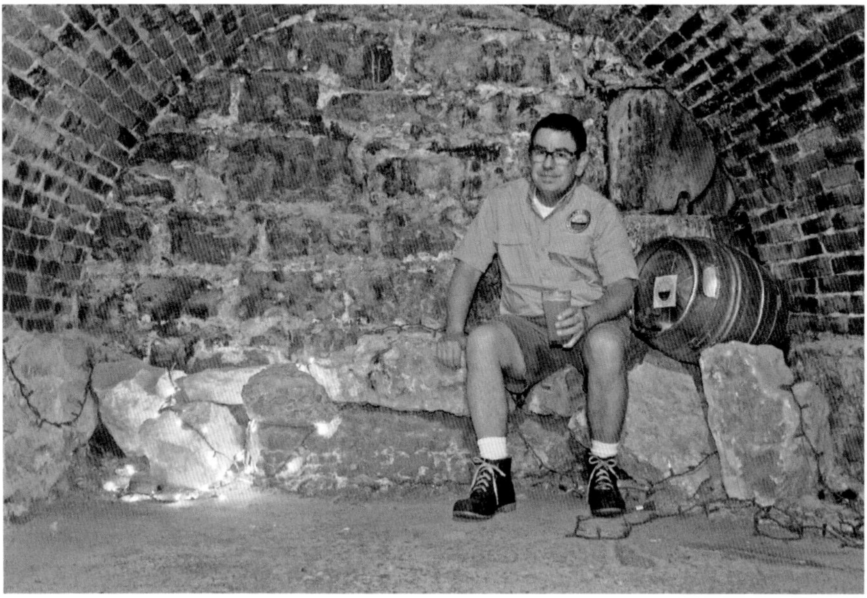

Angelo Signorino today in the basement at Barley's, 467 North High Street, in a vault that long ago ran under High Street. *Photo by the author.*

Increasingly, King Gambrinus's victory for localized beer would look more like a historical reset of the definition of "local." Gambrinus's heyday happened during the era of lagers, baseball, the wars and prosperity. Cold, refreshing, workaday beer was as much a part of that culture as the wild, tear-up-the-stylistic-rules beers of today are a part of the current hipster/foodie culture. A future generation was being born, eventually to undermine the idea of American beer as serviceable refreshment, which was the result of corporate interpretation and marketing of a style born of the traditional German palate.

As it has panned out, Gambrinus and its German predecessors may have had more in common, in terms of style and business attitude, with Anheuser-Busch than today's small, creative craft breweries. The earliest German brewers were only local because they were limited by slower transportation and the inability to preserve their beer. As soon as pasteurization and the railroads kicked in, they spread quickly into the larger region. At least at the start, most of the new craft brewers tend to value the creative as much as the business side.

Columbus Brew Adventures's Jim Ellison puts it succinctly: "The German brewers were a product of their era, the 1800s, and culture,

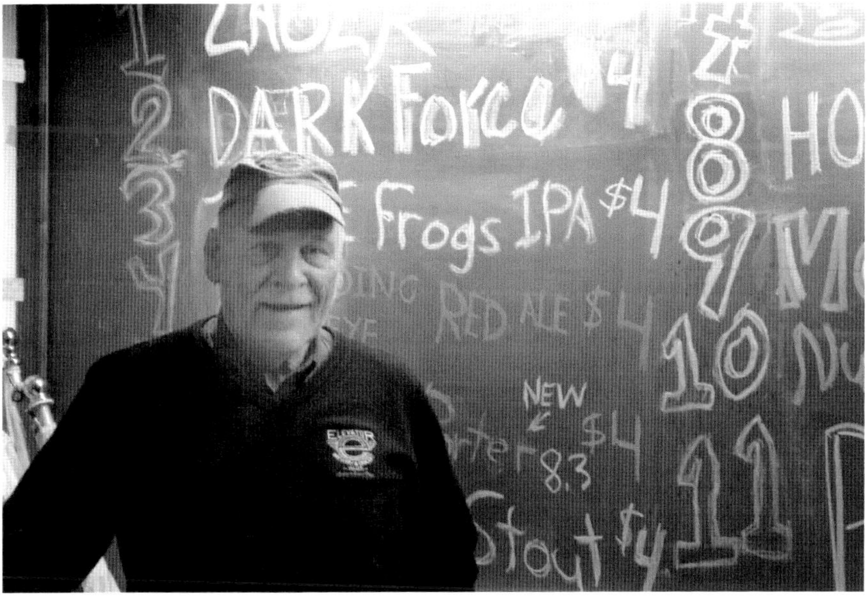

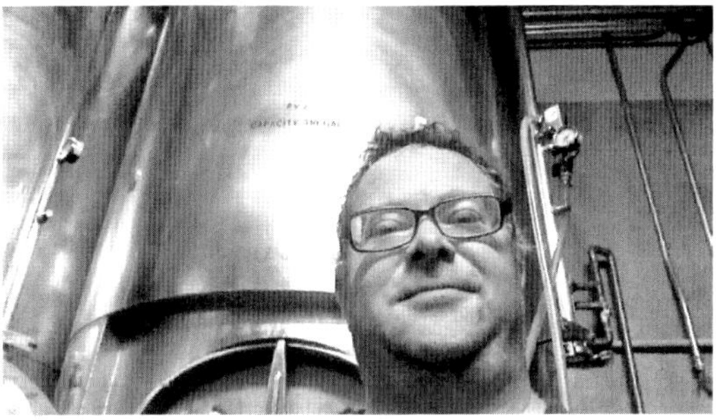

Above: Elevator founder Dick Stevens today in the taproom at the 165 North Fourth Street brewery. *Photo by the author.*

Left: Elevator's first brewer, Vince Falcone, today brewing in San Diego. *Photo by Falcone.*

including the Reinheitsgebot [German Brewing Purity Law]. The idea of pursuing a passion or brewing as an art would have been foreign to them."

Eric Bean, owner and brewmaster at CBC, agreed that the newer brewers tend to be more interested in creativity than in traditional craft. "The very newest guys," he said, "I think the motivations might be different....I think the real similarity of that [the old Germans] with today's craft brewer, is independence. Motivations versus creative versus the old craft. But really it's taking a skill set and being able to provide something that is important to people....I think the old German brewers saw that same opportunity to give something to people that they wanted every day....But I think for them it was a sense of independence from their Old World country and being able to have jobs. Here, it is a sense of working for a small independent company.

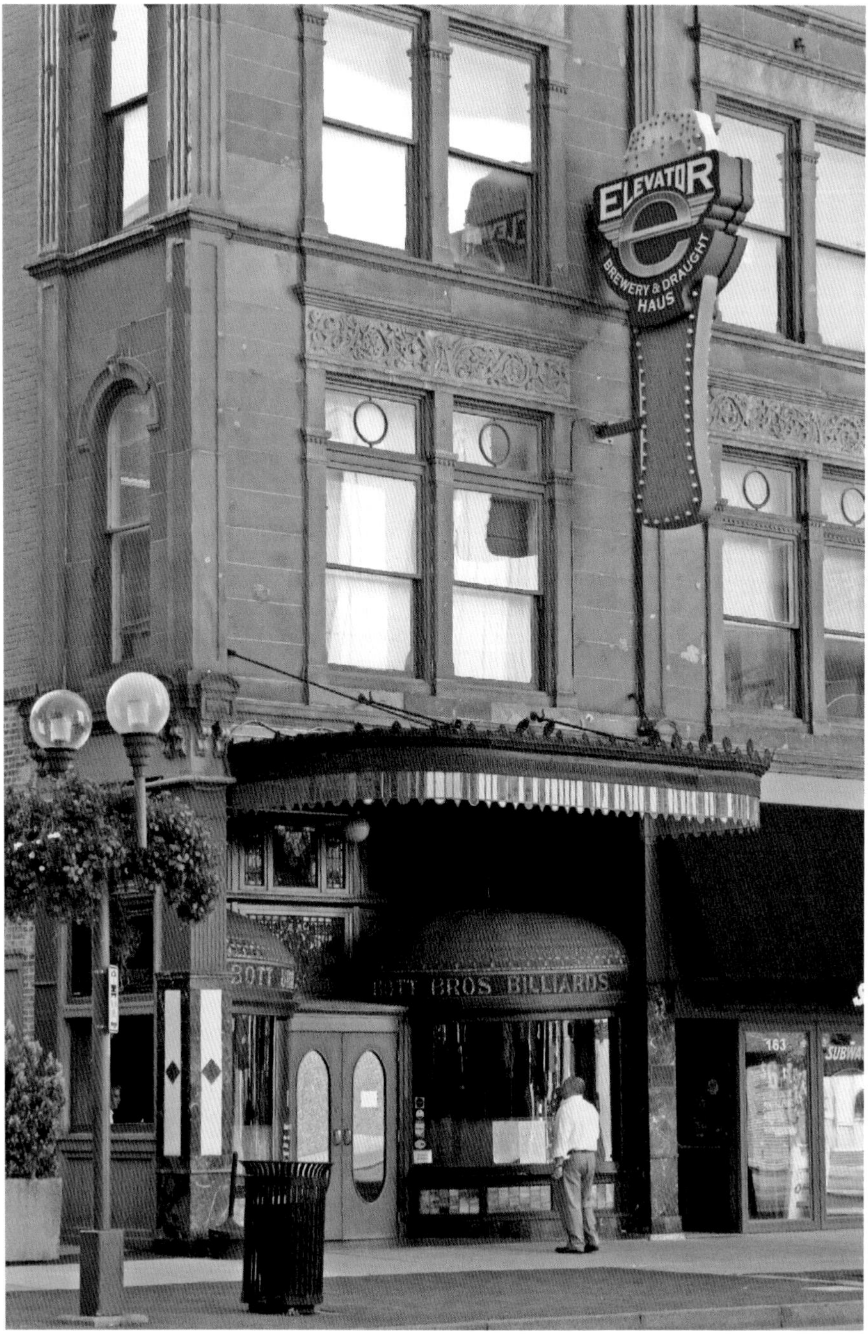

Elevator Brewery & Draught Haus, 161 North High Street, today. *Photo by the author.*

That's a big part of our industry, is that up until eighteen months ago, all the small [craft] breweries were owned by small businessmen."

Bean was referring to the spike in acquisitions and mergers going on in the national and international industry. With a few initial investments and outright purchases beginning way back in 1994 with Anheuser-Busch's 25 percent purchase of Seattle's Red Hook Ale Brewery, acquisition now has reached a fever pitch, with big beer merging and buying smaller conglomerations and individual breweries, with varying arrangements. Even equity investment companies are getting in on the act. Though the character of beer produced by those taken over has changed little thus far, the craft brew industry is watching with a suspicious eye.

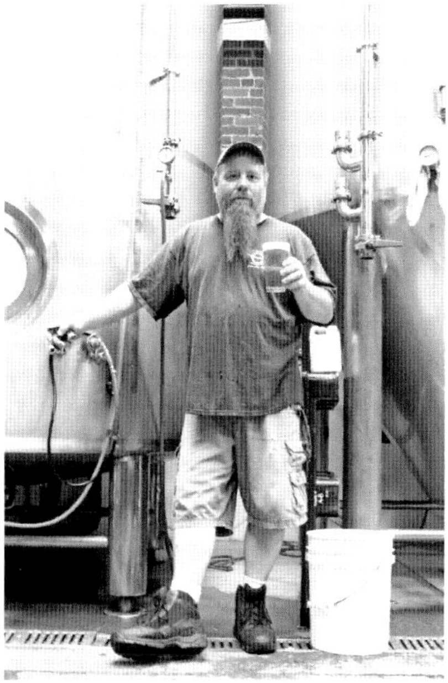

Vic Schiltz brewmaster until summer 2017, in Elevator Brewery's expanded North Fourth Street location in downtown Columbus. *Photo by the author.*

In the sense that the class of '89 was closer to the Old World brewers in employing traditional craft, Bean agreed that he and a couple of others are bridges to the newest wave. Scott Francis and CBC in 1989 represented a focusing on tradition, albeit English rather than German, as part of a nascent investigation of food and drink, its place in our lives and the creativity embodied in flavor, setting and cultural mix. Those who have run crazy with his lead today aren't as interested in recreating English ales or the classic lagers of Wagner and Hoster, as those beers were intertwined with the palate and the social life of their times. Instead, they are exploring flavor and innovation with an openness and unprecedented freedom.

By the time Columbus came back in line with the national growth trends in the second decade of the new century, a craft brew explosion was fully realized. From 2011 to 2015 in Columbus, more than a dozen new breweries opened, with five in 2012 alone. Not only did they cater to an audience that had expanded significantly from the previous decade, but they also stimulated a market that would continue to grow in the present.

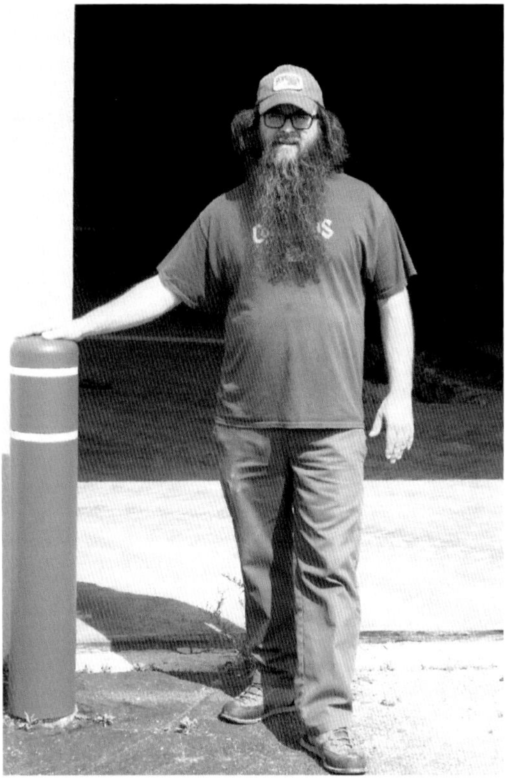

Left: Columbus Brewing Company owner/brewer Eric Bean during the building of the company's huge new brewery at 2555 Harrison Road in 2016. *Photo by the author.*

Below: Eric Bean and his wife, Beth, in front of the newly operational brewery's mash tun, 2016. *Photo by the author.*

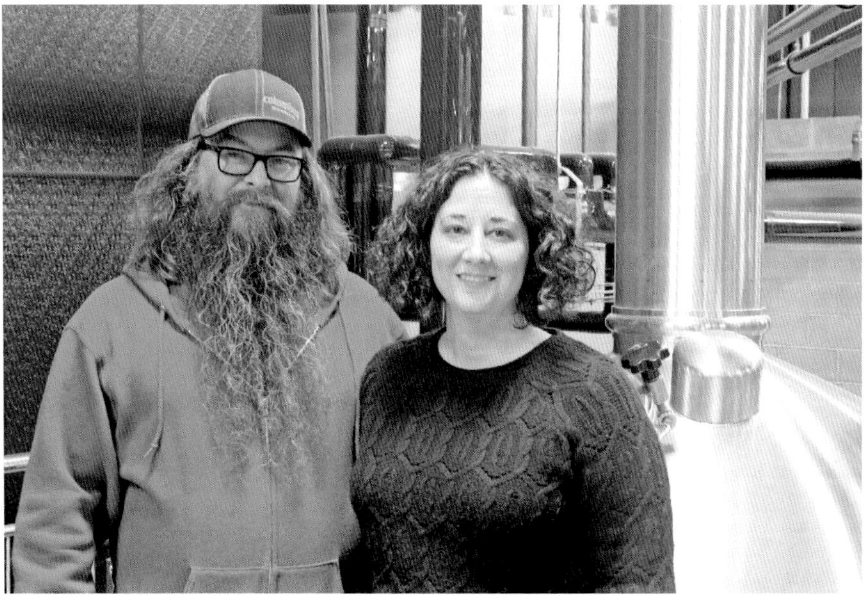

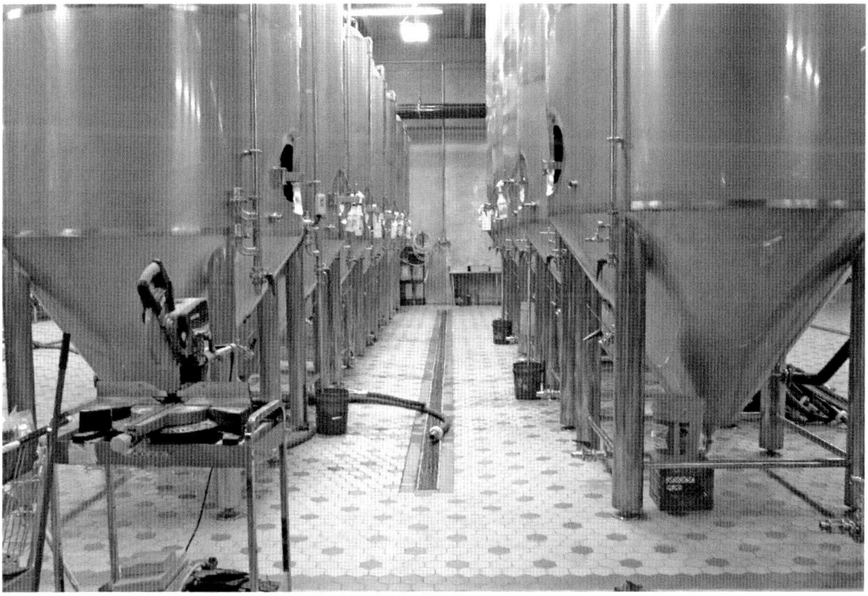

CBC fermenters, Harrison Road plant. *Photo by the author.*

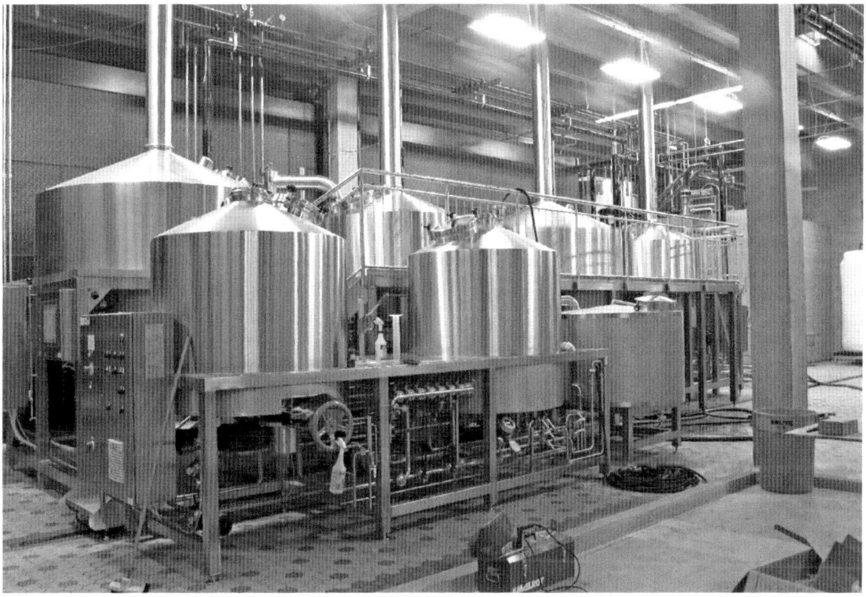

CBC pilot brewery, mash tuns and brew kettles, Harrison Road. *Photo by the author.*

The solid foundation for this growth didn't just move here from Seattle and Brooklyn nor arrive with the foodie-ing of local young people, though. It was built with the help of distribution, community support, increased media attention and professional apprenticeship.

Distribution of craft beer was off to a good start by the early '90s. Robins Wine & Spirits began with imports and West Coast crafts in the early '90s, with the marketing aid of tastings and retail offerings led by Robins rep Dan Tarpy's family beverage center in the Kingsdale shopping center. Ron Wilson opened Premium Beverage Supply in 1995, adding a distribution portfolio committed to craft breweries, both national and local.

All that distribution gradually took hold and joined the zeitgeist that was to reach its recent peak beginning in 2011. Helping earn an audience became the job, too, of carryouts, restaurants and bars. Places such as Pace-Hi carryout, Palmer's Beverage Center, North Market's Grapes Of Mirth, Weiland's Gourmet Market, the Wine Vault, Gentile's Wine Sellers, Colorado Cattle Company and even the now-closed Andersons General Store seemed like lone voices at the time, compared with the pervasive availability of local craft beer today, with the grocery chains jumping in and the fight for shelf space fully on. (Tom Griesemer, stores manager of Colorado Cattle Company and the mover for the bistro's beer menu, would go on to found the first craft roast coffee business in town, mirroring Alfred Peet's innovations, in Columbus in 1988 with Stauf's Coffee Roasters.)

The proliferation of bars and nightclubs that have many tap handles and lists of craft beer offerings makes it hard to remember how unique places such as Bernie's Distillery and Jerry Flaherty's Thirsty Ear bar and music club were.

Bernie's Bagels & Deli opened in 1975 and expanded in 1982, adding a bar in 1983. The bar received its own name, "The Distillery," according to longtime manager Jack Lefton, and an altered version of the venue's logo. When logo artist Larry Hamill gave a mug to Bernie's dancing bagel mascot and added the words "ale, stout, porter," Lefton and day manager Pete Hurlbut decided they needed to stock some of the many available from local distributors. They established the "Passport," a program rewarding patrons who sampled all of the bar's available imports and craft brews with a personalized pewter-colored mug, which hung on the wall behind the bar. The selection started with 80 or so beers, according to Lefton, and topped off at 120.

Flaherty's parents owned two carryouts on the west side of Columbus in the early 1970s. Jerry was a fan of Monty Python's Flying Circus, where there was frequent mention of Watney's Red Barrel Ale. Wishing to expand his horizons from the narrow range of imports then available, he convinced his dad to stock Watney's, Guinness and Bass. The latter two would become cornerstone inspirations to the new American brewers.

A music fan as well, Flaherty's Bent Back Records shop was just south of Scott Francis's homebrew business, the Winemaker's Shop. Flaherty became a homebrewer, fifteen years later tapping his love of craft beer when he opened the Thirsty Ear Tavern. Thirsty Ear had nineteen taps—more than anyone in central Ohio, according to Flaherty—and dozens of bottled beers. The idea was to allow patrons to sample a wide range of beer on draft and with single bottles. At the outset, imports figured strongly into the mix with new American brews. "We didn't call them 'craft' back then," he said. Flaherty's run at Thirsty Ear, now Woodlands Tavern, from 1997 to 2005, made it a significant player in the rise of craft beer in Columbus.

Homebrewing suppliers continued making a crucial contribution, especially Francis's Winemaker's Shop, which was the only game in town until Gentile's Wine Sellers began carrying ingredients and equipment in 1996. More recently, North High Brewery and Buckeye BrewCraft in Westerville next door to Francis's Temperance Row brewery have become suppliers for home brewers. Brew shops support the ever-expanding homebrew market, still the primary source for aspiring professional brewers. Among those inspired by the Winemakers Shop are Barley's Angelo Signorino, CBC's former brewmaster Ben Pridgeon, Weasel Boy's Jay Wince, Temperance Row's Alex Francis, Elevator's Vic Schiltz and Four String's Dan Cochran and Larry Horowitz.

Recently, ingredients for the professional brewer have started to be sourced locally. A *Columbus Business First* article reported that more than thirty Ohio brewers used Ohio hops last year. The Ohio Hops Growers Guild's website claims seventy-plus hops farms in Ohio, growing thirty-plus varieties. Haus Malts, the first new malting house in Cleveland since Prohibition, sources most of its barley from Ohio farms.

Founded in 2008, the Ohio Craft Brewers Association has been a boon to the local market as well. Its website currently boasts 135 Ohio members out of an Ohio brewery population of 173, with 39 opening last year. Their production in 2015 ranked Ohio fourth in the United States, according to the website. Mary MacDonald is the executive director, and the officers and board are made up of brewers statewide.

Giving the boom a boost, as well, is Jim Ellison's Columbus Brew Adventures, founded in 2013. A history buff and "non-practicing librarian,"

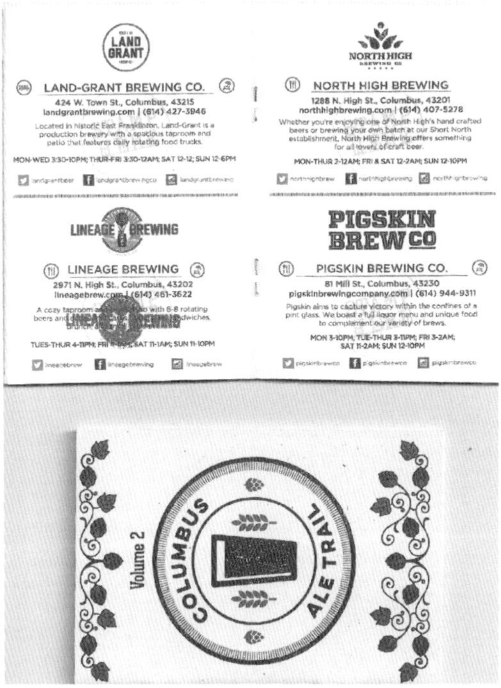

Columbus Ale Trail passport, Vol. 2. Volume 3 was released in the spring of 2017. *Scan. Thanks to Columbus Ale Trail.*

Ellison integrates tours of the Brewery District and other historical sites with stops at local breweries, distillers, a cider maker, wineries and bars. Walking tours are mixed with bus trips and stops in bars and bistros. "We are very focused on the stories and personalities of our local breweries and brewers," he said. "We do try to educate people—but not so much that it impairs their fun."

In conjunction with the local tourist bureau Experience Columbus, Ellison also started the Columbus Ale Trail program, which provides passports containing the names and info of local breweries, to be stamped upon a visit. There are rewards for completing the booklet, which was updated to a third volume in May 2017 and includes thirty-seven stops, including taprooms, brewpubs and production facilities.

The growth has not gone unnoticed in the local media. The *Columbus Dispatch* includes timely features, frequently in its business section, while the alternative weekly *Columbus Alive* runs features and news, as well as lifestyle pieces. Local free monthly *(614)* magazine has been very supportive, running features, news and interviews in its regular publication and a host more in its food and drink quarterly *Stock & Barrel*. *Great Lakes Brewing News*'s bimonthly tabloid is available at most local groceries, bars and breweries. Even the

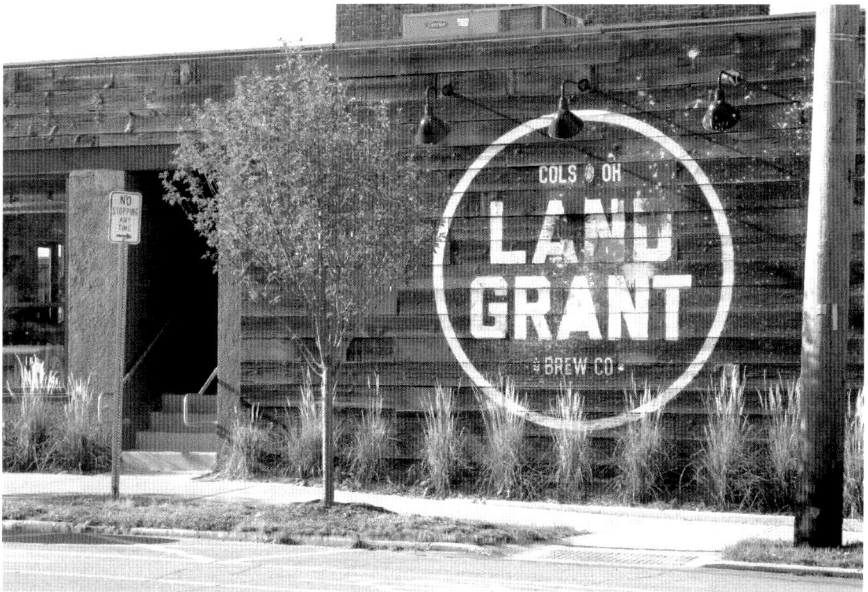

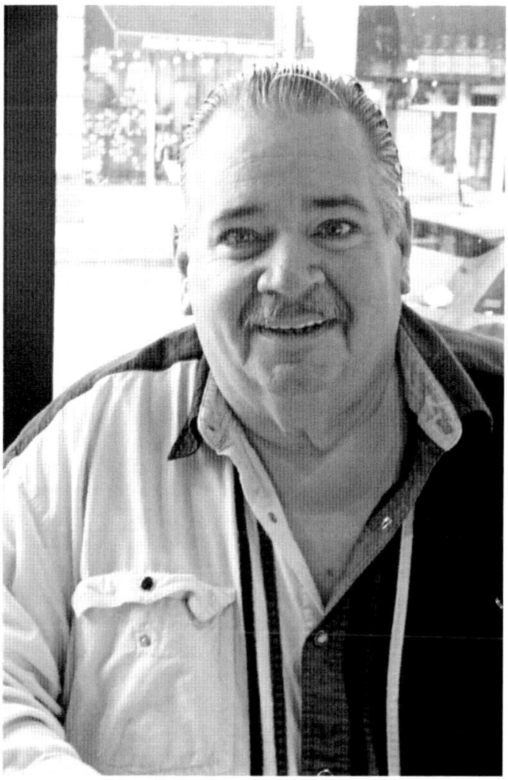

Above: Land Grant Brewing Company, opened in 2014. *Photo by the author.*

Right: David Foster caught in Uptown Deli/Temperance Row, December 2016. *Photo by the author.*

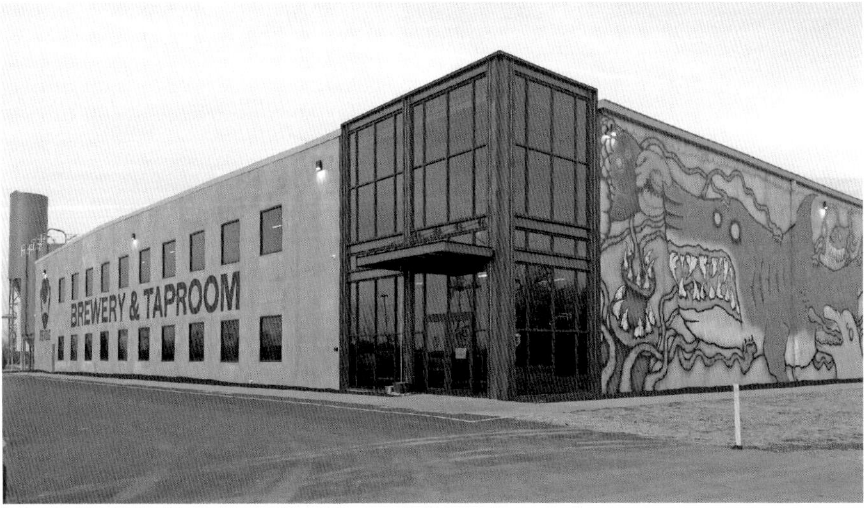

Main entrance to massive new BrewDog brewery, restaurant and U.S. headquarters, February 20, 2017, at the opening of its pub. Brewing was to begin a couple of weeks later. *Photo by the author.*

weekly *Columbus Business First* has gotten onboard, with staff reporter Dan Eaton seemingly making breweries his personal and professional mission.

All of this continues to fuel the explosion. By Columbus Ale Trail's count, there are thirty-seven breweries, brewpubs and micros in central Ohio as of September 2017. Ellison estimates that in a year there may be upward of forty-five. Where will it all end?

For a couple of months late in 2014, Columbus was abuzz with the potential of being chosen as the site for Stone Brewing's eastern and second gigantic craft brewery. The Escondito, California company was one of the largest craft brewers at the time, and it hoped to open a $74 million, 200,000-square-foot brewery, restaurant and garden in Columbus, in part because its CEO and cofounder, Greg Koch, is from Pataskala, just down the pike.

The company decided instead to build its expansion in Richmond, Virginia, thanking locals later by brewing a "Pataskala Red X IPA." Further, it put a bug in the ear of Scotland's BrewDog, a like-minded, similarly sized concern that wished to land a beachhead in the United States. So it went, and BrewDog U.S. opened its $30 million, 100,000-square-foot brewery in Canal Winchester on February 20, 2017. More than just a fabulous addition to the local craft scene, BrewDog is confirmation that central Ohio has unquestionably arrived on the national craft beer scene.

Appendix

COLUMBUS BREWERIES AS OF SEPTEMBER 2017

Actual Brewing Company
655 North James Road, Columbus, OH 43219
Website: actualbrewing.com
Phone: 614-636-3825
Brewmasters: Chris A. Moore, Jonathan Carroll, Zach Harper and Kris Fry
Actual might be the poster boy for the unruly, unbound new brewers. Founded by a refugee from the banking industry, the eastside brewery includes a taproom that looks like your college kid's apartment and a brewery put together in chunks. The results, though, have been unique, flavorful and successful enough for the company to make plans for a new taproom/satellite brewery in Clintonville, next to Lucky's Market in mid-2017.

Barley's Brewing Company
467 North High Street, Columbus, OH 43215
Website: barleysbrewing.com
Phone: 614-228-2537
Brewmaster: Angelo Signorino
This is the first English-style brewpub in town, established in 1992 by Scott Francis, the godhead of Columbus brewing, and ale fanatic Lenny Kolada. Barley's continues today under the brewing direction of Angelo Signorino, who came on board shortly after its opening and has expanded the creative offerings to include signature brews such as Blurry Bike IPA, Four Seas Imperial IPA, its great Auld Curiosity Ale, Angelo's Crooked Sky Rye Ale and the popular Barley's Scottish Ale.

THE BREW BROTHERS AT ELDORADO SCIOTO DOWNS
6000 South High Street, Columbus, OH 43207
Website: sciotodowns.com/dining/the-brew-brothers
Phone: 614-295-4700
Brewmaster: Ryan Torres
Brew Brothers, a chain brewery, is situated at the casino and longtime horse track and has its own brewing facility with a patio, restaurant, live music stage and ten taps, half of which serve the venue's own beer. Brewmaster Ryan Torres, who began at Barley's, works in full view, creating Carano Extra, a kolsch, Double Down Stout, Gold Dollar Pale Ale and Redhead Amber Ale.

BREWDOG
96 Gender Road, Canal Winchester, OH 43310
Website: brewdog.com
The Scottish brewery's planting its first American roots in Columbus is flattering and gives a high-profile boost to the town's national cred. Though it has made its biggest buck from its Punk IPA, which cashes in on the hoppy American iteration of a classic British style, its portfolio ranges wide and creative, inspiring great anticipation for its specialty and taproom contributions late in 2017.

BUCKEYE LAKE BREWERY
5176 Walnut Road, Buckeye Lake, OH 43008
Website: buckeyelakebrewery.com
Phone: 740-331-2898
Brewmaster: Dave Endicott
This is the brewery that gave us Mike Byrne, brewmaster and cofounder of Lineage. Owner Rich Hennosy says on the brewery's website that its aim was simply to offer fresh beer, created according to style, for the locale. Though he admits the focus on tradition has stretched a bit, the brewery's bottles and cans, clad in classic 1950s and '60s images, contain mostly straightforward lagers and ales.

COLUMBUS BREWING COMPANY
2555 Harrison Road, Columbus, OH 43204
Website: columbusbrewing.com
Phone: 614-224-3626
Brewmaster: Eric Bean

The craft brewery that started it all, founded by Scott Francis and beginning production in 1989 in a tiny space on Front Street, was followed in a few years by a move to the end of Short Street. The brewery's success with current owner Eric Bean at the helm soon outgrew that facility, thanks to the popularity of its pale, IPA and the much sought Bodhi Double IPA. Bodhi shortages should be rare, as the firm's new megaproduction facility will take it from a projected 25,000 barrels in 2016 to a capacity of 50,000 in a couple of years. The building can be fitted to brew 100,000 in the future.

COMBUSTION BREWERY
80 West Church Street, Suite101, Pickerington, OH 43147
Website: combustionbrewing.com
Phone: 614-362-8450
Brewmaster: Keith Jackson
Combustion inhabits a one-hundred-year-old creamery in Pickerington. Spearheaded by Gordon Biersch veteran Keith Jackson, the brewery has its beer-making chops in order, producing a variety of styles, including Wanderlust blonde ale, Combustion IPA, Now We're Talkin' double IPA and flavored offerings such as the Blueprint blueberry version of Wanderlust and Antidote, a coffee-infused Wanderlust. It is a hop, skip and jump away from Canal Winchester's Loose Rail and BrewDog.

COMMON HOUSE ALES
535 Short Street, Columbus, OH 43215
Website: commonhouseales.com
Phone: 614-638–4619
Brewmaster: Sam Hickey
Smokehouse Brewery's Lenny Kolada had a vision for extending the reach of his Dublin Road brewpub. It included a bit of community activism for his Certified B Corporation offshoot brewery. Purchasing the equipment and taking the space vacated by the Columbus Brewing Company, he began brewing beers that were an extension of those at the Smokehouse and inspired by his cofounding Barley's. One dollar of Common's flagship Six One for Good ale goes into common shares for community organizations, managed by the Columbus Foundation.

ELEVATOR BREWING COMPANY
165 North Fourth Street, Columbus, OH 43215
Website: elevatorbrewery.com
Phone: 614-679-2337
Brewmaster: Doug Beedy
Though production began in 1999 at Elevator, it is one of the founding breweries in Columbus's craft brew explosion. Working from defining styles established by first brewer Vince Falcone, former brewmaster Vic Schiltz creatively tweaked the company's wide range of brews. Dark Force is an award-winning lager produced for ten years, Bleeding Buckey is a tribute to Schiltz's alma mater and Big Vic is its sledgehammer IPA. New brewmaster Doug Beedy promises to add his own stamp. The brewery has a funky garage-like taproom.

ELEVATOR BREWERY & DRAUGHT HAUS
161 North High Street, Columbus, OH 43215
Website: elevatorbrewing.com
Phone: 614-228-0500
Brewmaster: Doug Beedy
As the stand-alone "pub" part of Elevator Brewing company, this fine restaurant has provided the primary conduit for Elevator's beers nearly from the beginning. In addition to offering dishes such as its trademark "Rock Filet" steak, it awards titles to experienced beer drinkers with its Masters of Beer Appreciation and Professor of Hearty Drinking degrees.

ENDEAVOR BREWING COMPANY
909 West Fifth Avenue, Columbus, OH 43212
Website: endeavorbrewing.com
Phone: 614-456-7074
Brewmaster: Cameron Lloyd
Endeavor is the former Zauber Brewery, renamed after a change in ownership and a shift toward new-ish brewer Cameron Lloyd's preferences. The accent is still partly German and Belgian, but English and other styles will work their way into the mix. The Exploer Club eatery has moved out, replaced by a rotating series of food trucks.

FOUR STRING BREWING COMPANY
Taproom: 985 West Sixth Avenue, Columbus, OH 43212
Phone: 614-670-7895

Website: fourstringbrewing.com
Brewmaster: Larry Horwitz
Dan Cochran's long history as a musician in Columbus was reflected in his initially casual approach to opening a brewery and marketing its product. The taproom at the original brewery location was the best place to find his beers, though, with the addition of canning and draft distribution, the business's visibility exploded.

Four String Brewing Company Production
660 North Hague Avenue, Columbus, OH 43204
Phone: 614-725-1282
Website: fourstringbrewing.com
Brewmaster: Larry Horwitz
The dizzying growth of Dan Cochran's brewery, especially after the addition of brewmaster Larry Horwitz, led to its building a huge new production facility on North Hague Avenue on the west side. Classic styles such as the company's Brass Knuckles Pale Ale and its terrific Payback Pilsener will not be in short supply for a long time, given the facility's capacity for growth from about eight thousand barrels today to fifty thousand down the road. If Payback led the local market in exploring lagers and lighter beers, its Hilltop Heritage Lager is the logical end, a refreshing, affordable craft beer that answers to the appeal of mainstream corporate brews. The facility recently added a taproom.

Gordon Biersch Brewery
401 North Front Street, Suite 120, Columbus, OH 43215
Website: gordonbiersch.com
Phone: 614-246-2900
Brewmaster: Keith Jackson
Gordon Biersch is part of a chain founded in 1988 that includes thirty-five restaurant/breweries. The brewpub makes clean, relatively style-strict German lagers and ales and Czech pilsners. The accent is on tradition and professional brewing techniques. Eric Bean, owner of CBC and a Biersch alumnus, credits the company with preparing him to run a successful production brewery. Styles include a Marzen, Pilsner, Golden Export, Schwarzbier and Hefeweizen.

HOFBRAUHAUS COLUMBUS
800 Goodale Boulevard, Columbus, OH 43212
Website: hofbrauhauscolumbus.com
Phone: 614-294-2437
Brewmaster: Robert Makein
Hofbrauhaus is a strict Munich brewhouse and restaurant, owned by the nearly five-hundred-year-old German company. Traditional Bavarian styles, including a Lager, Hefeweizen and Dunkel, are constantly on tap and perfectly fit the mood and food in the beer hall and garden. Seasonals are rotated the first Tuesday of every month. The brewery just began filling growlers and cans on the premises.

HOMESTEAD BEER COMPANY
811 Irving Wick Drive West, Heath, OH 43056
Website: homesteadbeerco.com
Phone: 740-358-0360
Brewmaster: Adam Rhodes
Homestead is located on the former Newark Airforce Base, and its beers reflect a respect for American tradition and history, as many are based on classic styles, including the Pioneer Ohio Pilsner and the Tenpenny Amber Ale. That said, some of them are pretty liberal interpretations, including the 1805 IPA and 3 MC's Double IPA. The beer has a strong local presence in stores.

HOOF HEARTED BREWING
300 County Road 26, Marengo, OH 43334
Website: HoofHeartedBrewing.com
Phone: 419-253-0000
Brewmaster: Trevor Williams
Hoof Hearted is at the extreme creative end of the brewing spectrum, mixing ingredients and styles as if throwing darts at a board, tapping loud combinations of extreme hops and experimenting constantly. From the fact that the brewers built their own brewery from scrap to the funky artwork and names that grace their myriad creations, this company aims to break the mold, any mold.

HOOF HEARTED BREW PUB AND KITCHEN
850 North Fourth Street, Columbus, OH 43215
Website: HoofHeartedBrewing.com

Phone: 614-401-4033
Brewmaster: Trevor Williams
Hoof Hearted's brewpub, in the Short North, gives it a local launchpad for its mayhem. Its Friday Night Flights and Bites features a wildly creative menu, which experiments with brew ingredients such as spent grain. The regular menu is nearly as creative, and the beers are rotated regularly.

ILL MANNERED BREWING COMPANY
30 Grace Drive, Powell, OH 43065
Website: illmanneredbeer.com
Phone: 614-859-6819
Brewmasters: Tom Ayers, Greg Dannemiller, Brian Mathias, Ryan Romer-Jordan
Ill Mannered is a cozy little nanobrewery with a tiny taproom in a small strip mall in Powell, Ohio, north of Columbus. There's nothing minor about the range of beers the brewery has on offer at any one time, though, from golden ale to strong Belgian, porter to IPA, witbier to rye ale, all with amusing names such as Argue the Toss and A Risky Ending.

KINDRED ARTISAN ALES TASTING ROOM & BARREL HOUSE
750 Cross Pointe Road, Columbus, OH 43230
Website: KindredAles.com
Phone: 614-626-4341
Brewmaster: Max Lachowyn
Kindred specializes in Belgian, wheat and German styles, with several Saisons, a traditional spiced Belgian wit and a tart Berliner weisse. But it mixes it up a bit with its Long Sleeves Red Rye IPA and the Salvage Porter. It does best when creating with the Belgian yeast, which appears to be the brewer's calling. The brewery and taproom feature a tasteful industrial design. Look for a proposed satellite brewery and eatery in Clintonville at Crestview and High.

KNOTTY PINE BREWING
1765 West Third Avenue, Columbus, OH 43212
Website: knottypinebrewing.net
Phone: 614-817-1515
This nanobrewery in Grandview sticks to what works, from the menu of burgers, salads and uncomplicated entrees to reliable beer styles. Stock offerings include Mirror Lake IPA, Cherrywood Black Porter, Snow Day

IPA, Buckeye Blonde, and the Ghost pumpkin beer. It also offers flavored variations and its own hard root beer ale, named 3rd and W, after its location.

LAND GRANT BREWING COMPANY
424 West Town Street, Columbus, OH 43215
Website: landgrantbrewing.com
Phone: 614-427-3946
Brewmaster: Jamie Feihel
Land Grant's founders are big sports fans. That shows in everything from the names of their beers to their PR. An impressive, comprehensive design sense accompanies it all, from the labels to the baseball cards for each brew that include essential data. The proof is in the tasting, though, and LG classics such as 1862 Ale (Kolsch), Son of a Mudder (brown) and Greenskeeper IPA (session) are clean, tasty interpretations of classics.

LINEAGE BREWING
2971 North High Street, Columbus, OH 43202
Website: lineagebrew.com
Phone: 614-461-3622
Brewmaster: Mike Byrne
Lineage has subtle fan themes running through its marketing, including beer, bikes and dogs. Situated in a beautifully repurposed old car wash, its open garage door is welcoming in the summer. So is the beer, which includes standards such as Spaceship #6 IPA, Loughran's Irish Stout, Kimmy Gibler (SF lager) and its Aunt Bernice Berliner Weiss, which is sometimes infused with fruit. The beer is accompanied by a small but creative menu.

LOOSE RAIL BREWING
37 West Waterloo Street, Canal Winchester, OH 43110
Phone: 614-834-7267
Brewmaster: Jonathan Woodruff
Loose Rail opened in Canal Winchester in May 2017 in a lovely historic building. Its beer styles are time tested, as well—in craft beer years, that is. Offerings include Full Steam saison, Dead Man's Throttle IPA, Ash Can amber, Go On Git double IPA, as well as the lighter John Henry dortmunder and Workingman's kolsch. In tandem with Pickerington's Combustion Brewing, Loose Rail forms a natural bar hop from Columbus to the city's BrewDog.

NORTH HIGH BREWING
1288 North High Street, Columbus, OH 43201
Website: northhighbrewing.com
Phone: 614-407-5278
Brewmaster: Jason McKibben
North High began in 2011 as a combination microbrewery and Brew on Premises program, where amateurs can brew a batch in-house with the oversight of a professional brewer. The success of its own beer has overshadowed the guest brewing, though, and the business has expanded ever since, with an off-premises production facility making enough beer to get its cans distributed statewide. In addition to fine variations of the basics, North High also creates a host of seasonal and limited releases.

PIGSKIN BREWING COMPANY
81 Mill Street Suite 150, Gahanna, OH 43230
Website: pigskinbrewingcompany.com
Phone: 614-944-9311
Brewmasters: Mike Rockwell, Nick Bailey, Vic Gonzales
A brewpub in Gahanna seemed a hard sell at first, which might explain the sports theme and motto "Victory in Every Sip." Variations of standards include Cream of the Crop cream ale, Laces Out hefeweizen, What's On Second session IPA, Highland Games Scottish and Undefeated American IPA. Pigskin recently opened its own kitchen serving pub grub such as flatbreads, wraps, salads and starters.

PLATFORM BREWING COMPANY
408 North Sixth Street, Columbus, OH 43215
Phone: 614-826-2285
Cleveland's Platform had a presence in Columbus for more than a year before its local branch opened. The brewers found the 120,000-square-foot Carfagna's production building and got it for a song, opening a three-barrel brewhouse to supply the pub through twenty-four taps. The location also serves as a warehouse for the local distribution of its canned beer, all produced in Cleveland.

RESTORATION BREW WORX
25 North Sandusky Street, Delaware, OH 43015
Website: restorationbrewworx.com
Phone: 740-990-7120

Brewmaster: Frank Barickman
Primarily serving Ohio Wesleyan University students, Restoration holds down a key location in downtown Delaware, the classic college town. Its beer offerings range wide, from American, double and Belgian hybrid IPAs to English and Scottish ales, to Belgian wit and American-style barleywine. Pub grub includes a nice selection of sandwiches, starters and salads.

ROCKMILL BREWERY
5705 Lithopolis Road Northwest, Lancaster, OH 43130
Website: rockmillbrewery.com
Phone: 740-205-8076
Brewmaster: Matthew Barbee
When it comes to Belgian ales, nobody in central Ohio makes them with the sophistication, attention to detail and eye for tradition that Rockmill employs. The brewery is built in a barn on an old horse farm outside Lancaster, chosen because its spring water is remarkably like that in Belgium. An amazing range of creations flows from the little brewhouse, packaged in "bomber" bottles and available, along with uncommon hospitality, in the location's taproom.

ROCKMILL TAVERN
503 South Front Street, Columbus, OH 43215
Phone: 614-732-4364
Website: rockmillbrewery.com/tavern
Late in 2016, Rockmill opened a tavern in the historic Brewery District, in the Worly building, which housed Hoster Brewery's horses in the nineteenth century, radio station CD101FM in the late nineteenth and into the twentieth, and World of Beers for a short time after that. Belgian ales are famous for their copacetic pairings with food, and the tavern serves a small but sophisticated selection of small and large plates. The beer is the attraction, though, served from tap and bottle. All Belgian, it is a bountiful selection of rich, world-class incarnations.

SEVENTH SON BREWING COMPANY
1101 North Fourth Street, Columbus, OH 43201
Website: seventhsonbrewing.com
Phone: 614-421-2337
Brewmaster: Colin Vent

To the list of breweries built in cool, vintage digs, add Seventh Son, opened in a repurposed tire dealer, retaining its garage feel. To that, add a team of brewers that knows both how to pay the rent with its portfolio and how to keep it dynamic. Seventh Son maintains a solid lineup of four flagship beers, including Seventh Son American Strong Ale, Stone Fort Oat Brown Ale, The Scientist IPA and Humulus Nimbus Strong Pale Ale. An attachment to the beer selection on its website lists another seventy-five, some rotated, some perhaps one-offs. A major expansion of its brewery and taproom is scheduled for late 2017.

SIDESWIPE BREWING COMPANY
2419 Scioto Harper Drive, Columbus, OH 43204
Website: sideswipebrewing.com
Phone: 614-719-9654
Brewmaster: Craig O'Herron
How small is small? How about a shotgun-shaped space in an industrial park that—with recent improvements—is about three thousand square feet, including the brewery and taproom, and has space for about forty people. But Sideswipe has loyal fans, among them Actual Brewing Company's Fred Lee, who, according to a *Dispatch* news story, called the brewery's O'Herron's Pixelated Sun wheat beer "the most underrated beer in Columbus."

SMOKEHOUSE BREWING
1130 Dublin Road, Columbus, OH 43215
Website: smokehousebrewing.com
Phone: 614-485-0227
Brewmaster: Alex Kolada
When Barley's Smokehouse & Brewpub, Ale House No. 2 opened in 1998, it was a culinary iteration of Barley's on High Street, its beers remaining very similar. Years later, though, under Lenny Kolada's exclusive ownership and new brewer Sam Hickey, it became a creative dynamo of experimentation with standards including IPAs, barleywines, Belgians and many more. Under Hickey, the brewery made sixteen new beers in 2015 alone. With Hickey moving to Kolada's new Common House, his son has taken the brewing reigns at Smokehouse.

STAAS BREWING COMPANY
31 West Winter Street, Delaware, OH 43015
Website: staasbrewing.com

Phone: 740-417-4690
Brewmasters: Donald and Liz Staas
Staas small-batch brews are rotated regularly, guaranteeing optimum freshness. It is particularly important, given the brewers' insistence on maintaining strict style guidelines, especially with its English and Belgian ales, which dominate its stalwarts list. Those include the Evangelist Belgian Quadruple, Wildcat Sally Saison Farmhouse Ale, Flood Water English Coffee Stout, Golden Delicious Belgian Golden Strong and The Runner Up English Extra Special Bitter. There are concessions, though, to the current market, with an American IPA and double IPA.

TEMPERANCE ROW BREWING AT UPTOWN DELI
41 North State Street, Westerville, OH 43081
Website: uptowndeliandbrew.com
Phone: 614-891-2337
Brewmaster: Scott Francis
Temperance Row marked Columbus brewing godhead Scott Francis's return to action with its opening at the end of 2014, after the brewer went three years without a gig. The brews, predominately the traditional English styles with which Francis jump-started the craft brew movement in Columbus in 1989 at CBC, were as familiar as old friends. The Scofflaw Scottish Ale, Hatchetation Pale Ale and Contradiction ESB are special treats. The brewery's Macedonian Imperial Stout is spectacular. Uptown Deli, which fronts the brewery, features high-quality, classic deli offerings.

THREE TIGERS BREWING COMPANY
140 North Prospect Street, Granville, OH 43023
Website: threetigersbrewing.com
Phone: 740-920-4680
Granville's Three Tigers connects with its community in a couple of rather unique ways. The brewery and taproom, which serves bar snacks and has a cooperative arrangement with Mai Chau Restaurant next door, also presents live music and hosts a homebrew competition. Its house beers have a nice range, including a Belgian strong ale, an American IPA, a Kolsch, Hefeweizen, oatmeal stout and a double IPA.

TWO TONES
145 North Hamilton Road, Whitehall, OH 43213
Website: 2tonesbrewingco.com

Brewmasters: Tony McKeivier, Tony Hill
The two tones in question began home brewing as students at Ohio State, out of the blocks, creating a 10 percent oatmeal imperial stout. The flagship beers for their new brewery are a little bit less ambitious, but one of them is a little unusual. The IPA is pretty standard; Uncle Joe's Irish Red Ale, though, aims to echo the gin loved by McKeivier's Irish uncle, with juniper berries added at the end of the boil. Other brews include a couple Kolsches, a porter and a pumpkin ale. The brewery sells dog treats made from its spent grain.

Weasel Boy Brewing
126 Muskingum Avenue, Suite E, Zanesville, OH 43701
Website: weaselboybrewing.com
Phone: 740-455-3767
Brewmasters: Jay and Lori Wince
When he began home brewing, Jay Wince learned from the best, buying ingredients and getting advice from Scott Francis, Nina Hawranick and Angelo Signorino at the Winemakers Shop, ground zero for the craft beer movement in Columbus. The result is Weasel Boy in Zanesville, founded with his wife, Lori, in 2007, the first brewery in that river city since Prohibition. Critters inhabit the names of its brews, including Plaid Ferret Scottish Ale, Ornery Otter Blonde Ale, Brown Stoat Stout and Dancing Ferret IPA, all of which lend a subtle twist to their signature styles.

Wolf's Ridge Brewing
215 North Fourth Street, Columbus, OH 43215
Website: wolfsridgebrewing.com
Phone: 614-429-3936
Brewmaster: Chris Davison
The full and impressive menu at Wolf Ridge always vies for attention with its in-house crafted beers. Both are basic but sophisticated in their production. The menu, which includes no wild cards, is expertly prepared, fine dining without all the long names and fusion dazzle. The beers are solid, as well, the current list including twenty of the brewery's own creations, including its eminently drinkable Clear Sky cream ale, Dire Wolf Imperial Russian Stout, L'Abondance Saison and Howling Moon Imperial IPA.

ZAFTIG BREWING COMPANY
7020 A Huntley Road, Worthington, OH 43229
Website: drinkzaftig.com
Phone: 614-636-2537
That one of its flagship brews is the 9 percent ABV strong ale Shadowed Mistress speaks volumes about Zaftig, the tiny brewery in the shadow of Anheuser-Busch. Full-bodied and mind-altering brews include stouts, IPAs, a big wit and a barleywine. The beers reflect the boldness suggested by the brewery's name, which in Yiddish describes a woman of full, rounded figure. Zaftig just opened a taproom, so consult the website for times and offerings.

BIBLIOGRAPHY

Books

Acitelli, Tom. *The Audacity of Hops: The History of America's Craft Beer Revolution*. Chicago: Chicago Review Press, 2013.

Arnold, John P. *Origin and History of Beer and Brewing*. 1911. Cleveland, OH: BeerBooks.com, 2005.

Baron, Stanley. *Brewed in America: A History of Beer and Ale in the United States*. 1962. Cleveland, OH: BeerBooks.com, 2006.

Behr, Edward. *Prohibition: Thirteen Years That Changed America*. New York: Arcade, 2011.

A Centennial Biographical History of the City of Columbus and Franklin County Ohio. Chicago: Lewis Publishing Company, 1901.

Cole, Charles C., Jr. *A Fragile Capital: Identity and the Early Years of Columbus, Ohio*. Columbus: Ohio State University Press, 2001.

Darby, Jeffrey T., and Nancy A. Reechie. *German Columbus*. Charleston, SC: Arcadia Publishing, 2005.

Fancelli, Frank. *The Wasserstrom Company, 1902–1997: The First 95 Years*. Columbus, OH: Wasserstrom Company, 1998.

Fitzpatrick, Stephen A., and U.S. Morris. *History of Columbus Celebration, Franklinton Centennial; 1797–1897*. Columbus, OH: Press of the New Franklin Print Company, 1897.

Franklin County at the Beginning of the Twentieth Century. Columbus, OH: Compiled and published by the Historical Publishing Company, 1901.

Gaston, Paul L. *Ohio's Craft Beers: Discovering the Variety, Enjoying the Quality, Relishing the Experience*. Kent, OH: Black Squirrel Books, 2016.

Henderson, Andrew. *Forgotten Columbus*. Charleston, SC: Arcadia Publishing, 2002.

Herbst, Henry, Don Roussin, Kevin Kious and Stefene Russell. *St. Louis Brews: The History of Brewing in the Gateway City*. St. Louis, MO: Reedy Press, 2015.

Hooper, Osman Castle. *History of the City of Columbus Ohio*. Columbus, OH: Memorial Publishing Company, n.d.

Lee, Alfred E. *History of the City of Columbus, Capital of Ohio*. 2 vols. Chicago: Munsell and Company, 1892.

Martin William T. *History of Franklin County*. N.p.: Follett, Foster & Company, 1858.

Musson, Robert A. *Brewing Beer in the Buckeye State*. Vol. 1. *A History of the Brewing Industry in Eastern Ohio from 1808–2004*. Medina, OH: Robert A Musson/Zepp Publications, 2005.

———. *Brewing Beer in the Capital City, A History of the Brewing Industry in Columbus Ohio*. Vol. 1. *The Hoster Story*. Medina, OH: Robert A Musson/Zepp Publications, 2011.

———. *Brewing Beer in the Capital City, A Pictorial History of the Brewing Industry in Columbus Ohio*. Vol. 2: *The Gambrinus/August Wagner Breweries*. Medina, OH: Robert A. Musson/Zepp Publications, 2013.

———. *Brewing Beer in the Capital City, A Pictorial History of the Brewing Industry in Columbus Ohio*. Vol. 3. *Franklin, Washington, Ohio, Anheuser-Busch, and Craft Brewers*. Medina, OH: Robert A Musson/Zepp Publications, 2015.

Okrent, Daniel. *Last Call: The Rise and Fall of Prohibition*. New York: Scribner, 2010.

100 Years of Brewing. Chicago: H.S Rich & Company, 1903.

Randall, Emilius Oviatt, and Daniel Joseph Ryan. *History of Ohio: The Rise and Progress of an American State*. New York: Century History Company, 1912.

Schlegel, Donald M. *Lager and Liberty: German Brewers of Nineteenth Century Columbus*. 2nd ed. Columbus, OH: Donald M. Schlegel, 2014.

Stream, Curt. *Brewing in Seattle*. Charleston, SC: Arcadia Publishing, 2012.

Magazines and Newspapers

All About Beer 26, no. 2 (May 2005).

Brown, T.C. "Bubbling Over: Local Craft Beer Business." *Columbus CEO* (March 2015): 46–54.

Croyle, Steve V. "Big Beer Made Here?" *Stock and Barrel* (Summer 2016): 94–107.

Davis Noah. "The Craft Beer Market Has Exploded, and Now Brewers Are Worried about a Collapse." *Business Insider*, December 14, 2013. http://www.business insider.com.

Great Lakes Brewing News: Celebrating a Region's Beer and Culture 20, no. 5 (October/November 2016).

Hieronymus, Stan. "The Class of 88: Looking Back at a Quarter Century of Business, Beer, and People." *All About Beer* (January 2014). http://allaboutbeer.com.

Hoster, Jay. "How Beer Brewing on Columbus Dwindled to One Big Fish." *Columbus Monthly* (November 1976): 63–74.

Kilbourn, John. *The Ohio Gazetteer or Topographical Dictionary*. N.p.: John Kilbourn, 1829.

"The Land-Grant Brewing Company. Land-Grant Brewing Company Announces Partnership with Columbus Crew SC." LandGrant.com. April 27, 2015. http://landgrant.com.

Lovelace, Craig, "Shaping Columbus: Louis Hoster, Brewery District Pioneer." *Columbus Business First* (May 2012). http://www.bizjournals.com/columbus/print-edition/2012/05/18/shaping-columbus-louis-hoster.html.

Malone, J.D. "Columbus Brewing Launching Larger Brewery, New Branding." *Columbus Dispatch*, April 14, 2016. http://columbusdispatch.com.

Matthews, Katherine. "The New Beer-makers and Their Gourmet Brews." *Columbus Monthly* (May 1990): 99–102.

Norman, Michael. "Risky Business in the Brewery District." *Columbus Monthly* (February 1989): 26–34.

Poulson, Andrew. "Land-Grant Brewing Company, Columbus." *Ohio Magazine*: *Craft Beer Issue* (February 2017): 58–59.

Williams, Brian. "Business Is Hopping." *Columbus Dispatch*, March 3, 1997, 1–2.

Magazines and Newsletters

All About Beer
Columbus Monthly
Crate and Barrel
Great Lakes Brewing News
Ohio Tavern News
614 Magazine
Western Brewer (from archives)

Newspapers

Capital City Fact
Columbus Alive
Columbus Citizen
Columbus Citizen-Journal
Columbus Dispatch
Columbus Evening Press
Ohio State Journal
Ohio State Journal and Columbus Gazette
Western Intelligencer
Western Intelligencer and Columbus Gazette

Websites

American Brewiana Association. https://www.americanbreweriana.org.
BeerHistory.com. https://www.beerhistory.com.
Brewers Association. https://www.brewersassociation.org.
Drink Up Columbus. https://drinkupcolumbus.com.
Metropolitan News Company. https://mnc.net.
Michael Jackson's Beer Hunter. https://beerhunter.com.
Ohio Brewiana. https://www.ohiobrewiana.com.
Ohio Craft Brewers Association. http://www.ohiocraftbeer.org.
Ohio Hop Guild. http://ohgg.org.
OldBreweries.com. http://oldbreweries.com.
Rustycans.com. http://rustycans.com.

Documentaries

The Beer Hunter. Discovery Channel. Showtime. 1993.
Beer Hunter: The Movie. 2013. www.beerhuntermovie.com.
Beer Wars. Gravitas Ventures LLC, 2009.
Columbus Neighborhoods, Franklinton, *German Village* and *Worthington*. PBS. 2013.
Prohibition. PBS. 2011.

Interviews

Eric Bean
Victor Ecimovich III
Jeff Edwards
Jim Ellison
Vince Falcone
David Foster
Scott Francis
Jay Hoster
Alex O. Hostettler
Chris Hostettler
Lenny Kolada
Ben Pridgeon
Angelo Signorino
Dean Skillman
Dick Stevens
Dan Tarpy
Ron Wilson
Allen Young

Other Resources

Columbus Metropolitan Library
German Village Society, August Wagner Collection
Ohio History Connection
Westerville Public Library and Anti-Saloon League Museum

INDEX

C

D

E

F

G

W

Y

Z

ABOUT THE AUTHOR

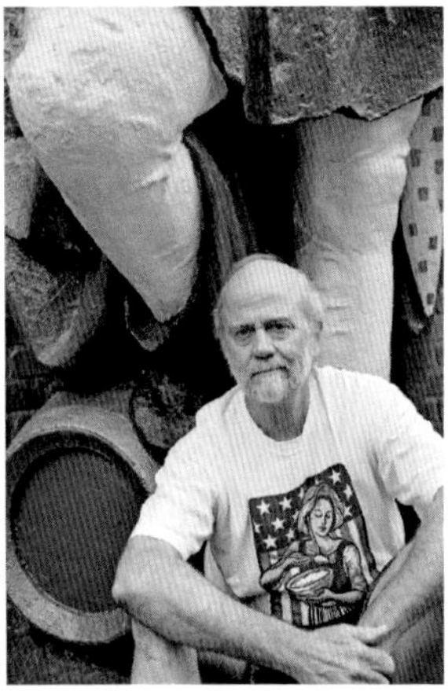

Author Curtis Schieber brewed his first batch of beer on January 18, 1992, with malt extract and dried yeast. With the second batch, he graduated to liquid yeast, and by the seventh, all grain and fresh, whole hops. He has never looked back. Brewing was an extension of the passion he has had for flavorful beer since the mid-1970s, beginning with British ales such as Bass and Guiness, early craft brewer Anchor Steam and, later, Belgian ales including Chimay. Today, he favors saison, German alt and dunkel and barley wines.

Most of his work hours during the last forty-two years, though, have been spent in or around the music business. He owned a record store for most of the 1980s and promoted concerts and released records on his independent label for six years. Though he was published frequently in the *Monthly Planet* in the late 1970s, he began writing for something like a living in 1989, a year after he closed the record shop. He freelanced and then became music editor for *Columbus Alive!* and, later, a reviewer and columnist for the *Columbus Guardian* and the daily *Columbus Dispatch*, to which he continues to contribute after more than twenty-five years. He has hosted a specialty radio show on commercial alternative radio station WWCD, CD102.5FM since January 1991. The year 2017 marks the fifteenth he has made his "day job" at Barnes & Noble Booksellers.

Though he spent six formative childhood years in Mexico City, he is happily settled with his wife and two children in Columbus, Ohio, a significant market in the craft brewing movement.